BOWIE IN BERLIN
A NEW CAREER IN A NEW TOWN

David Bowie and
Iggy Pop at Copenhagen
Central station,
April 1976.

BOWIE IN BERLIN

A NEW CAREER IN A NEW TOWN

Thomas Jerome Seabrook

BOWIE IN BERLIN
A NEW CAREER IN A NEW TOWN

Thomas Jerome Seabrook

A GENUINE JAWBONE BOOK
First edition 2008
Published in the UK and the USA by Jawbone Press
Office G1
141–157 Acre Lane
London SW2 5UA
England
www.jawbonepress.com

ISBN: 978-1-906002-08-4

Editor: John Morrish
Design: Paul Cooper Design

Printed by Short Run Press, Exeter, Devon

7 8 9 10 28 27 26 25

CONTENTS

Clockwise from top left: Bowie on the set of *The Man Who Fell To Earth*, July 1975; onstage at the Falkoner Teatret, Copenhagen, Denmark, April 1976; at the Wembley Empire Pool, London, England, with Carlos Alomar (right) and Tony Kaye (centre), May 1976; with Rip Torn in a scene from *The Man Who Fell To Earth*.

Bowie, Tony Visconti, and Brian Eno during the *Low* sessions at the Château d'Hérouville, September 1976; Iggy Pop reveals his more thoughtful side during a break from the Station To Station tour in New York, March 1976.

Bowie and Iggy take a ride through Berlin-Tegel International Airport, April 1977; Iggy at the Rainbow Theatre, London, England, March 1977; at the same venue with Ricky Gardiner on guitar and Bowie on keyboards.

Robert Fripp (left),
Brian Eno (centre),
and Bowie at Hansa
Tonstudio 3, Berlin,
Germany, July 1977;
Bowie performs an off-
the-cuff duet with Marc
Bolan at the Granada
Television studios,
Manchester, England,
September 1977.

Bowie and Bing get ready to sing their famous festive duet, September 1977; a still from *Just A Gigolo*, Bowie's "32 Elvis Presley movies contained in one"; at the *Gigolo* premiere at the 31st International Cannes Film Festival, May 1978; backstage at Max's Kansas City, New York, with Jerry Casale of Devo, December 1977.

Bowie at Madison Square Garden, New York, in April 1978, the final date of the American leg of his Low / "Heroes" tour.

INTRODUCTION

C onsider this: it's Monday, probably, and if there's a greasy pipe to be slithered down, David Bowie has slithered down it. He is, by his own admission, lucky to be alive, having come so close to exploding in a coke-fuelled supernova during his recent yearlong stay in Los Angeles. Since then he has relocated to Berlin, in the vain hope of 'cleaning up', and now finds himself behind the wheel of an open-topped Mercedes-Benz Ponton, cruising the city's ripped backside with Iggy Pop, once of The Stooges, in the passenger seat.

This unlikely double-act has been joined at the hip since the start of the year, united by a desire to curb their prodigious chemical appetites and an uncertainty about how on earth to go about it. Some days are better than others. "There's seven days in a week," Iggy would later recall: two for bingeing, two for recovery, and three more for "any other activity". Sometimes that meant painting, reading, or visiting art galleries; sometimes drinking the night away in dimly lit sidestreet clubs, watching women dressed as men dressed as women sing ancient songs of love, loss, and war. On other occasions it meant pulling the top down and putting your foot to the floor, doing laps of the city in search of something better to do.

That, in fact, is what these dum dum boys are up to tonight:

riding and riding, in Iggy's words, or "going round and round" in Bowie's. Pulling into the Kurfürstendamm, one of the main arteries of West Berlin's zigzagging network of roads, they spot someone they know, parked by the side of the road – not a friend, mind you, but a drug dealer, whom Bowie is pretty sure has pulled a fast one on them. What can we do about this? he wonders. Stepping out of the car and resolving the situation in gentlemanly fashion isn't an option. Someone, as he might later sing, could get killed. No, there's only one thing for this, he thinks, as he rams the front grille of the Mercedes into the back of the dealer's car – and then reverses, and does it again.

"I rammed him for a good five to ten minutes," Bowie later recalled, between songs at a BBC concert in 2000. "Nobody stopped. Nobody did anything." In the end, confident that he's made his point clearly enough, he drives away, but the incident is far from over. Having broken so dramatically out of the state of catatonic inertia that has dogged him for the past few months, the horror of what he has just done begins to dawn on him. Later the same evening, he finds himself in the basement car park of the hotel in which he and Iggy have been staying, driving round in circles, pushing close to 100 miles per hour and giving serious thought to the idea of bringing a definite close to this sorry charade by ramming the car into a wall. Until, that is, it runs out of gas. Crisis averted, this time.

A couple of weeks later, Bowie is in Hansa Tonstudio 2 with Tony Visconti, putting the finishing touches to the last song to be completed for *Low*, his newest and most groundbreaking album yet. The song, untitled when Bowie and his band laid down the musical tracks in September, is now called 'Always Crashing In The Same Car', and takes as its main lyrical inspiration those hair-raising moments underneath the Hotel Gehrus.

This incident is remarkable enough simply as an indication of the depths to which David Bowie, the greatest musical star of the 1970s, had fallen. But it is even more extraordinary to consider that, at a time of such incredible personal turmoil, he was able not just to continue working, but to create some of the most striking, moving, and groundbreaking work not just of his career but in the history of popular music. His return to Europe after a two-year, self-imposed exile in America precipitated a rush of intensive creativity equalled only by a handful of other musical acts: The Beatles and Bob Dylan in the 1960s, Stevie Wonder in the 1970s, and Prince in the 1980s.

But despite the wealth of innovative and imaginative music Bowie made between 1976 and 1979, his career is generally measured not by this but by the more theatrical, extravagant records he produced earlier in the 1970s, or by the much more commercial, pop-orientated phase he entered into in the 1980s. For so many listeners, even those who have a soft spot for him, Bowie will never be much more than a red-headed, bisexual glam-rocker with eyes of different colours, or the bequiffed, besuited crooner of 'Let's Dance' – by his own estimation a much more "humanistic" record than some of his others, but also one that lacked something of the trailblazing vitality of his late 1970s output (which encompasses not just his own *Low*, *"Heroes"*, and *Lodger*, but also the two albums he co-wrote and produced for Iggy Pop, *The Idiot* and *Lust For Life*).

Even in the midst of this period, Bowie still struggled to shake off the spectre of Ziggy Stardust. During an interview for British television a few months before the release of *Lodger*, Bowie's interrogator, Valerie Singleton, confessed to "immediately associat[ing] you with that particular period". She wasn't alone then, and isn't now. But perhaps it's time to think of him instead in the context of this later and most incredibly fertile phase of his working life, and the circumstances through which he arrived at it.

PART 1
SPEED OF LIFE

BLACK NOISE

During the 1970s, David Bowie was British pop's most talismanic, chameleonic character. Having announced himself in 1969 with his rush-released, zeitgeist-encapsulating 'Space Oddity' – a tale of interstellar adventure and communication breakdown that hit Number Five on the UK singles chart just in time for the Apollo 11 moon landing – the singer, songwriter, and trendsetter spent the following decade weaving his way through most of rock and pop's major strands, breaking ground at a pace few could ever match.

Bowie's first album release of the 1970s, *The Man Who Sold The World*, may not have captured too many imaginations at the time, but it did establish several key patterns for what was to follow. Its Led Zeppelin-like hard-rock sound was markedly different to the gentler, acoustic songs on the album that preceded it (which has been known since 1972 as *Space Oddity*, because of the popularity of the title song, but was originally called *David Bowie* in Britain and *Man Of Words / Man Of Music* in the United States). Just as importantly, the album's cover image – the singer draped across a velvety chaise longue, wearing what he later described as a "man's dress" – gave an early indication of the theatrical androgyny he would cultivate in the coming years. Alongside an undeniable gift for popular song and a keen sense of the next big thing, what set Bowie apart from the majority of his 1970s peers was his ability to shock and awe in the same breath.

The next couple of years marked David Bowie's ascent to the top of the pop world in Britain and mainland Europe. Like *The Man Who Sold The World*, the next album, *Hunky Dory*, was not an immediate commercial success on its release in the final weeks of 1971; but a song-cycle of such quality was unlikely to be ignored for long. The first bona fide 'classic album' in the Bowie canon, its strengths are its masterful marriage of high and lowbrow art, and a pop sensibility doused in cabaret, sexual ambiguity, and lyrics inspired by Nietzsche. Song titles that name-check Andy Warhol and Bob Dylan give a good indication of this set's musical bent, which is much closer to *Space Oddity*'s dreamy pop than the previous year's proto-metal stylings. The mood is playful right up until the final song, 'The Bewlay Brothers', noted by Roy Carr and Charles Shaar Murray as the singer's "densest and most impenetrable song,"[1] and often taken to concern David's schizophrenic stepbrother, Terry.

The opener, 'Changes', now held to be among Bowie's greatest songs, was, surprisingly, not issued as a single in the UK until 1975, but did give the singer his first success on the *Billboard* chart – albeit a lowly Number 66. Another piano-led instant classic, 'Life On Mars', was also held back for single release until later on in the singer's career. In fact, what truly made David Bowie a star did not arrive on a seven-inch or 12-inch slab of vinyl, but in the January 22nd 1972 edition of *Melody Maker*. Much has been made over the years of the veracity of Bowie's announcement, to the journalist Michael Watts, of his bisexuality. Ultimately, it matters not whether his homosexual leanings were exaggerated. What does matter is that, in making this claim, he hauled himself up way beyond the level of modern-day minstrel to become something else entirely.

Bowie completed this transformation with what remains the canniest move in a career full of bright, bold steps. *The Rise And Fall Of Ziggy Stardust And The Spiders From Mars* is not by any stretch of the imagination David Bowie's finest musical achievement. The albums that preceded and follow it, *Hunky Dory* and *Aladdin Sane*, are at the very least its equal. But, of course, *Ziggy Stardust* was more than just an album. In his most celebrated act, Bowie became the concept album's day-glo title character: and not just on record, but on and off stage, too, in interviews and beyond. Ziggy Stardust pioneered the idea of the larger-than-life rock star, but it also whipped up an ever-quickening whirlwind around its creator.

David Bowie was certainly not the only musician of the time to find himself struggling to adjust to the pressures of fast-growing fame and the demands of a devoted, hysterical fan base. But where Elton John could, if he wished, go home, put his feet up, and be plain old Reg Dwight for the night, there was, by the end of 1972, little to differentiate between Bowie and Ziggy. "That fucker would not leave me alone for years," Bowie later recalled. "That was when it all started to sour…. And it took me an awful time to level out. My whole personality was affected."[2]

The following year, 1973, saw the release of two more albums – *Aladdin Sane*, a refinement of *Ziggy Stardust*'s glam-rock, and *Pin Ups*, a collection of 1960s songs such as Them's 'Here Comes The Night' and 'See Emily Play' by Pink Floyd – between which Bowie called time on the *Ziggy Stardust* era at the close of a performance at London's Hammersmith Odeon on July 3rd, 1973. His famous declaration – "Not only is this the last show of the tour, but it's the last show we'll ever do" – did not, as was originally thought, mean the end for David Bowie, just his crimson-haired alter ego. He had grown tired both of the strain of *being* Ziggy, and of his somewhat rudimentary backing trio, with whom he had been playing since the start of the decade – an age for someone with so constant a need to evolve as Bowie.

Despite bringing the curtain down on Ziggy Stardust and dismissing his well-loved backing group, The Spiders From Mars, David Bowie remained as popular as ever in Britain in 1974, and began to achieve much greater success in the USA. The last of his three glam-rock albums, *Diamond Dogs*, had its roots in an ambitious plan to stage a musical based on George Orwell's *Nineteen Eighty-Four*, and was accompanied by a lavish, theatrical US tour and a new role as Halloween Jack. The biggest live draw of Bowie's career in America, the tour also demonstrated the effects of his fame, its various trappings and excesses, and the very speed of life he felt compelled to pursue in order to keep up with his creative impulses. "I didn't really use [drugs] for hedonistic purposes," he explained 25 years later. "I would work for days in a row without sleep. It wasn't a joyful, euphoric kind of thing. I was driving myself to a point of insanity."[3]

As the tour, and the year, wound down, it became clear that Bowie was not, by any stretch of the imagination, in a good way. Exhausted and ravaged by increasingly severe cocaine abuse, Bowie had become a ghoulish shadow of the elaborate characters of old. Midway through his trek across America, he decided to abandon the extravagant stage sets, costumes, and choreography and, moreover, the rock'n'roll sound that had brought him his biggest successes, in favour of what he called 'plastic soul'. The Diamond Dogs tour became the Philly Dogs tour; out went another band, and in came a wider pool of mostly black musicians, including guitarist Carlos Alomar, who would stay in Bowie's band until 1987, and a quartet of backing singers, among them Ava Cherry – Bowie's not-so-secret girlfriend of the time – and a pre-fame Luther Vandross. To some, this was yet another outlandish stylistic leap; others, such as the noted rock critic Lester Bangs, realised that Bowie had "just changed his props" again. The "ultimate vibe" here, according to Bangs, was "Johnny Ray on cocaine singing about 1984".[4]

But with a grim irony, this look, the most stripped-back yet, seemed only to render Bowie more alien – or, at least, less human – than before. The cover of the live album he released in October 1974, *David Live*, shows the full extent of his physical deterioration. The music contained within is unspectacular, and was already out of date on its release, having been recorded in July, at the Tower Theater in Philadelphia, before the tour had shifted focus from glam to soul; in interviews to promote the album, Bowie seemed more keen to talk up his next project – a half-finished *Young Americans* – which could "tell you more about where I am now than anything I could say".[5] The photograph on the front of *David Live*, however, was an apt portrait of the singer as 1974 tumbled into 1975. As Bowie himself would later remark, "It looks as if I've just stepped out of the grave".[6]

A pair of high-profile television appearances, on either side of the Atlantic, confirmed the weakened state of Bowie's body and mind. The first of these was a spot on *The Dick Cavett Show*, which aired on NBC in the USA on December 4th, 1974. Bowie began by performing two songs: the first, '1984', bridges the gap between his old and new musical styles; the second is a premiere of 'Young Americans', the title track from his as-yet unreleased 'plastic soul' record. Both are decent-enough readings of fine material; what follows makes for uncomfortable viewing even now, 30-odd years after the fact. Sitting across from the mild-mannered, all-American Cavett, a ghoulish Bowie spends most of the interview tapping and twirling a cane that had been handed to him, somewhat unadvisedly, at the end of the musical segment, and sniffing loudly while stumbling through polite but evasive, fragmented answers.

For the most part, Cavett does his best to ignore Bowie's obvious discomfort and focuses instead on fairly routine enquiries about the differences between the singer's on and offstage demeanour, and his friendship with Mick Jagger. At one point, Cavett asks if being asked to sit, away from his band, and "chat a little bit" makes Bowie nervous. The response is telling: "Oh ... let's carry on talking. Don't ask me that. Otherwise I'll wonder." Clearly, this is not the Starman of 1971–3. Here Bowie alludes to feeling "cocooned" during the Ziggy Stardust phase of his career, before heading off on a strange tangent about "black noise", which, he tells Cavett, "is the register within which you can crack a city or people ... it's a noise ... bomb". Cavett wonders if this could possibly be true. "Oh yeah, it is," Bowie replies. "It was invented in France ... up until last year you could buy the patent for it in the French patent office for about three-to-four dollars.... A small one could probably kill about half the people here. But a big one could ... destroy a city. Or even more ..."

This kind of paranoid, drug-fuelled rambling would become typical of David Bowie interviews over the next 18 months. In February 1975, *Creem's* Bruno Stein reported on an evening spent in an unspecified American hotel room with the singer and his entourage. Bowie talks at length – to others in the room, rather than Stein, who, it seems, is merely an observer – about watching for UFOs ("I made sightings six, seven times a night for about a year"), Mayan civilisation, media control and "cultural manipulation", and Nazism, in which Bowie was beginning to develop an unhealthy interest that would manifest itself, a year later, in one of the most notorious incidents of his career.

Around the same time as the *Creem* article hit the news-stands in America, the most thorough portrait of Bowie to date, *Cracked Actor*, aired on British television as part of the long running *Omnibus* documentary series. Filmed on the east and west coasts of the USA in mid 1974, it captures Bowie at a critical juncture: between sounds, between images, and – from the look of him – in the midst of succumbing to a deep drug addiction. Taking its name from a track on *Aladdin Sane* (itself a meditation on the downside of fame, written, fittingly, in Los Angeles), *Cracked Actor* is split between live and backstage footage and insightful interview material.

Bowie talks mostly to the documentary's narrator and producer, Alan Yentob, about the (mostly negative) effects of fame, and of 'becoming' his creations. He makes several references to schizophrenia, and to not knowing "whether I was writing the characters or the characters were writing me". At one point he asks if Yentob knows "that feeling you get in a car when somebody is accelerating very fast when you're not driving? And you get that feeling in your chest like 'ughh' and you're pulled backwards, and you're not sure whether you like it or not.... That's what success was like.... It was very frightening for me, and coping with it was something that I tried to do ... some of those albums were me coping, taking it all very seriously." Most telling, however, is the moment when, driving through L.A. in the backseat of a limo, Bowie mutters that he "hope[s] we're not stopped" after hearing distant police sirens, and lets out a loud, powdery snort.

By the time *Cracked Actor* aired, on January 26th 1975, Bowie had completed his seventh studio album of the 1970s: *Young Americans*. The album was recorded in three stages. Work began during a two-week stint at Sigma Sound in Philadelphia in August 1974, between the first and second legs of the Diamond/Philly Dogs tour, which resulted in what, for a while, was considered to be a finished record, and was set to be called *Somebody Up There Likes Me*. In the event, only four of the nine songs recorded at this point made the final cut (the other five, including a funked-up remake of 'John I'm Only Dancing,' have all since emerged on reissues and compilations). Two more songs were added in November, at which point producer Tony Visconti returned to London to mix the project. In January, midway through mixing, he was informed to his dismay that Bowie had recorded (and mixed) two further songs without him at Electric Lady Studios in New York: a throwaway cover of The Beatles' 'Across The Universe', and an off-the-cuff collaboration with John Lennon, 'Fame', which borrowed liberally from 'Footstompin'' by The Flares, a song Bowie had been performing regularly on tour.

As well as being a fine album in its own right, despite the jarring and somewhat baffling inclusion of these two late additions, *Young Americans* marks an important phase in the evolution of Bowie's music. It was the first of his albums to abandon, almost entirely, rock'n'roll in favour of something funkier and more soulful. And it introduced two musicians who would play on all of Bowie's albums right through to 1980's *Scary Monsters (And Super Creeps)*: guitarist Carlos Alomar and drummer Dennis Davis. Alomar, who had until then been playing in the RCA Recording Studios house band, was first called upon to play on Lulu's Bowie-produced cover of 'The Man Who Sold The World'.

He and Bowie quickly hit it off, and, over the next half-decade, Alomar became as crucial a figure as any in helping to realise the singer's musical ambitions. And when Bowie needed a new drummer, Alomar knew just the guy. "When he heard Dennis [Davis]," Alomar later recalled, "[Bowie] was like, 'That's it, it's over, the door's closed.'"[7]

Just as importantly, *Young Americans* brought Tony Visconti back into Bowie's orbit. Although he had co-mixed *Diamond Dogs* and helped salvage the badly recorded *David Live*, Visconti had not worked on a Bowie album from the ground up since he produced *The Man Who Sold The World* in 1970. Having produced most of *Young Americans*, he would later play a defining role, alongside Bowie and Brian Eno, in shaping the sound of *Low*, *"Heroes"*, and *Lodger*.

The release of *Young Americans* was delayed by Bowie's decision, in late January, to fire his manager, Tony DeFries. Bowie cited as his primary motivation his dissatisfaction with the terms of the contract he had signed with DeFries's MainMan company in 1972, by which he was entitled to only a small advance on each of the records he made. It seems likely, however, that Bowie's decision had just as much to do with the state of drug-induced depression and paranoia he was fast falling into, not to mention a growing need for cash to fund his cocaine dependency. (The advice of John Lennon, who was himself still fighting legal action from former Beatles manager Allan Klein, was another contributing factor.) As miserly as the MainMan contract might have seemed, it was fairly common for recording artists of the time not to see much in the way of financial return for their work.

When *Young Americans* eventually came out, in March 1975, it cemented Bowie's rising stardom in the USA and gave him his first Top 10 studio album on the *Billboard* chart. Some of Bowie's British admirers, already unsure about the 'Americanisation' of several tracks on *Diamond Dogs*, were further put off by this latest stylistic revamp. But for every *Ziggy*-era fan who didn't buy *Young Americans*, at least one new listener did; disco was making inroads into the UK charts in early 1975, so Bowie's new album fitted the mood perfectly.

Bowie chose not to tour in support of *Young Americans*. There had originally been plans for the Philly Dogs band to play on through the early months of 1975, first in South America and then in Europe, but these were curtailed by Bowie's problems with DeFries and MainMan. In fact, he made very few public appearances at all in 1975, and only one that coincided with the release of *Young Americans*.

On March 1st, a week before the UK release of the album (it would not hit the shelves in the USA until April), Bowie was invited to present the award for Best Rhythm & Blues Vocal Performance at the Grammys, which were held at the Uris Theatre in New York. He made a rambling, three-minute speech about the winner, Aretha Franklin, which didn't seem to do much to endear him to her (she, like a lot of other Americans, still seemed to view Bowie as a strange, gay glam-rocker from another planet). The one time Queen Of Atlantic Soul snatched the trophy out of his hands before announcing: "I'm so happy, I could kiss David Bowie!"

And that was it, as far as the public was concerned, until the closing months of 1975. There would be no new tour, and only a smattering of media appearances. Instead, Bowie spent the rest of the year becoming ever more delusional, and ever more dependent on cocaine, but he also threw himself into two new projects that, when unveiled in 1976, would stand among his most important and captivating artistic statements to date.

THE YEAR OF MAGICAL THINKING

L os Angeles has always had an untidy relationship with music. While its near neighbour, San Francisco, has managed over the years to cling to a reputation for free-thinking and perennial creativity, L.A. has often seemed stifled by the glitz and glamour of Hollywood, and the lure of filthy lucre. It might be the home of the music industry, but it has never truly been the home of music. For a brief period during the mid 1960s every street corner seemed to throw up a band for the ages – Love, The Doors, and The Byrds, to name but a few – but very few of these groups hung around for long, their principals having either departed the scene altogether or retreated into a fog of self-indulgence in Laurel Canyon.

In April 1975, having completed a three-year cycle of relentless touring and record-making, David Bowie became the latest coked-up singer-songwriter to drop anchor in L.A. He had been living out of a New York hotel room since December, but the fallout from his sacking of Tony DeFries and MainMan convinced the singer that he needed to relocate. New York had begun to "close in on me," he told *Rolling Stone* magazine's Cameron Crowe later in the year. (Crowe, still only 17, was one of the few music journalists able to get more than a fleeting glimpse of Bowie at this point in his career.) After three months of tense negotiations, Bowie and DeFries reached a settlement: in order to extract himself from his MainMain contract, Bowie had to agree to pay his former manager half of any revenue from *Hunky Dory*, *Ziggy Stardust*, *Aladdin Sane*, *Pin-Ups*, *Diamond Dogs*, and *David Live*, and 16 per cent of his gross earnings until 1982. Upon hearing these terms, Bowie reportedly broke down at the conference table, and spent the next week in a state of shock. (Publicly, he was keen to assert the positive aspects of the split. "It's not going to bother me," he told Crowe. "I'll survive. I'm far from broke. I'm free."[1])

Prior to leaving New York, Bowie completed another important piece of business – one that would open up a whole new career path. In February, he met with the British film director Nicolas Roeg, who was interested in casting Bowie in his big-screen adaptation of the Walter Tevis novel *The Man Who Fell To Earth*. Roeg originally had Peter O'Toole in mind to play Thomas Jerome Newton, the humanoid alien at the centre of the story; he also considered casting Michael Crichton, the actor-turned-writer now best known for writing *Jurassic Park* who, at six foot nine, matched the physical criteria of the towering Newton in Tevis's novel. But when Roeg decided he would prefer a more frail-looking Newton, his casting agent Maggie Abbott immediately suggested Bowie, whom she later described as having "just the charisma the character required".[2]

Roeg was not totally convinced to begin with, but made his mind up after seeing *Cracked Actor*. He was particularly taken by the rambling, drug-addled scenes in the back of Bowie's limo, in one of which the singer, already beginning to sound like Newton, compares himself and his experiences in America to "a fly floating around in my milk … it is a foreign body and it's getting a lot of milk. That's kind of how I felt – a foreign body, and I couldn't help but soak it all up." So taken was Roeg by this that he ended up recreating the scene in his own film.

Having spent the early part of the 1970s playing a rock star who had fallen to earth, Bowie was perfect for the role. It came as little surprise that rock'n'roll's most theatrical character, who had in recent years taken to calling himself 'the Actor', would turn up on the silver screen; he had in fact already made a series of low-key film and television appearances, including a pre-fame cameo in a 1968 BBC costume drama, *The Pistol Shot*. Roeg, meanwhile, was certainly not averse to casting musicians in his films, having given a certain Mick Jagger a leading role in his big-screen breakthrough, *Performance* (1968). He would later cast Art Garfunkel in *Bad Timing* (1980).

Bowie's meeting with Roeg very nearly didn't happen, in a manner that was typical of the singer's behaviour of the time. He arrived eight hours late – he had first forgotten that he was supposed to meet Roeg, and then assumed that the director would not have bothered waiting, so busied himself elsewhere. Eventually, Bowie returned to his rented New York residence in the early hours to find Roeg sitting at the kitchen table. The pair spent a further eight hours talking about the project, right through to the following afternoon (by which time they had been joined by film producer Si Litvinoff). Their rapport was instantaneous; Roeg had found his alien, and Bowie had found a film director with a similarly instinctual creative streak and artistic bravery. As Bowie would remark of Roeg a few months later, "It didn't take long for me to realise the man was a genius. I was and still am in awe of Roeg. Total awe."[3] Roeg returned the compliment, praising Bowie's "sense of mime and movement" and "amazing kind of self-discipline".[4]

The Actor's decision to take on his first major film role more than likely contributed to his choice of Los Angeles, the focal point of the movie industry, as his new home. The city's air of faded glamour would have appealed to him, too. The Sunset Strip area, which had, according to the writer Domenic Priore, given birth a decade earlier to a "fascinating artistic Mecca",[5] now had a seedy, insidious feel, its folk-rock coffeehouses replaced by shops selling occult paraphernalia.

Bowie arrived in the city in April, following a long train journey from New York, whereupon he moved into the home of his friend Glenn Hughes, the bassist in Deep Purple. With Deep Purple away on tour, Bowie shared the house with Hughes's housekeeper and the occasional hanger-on. He would be visited regularly by his assistant, Corinne 'Coco' Schwab, and less frequently by his wife, Angela, with whom he just about still shared a marriage that was incredibly open even by rock'n'roll standards. It had been several years since they had lived together for any appreciable amount of time, and neither was in any way discreet about their extra-curricular proclivities.

Even so, Angela, like Schwab, was concerned about the state of the singer's health, and with good reason. Los Angeles was the worst place a musician teetering on the edge of mental and physical collapse could have chosen to 'settle'. As Bowie himself had told Alan Yentob a year earlier, but had seemingly now forgotten, "There's an underlying unease [in L.A.]. You can feel it in every avenue.... And ever since [I first came here], I've always been aware of how dubious a position it is to stay here for any length of time."[6] Bowie's drug use continued to escalate while he lived in L.A., leaving him in a state of psychosis that bordered on schizophrenia. He had, in addition, taken to not sleeping for as many as six days at a time – something he would boast about at the time in interviews with journalists who didn't seem to realise, or want to realise, the extent of his problems – and was existing on a diet of milk and green and red peppers, which had caused him to become painfully thin. (Schwab was anxious to improve his diet, but could do no more than encourage him to drink fuller-fat milk.)

There have, over the years, emerged numerous outlandish stories about David Bowie's mental health and general behaviour during the time he spent in Los Angeles, some of which bear more relation to the truth than others. Many are tied to what was, undeniably, a deep obsession with black magic, which only exacerbated his already troubling paranoia. Among the most regularly cited of these stories suggests that Bowie kept his urine in jars in his fridge, for fear that some malevolent magician or other might use it to put a hex on him. In her autobiography, *Backstage Passes*, Angela Bowie notes that she "never saw any jugs, jars, vials, or any other containers full of urine or anything else resembling it", but adds that it wouldn't exactly have been out of character.

Backstage Passes also touches on a number of other well-known tales told about David Bowie's time in Los Angeles. Angela recalls taking a frantic, transatlantic telephone call from her husband, who had apparently been kidnapped by "a warlock and two witches" with evil intentions. She also details a later incident when, having joined David in L.A., she was asked by him to arrange an exorcism. Angela Bowie is not the most reliable of witnesses – she published her salacious memoir immediately after the expiry of a gagging clause in her divorce settlement, and makes little attempt to raise the tone above the opening sentence's recollection of "exactly where and when David Bowie and I first slept together". But enough stories such as these have circulated over the past 30 years to suggest that, even if only a fraction are true, something must have been very wrong with Bowie at this point in his life.

Cameron Crowe's February 1976 story for *Rolling Stone* confirms the singer's tendency to lapse at any moment into paranoid delusion: "Suddenly – always suddenly – David is on his feet and rushing to a nearby picture window. He thinks he's seen a body fall from the sky. 'I have to do this,' he says, pulling a shade down on the window. A ballpoint-penned star has been crudely drawn on the inside. Below it is the word 'Aum.' Bowie lights a black candle on his dresser and immediately blows it out to leave a thin trail of smoke floating upward. 'Don't let me scare the pants off you. It's only protective. I've been getting a little trouble from … the neighbours.'"

Other press reports of Bowie's time in L.A. described similarly peculiar behaviour, but all stopped short of passing final judgement on his condition: that he had suffered, or was on the verge of suffering, a nervous breakdown, and that he was perpetuating severe mental and physical ill health through drug abuse and malnutrition. They seemed more keen to focus on impressive, exaggerated boasts that the singer had "written nine films"[7] in the past year alone, and could "write an album in a month … I've already got two new albums in the can",[8] or on bold pronouncements such as that "rock'n'roll is dead … It's a toothless old woman".[9]

More telling are the brief allusions to days and nights spent "huddled in a room drawing pentangles, burning candles, chanting spells".[10] This, it seems, is how Bowie spent much of his time in L.A. Shortly after the incident with the 'witches' (who, it turned out, were merely a pair of coked-up groupies), Bowie moved into the home of his new lawyer-cum-manager, Michael Lippman, who tried, unsuccessfully, to coax the singer out of his troubled, anxious state. Lippman found himself able to do no more for Bowie than Coco Schwab had tried in recent months: to keep watch on him, and encourage him to eat. According to Angela Bowie, any suggestion that her husband ought to curb his drug intake was routinely met with a curt "Don't tell me what to do!" and a retreat into his locked bedroom, swiftly followed by "sniffing noises" and more time spent drawing occult symbols in the dark.

After a brief stay with the Lippmans, Bowie moved, with his wife, into a rented house on Doheny Drive, which he later described as having an Egyptian theme. "It appealed to me because I had this more than passing interest in Egyptian mysticism, the Kaballah, all this stuff that is inherently misleading in life."[11] These interests were not new to him, but had certainly been exacerbated, and darkened, by cocaine. Two songs from 1971's *Hunky Dory*, 'Oh You Pretty Things' and 'Quicksand', make reference to both occultism and Nietzschean proto-fascism, his two main areas of interest in 1975. 'Pretty Things' refers to Edward Bulwer-Lytton's 1871 novel, *The Coming Race*, which concerns an underground society and their attempts to harness the power of 'Vril-ya'; 'Quicksand' name-checks the infamous occultist Aleister Crowley and the organisation of mystics to which he belonged, the Hermetic Order Of The Golden Dawn. There are similar references in even earlier songs, such as 1969's 'Cygnet Committee'. By 1975, however, Bowie was not just writing songs about these things (although he continued to do that, too); they had pervaded his life, and were having a pronounced degenerative effect on him. Where once he would merely sing about 'The Supermen', he was now reportedly building 15-foot polyethylene sculptures of them in his back garden.

The spark of this renewed and more obsessive interest seems to have been a meeting with the underground filmmaker Kenneth Anger, best known for the occult-themed *Lucifer Rising*, in New York. In Los Angeles, Bowie spent long days and nights with the blinds pulled tightly shut, reading ever more obscure literature: *The Morning Of The Magicians* by Louis Pauwels and Jacques Bergier, for instance, or the writings of Madame Blavatsky, the founder of a late 19th century proto-New Age group, the Theosophical Society. Ever more fearful of what evil-doers might attempt to inflict upon him, he wore a large gold crucifix, given to him by Lippman, at all times. (Hedging his bets somewhat, he also asked Lippman for a mezuzah.) He is even reported to have regarded Led Zeppelin guitarist Jimmy Page, another musician with an interest in Crowley and black magic, as "a malevolent force out to get him".[12]

David Bowie's life on Doheny Drive consisted mostly, according to Angela Bowie, of sleeping until mid-afternoon, and then spending the evening, night, and early hours of the morning receiving a succession of visitors who were, for the most part, either roadies of other groups charged with delivering "fat packages of best Peruvian flake" or "semi-famous showbiz coke whores".[13]

These months in the middle of 1975 marked the first extended period for some years during which Bowie was not actively engaged in either recording or promoting his music. For all his protestations about being able to write songs in mere minutes, and having stacks of material ready for release, or that he had been busy writing screenplays, he was simply not in the right frame of mind.

Bowie's last foray into the recording studio had been in January, when he recorded a pair of somewhat throwaway late-additions to *Young Americans*. He would not begin work on his next album, *Station To Station*, until October. In between times, his only stint in the studio was a single day in May at Hollywood's Oz Studios, which came as a result of an aborted attempt by Bowie to resuscitate the career of his even more troubled friend Iggy Pop, the former Stooges frontman.

Iggy had little input into the musical direction of the session, according to Cameron Crowe, who watched as Bowie spent nine hours "composing, producing, and playing every instrument" on an "ominous" and "dirgelike" song, apparently called 'Drink To Me'. Iggy then added an improvised vocal (which rhymed "door" with "whore" and asked "Are you really that dumb?") before skulking off, pausing only to declare his performance "the best thing I've ever done".[14]

After Iggy's departure, Bowie wrote and recorded a demo of something called 'Movin' On' before retiring from the studio. Neither 'Movin' On' nor 'Drink To Me' was ever released; and when Iggy failed to turn up at the studio (for reasons that would become clearer over time) the following day, Bowie cancelled the remaining time booked at Oz. With little else on the immediate horizon, Bowie returned to his house on Doheny Drive, to read up on fascism, occultism, and the Kaballah, and to -do battle with his demons, real and imaginary.

In June it was officially announced, in the pages of *Variety* and the rest, that David Bowie had been cast as Thomas Jerome Newton in *The Man Who Fell To Earth*. Production of the film had been curtailed for some months when the original backers at Columbia dropped out upon discovering that their choice of leading man, Robert Redford, would not be considered for the role of Newton. Now, with the recently formed British Lion company taking Columbia's place, shooting commenced in New Mexico.

Unwilling, as ever, to fly, Bowie travelled the 800 miles between Los Angeles, California, and Albuquerque, New Mexico, on the Super Chief train. Introduced in 1936 by the Atchison, Topeka, and Santa Fe Railway, the Super Chief ran from Chicago to L.A., and soon established itself among the most efficient and luxurious modes of travel in the United States. Initially only running once per week in each direction, it became known as the 'Train Of The Stars' when a litany of film actors began to use it for journeys to and from Hollywood. Although it has since been swallowed up by the Amtrak corporation and renamed the Southwest Chief, the train remains sufficiently famous that it is possible to buy a Lego model of it.

Having arrived in Albuquerque, Bowie was driven to nearby Lake Fenton, where principal shooting was to take place. According to Nicolas Roeg, Bowie turned up in "the same limo as in *Cracked Actor*".[15] Both the limo and its driver, Tony Mascia, were duly cast in the film – a canny move by a director who, aware of Bowie's recent troubles, was keen to make life as comfortable as possible for his star. (With *Cracked Actor* still very much in mind, Roeg even went so far as to integrate an eerie restaging of Bowie's backseat paranoia into *The Man Who Fell To Earth*.)

Starring in *The Man Who Fell To Earth* came as a much needed respite for Bowie. It provided him with an important and artistically rewarding new project on which to focus, but one also that he did not have to direct (in the wider sense of the word) himself – which, it seems, might well have been beyond him at this point. By all accounts, he was in much better mental and physical shape during the three months he spent as Thomas Jerome Newton in New Mexico than he had been behind the shutters of his various Los Angeles homes. The change of location seemed to suit him: during a break from shooting, an apparently affable and relaxed Bowie spoke of how he found New Mexico to be "so clean and pure – and puritanical, too – not just the people, but the land…. This is the way I'd like [the rest of] America to be."[16] When not required on set, he spent his time back at the Albuquerque Hilton Inn with a small entourage that included Coco Schwab and, on occasion, his four-year-old son Zowie, learning to use a 16mm newsreel camera given to him by Roeg or jotting down fragments of ideas for films and books (including an aborted attempt at an autobiography, *The Return Of The Thin White Duke*). He also read avidly, as ever, having apparently brought 400 books with him for the 11-week shoot.

Most reports suggest that Bowie cleaned up his act significantly while in New Mexico. Executive producer Si Litvinoff later recalled that the singer had promised "not to do any cocaine during the shoot", although he was still managing to stay up half the night working on a prospective soundtrack. For his part, Nicolas Roeg had decided early on "not to do anything or say anything" about Bowie's cocaine usage, on the grounds that "I'm not into the guilt thing or trying to cure anybody of their humanity". Bowie was still worryingly thin, however, and seemed to be living on little more than ice cream. According to Candy Clark, who was Bowie's love interest on screen and Roeg's off it, the singer-actor was unable to turn up for the filming of one particularly memorable scene – the point at which he reveals his true, alien self to Clark's Mary-Lou – because "he'd drunk some milk and got sick".[17] Still wary of warlocks and wizards, Bowie found this incident very troubling indeed.

The Man Who Fell To Earth is often referred to, for convenience's sake, as a science fiction film (usually with the words 'cult' and 'classic' thrown in for good measure), but bears little relation to other landmarks of the genre. Bowie's character might be an alien, but it would not have made much difference to the story had he been, as another character wonders of him at one point, Lithuanian instead. This is an allegorical tale of dislocation and helplessness; of power, corruption, and lies. Bowie himself, interviewed on set by *Creem* magazine, called it a "very sad, tender love story", summing his character up as "man in his pure form ... brought down by the corruption around him".[18] There are allusions to the lives of Christ (when Newton is betrayed by the Judas-like Nathan Bryce) and Howard Hughes, a real-life take on Newton's obsessive, brilliant, pioneering, and reclusive character; there are hints, too, of Bowie himself, the 'alien' profiting from America but feeling very much an outsider there. But perhaps most notable are the intimations of Icarus, the Greek mythological character who flew too close to the sun in what is most often interpreted as a metaphor for societal collapse. That this is intentional is confirmed when Bryce lingers, while thumbing through an art book, on a print of Brueghel's *The Fall Of Icarus*, reproduced beside W.H. Auden's poem 'Musée Des Beaux-Arts', itself directly inspired by Brueghel's painting and another retelling of the Icarus myth.

Thirty years on, *The Man Who Fell To Earth* remains an intriguing, original take on the often formulaic science fiction genre. It is still considered among Nicolas Roeg's finest films, and is almost universally regarded as David Bowie's greatest performance as an actor. This, perhaps, is because he barely had to act at all. "My one snapshot memory of that film is not having to act," he later confessed – which is just as well, for where Bowie is required to do more than just 'be otherworldly', there is a certain stilted awkwardness to it.

The rest of the cast is strong and well chosen: Candy Clark wisely made the lonely, neurotic Mary-Lou "as false as Thomas Jerome Newton, with the false fingernails, eyelashes, and wig"; Rip Torn brings a sleek, cold detachment to college professor-turned-scientist Nathan Bryce; and Buck Henry is assured and understated as the patent lawyer Oliver Farnsworth.

The film is hard to fault visually. Roeg is equally adept at capturing the desolate beauty of the landscape of New Mexico as he is at imagining Newton's arid homeland. Roeg's rendering of this alien world is fairly conventional by comparison with other sci-fi – perhaps, as film critic Graham Fuller suggests, because the director is keen to show "how life on Earth is stranger and more disconcerting than anything in outer space."[19] Despite its fantastical pretext, *The Man Who Fell To Earth* covers many of the same themes as Roeg's other films: a lack of communication and emotional intimacy between lovers, a sense of dislocation in a foreign land, and a woozy feeling of temporal displacement. (The viewer is aware of lengthy gaps in the narrative, and of time tumbling by at varying speeds, but is never able to fully reconcile or quantify either.) The frequent sex scenes are typically 'Roegian' – visceral, voyeuristic, and ripe with oblique meaning. (At one point the sexless, alien Newton aims a pistol at Mary-Lou; she is terrified until he fires a blank in a not-so-subtle nod to his own feelings of impotence.)

The film's opening scenes are studied and enigmatic – two qualities typical of Nicolas Roeg's work. We see Newton's spacecraft hurtling through space and crash-landing in Lake Fenton, then Newton himself, stumbling into the two-horse village of Haneyville, where he sells what appears to be his wedding ring for $20 (even though, we soon discover, he has a pocket full of identical rings, and a wrap of $100 bills), announces himself to be British, drinks ravenously from the edge of the lake, and seems generally bewildered by his surroundings (which include an oversized blow-up head bouncing in the wind and a truck carrying sheep). There is, to begin with, almost no dialogue: the first vocal utterance, four minutes in, is the deep and somewhat threatening retch of a roadside tramp.

Seemingly more comfortable, but still undeniably guarded, Newton next pays a late-night visit to Oliver Farnsworth in New York. He shows Farnsworth nine 'basic' electronic patents, which he is unwilling to let out of his sight, but is eager for the lawyer to read immediately. Farnsworth is astonished by the content of the patents, which he claims will be worth $300 million within three years. Newton is disappointed at this figure, but nonetheless invites Farnsworth to be president of his World Enterprises corporation, telling him: "I don't want to have contact with anyone but you."

As World Enterprises continues its inexorable rise, its products – particularly a self-developing photographic film – pique the interest of Nathan Bryce, a bored, middle-aged, Chicagoan chemistry professor played by Rip Torn. When Bryce is reprimanded for neglecting his teaching and devoting his energies, instead, to his female students, he resolves to get a job working for World Enterprises. Newton, by this stage, is on his way back to New Mexico, where he checks into the Hotel Artesia under the alias 'Mr. Sussex'. There, after passing out in the elevator, he meets the kind-hearted but emotionally unstable chambermaid Mary-Lou. She and Newton become friends, first, and then lovers; she also introduces this hitherto uncorrupted man to sex and alcohol, and facilitates his obsession with television.

A year or more passes; an ever-more reclusive Newton, now living with Mary-Lou, spends his days staring at multiple television sets, while

Bryce's persistence in writing to World Enterprises has paid off, and he is now working in the fuel research department on an as-yet unspecified new project, which Farnsworth calls a "space program". We begin, meanwhile, to see slow flashes of life on the arid, desolate planet Newton has left behind and to understand why he has come to Earth: he is, as a much later Bowie song would have it, looking for water.

While the first half of *The Man Who Fell To Earth* is concerned mostly with the rise to power and influence of Thomas Jerome Newton and his World Enterprises, the second half charts his susceptibility to very human vices, the uncovering of his true identity, and the inevitable failure of his attempt to return home. Newton's space program, into which he has ploughed all of WE's resources, is taking longer than expected, and his relationship with Mary-Lou is beginning to disintegrate. Still devoted to his other family "back home," he is unable to engage himself emotionally with her. When, in the film's most memorable scene, he finally reveals his true, androgynous, alien self to her, it only furthers their emotional estrangement. (Bryce meanwhile discovers the truth about Newton by his own means, having taken x-ray photographs that reveal Newton's alien form.)

Newton is kidnapped on the eve of the space program's completion, after which World Enterprises is taken over by rival corporations, led by a man known only as Peters, who has Farnsworth thrown from the window of his New York apartment. Newton is held in a deserted hotel suite, and subjected to a battery of painful medical tests, for what appears to be a number of years. His only respite is television and the occasional visit from Mary-Lou (who nonetheless ends up marrying Nathan Bryce). Eventually, interest in Newton abates and he is able to leave the hotel and disappear into a life even more reclusive than before. At the film's close, he is tracked down by a curious, aging Bryce, who has found a record Newton had made – in the hope that his family might hear it – called *The Visitor*. Newton himself seems not to have aged at all, but has fallen into an alcoholic despondency driven by his failure to complete his mission and save his family. Bryce wonders if Newton is bitter about how things ended up. "No," he replies. "We'd have probably treated you the same if you'd come over to our place."

Shooting of *The Man Who Fell To Earth* wrapped towards the end of September, but Thomas Jerome Newton stayed with Bowie for much longer. Nicolas Roeg (who would spend the next nine months editing the film) reportedly warned Bowie of this before the film went into production, but was perhaps thinking only in terms of the singer being typecast. In fact Bowie, who had seemed to Roeg and others to have 'become' Newton rather than merely playing him during the making of the film, remained in character after leaving New Mexico and returning to Los Angeles. He retained Newton's wardrobe – which, as part of his contract, he had a hand in choosing for the film – and his striking dyed-red, centre-parted hairdo. Newton's air of lonely dislocation and icy paranoia stuck with him, too, and clearly informed Bowie's next (and final) onstage character, The Thin White Duke.

Bowie thrust himself into his next musical project almost as soon as he got back to Los Angeles – this time to another rented house, found for him by Coco Schwab, on Stone Canyon Drive, just north of W. Sunset Boulevard in the Bel Air district of the city. But for his brief attempt at writing and producing solo material for Iggy Pop in May, Bowie had not entered a recording studio since January, and that in itself was only to cut a couple of off-the-cuff tracks that were tacked onto *Young Americans*. You had to go back to the previous November to find Bowie's last proper, organised recording sessions. For a man preparing to make his eighth studio album in just over five years, this was a long time indeed.

During the first half of 1975, for reasons discussed already, Bowie was simply not in a fit state to make a record. But while shooting *The Man Who Fell To Earth*, he had begun to formulate ideas – albeit rather vague ones – about the direction his next musical work might take. At the end of September, he assembled a band that included four of the musicians he had worked with on *Young Americans*: rhythm guitarist and bandleader Carlos Alomar, lead-guitar player Earl Slick, drummer Dennis Davis, and backing vocalist Warren Peace. The line-up was completed by two new recruits. George Murray, who replaced Willie Weeks on bass, had previously played with Davis alongside Roy Ayers. Roy Bittan, a member of Bruce Springsteen's E-Street Band, came in on piano, replacing Mike Garson, who had until then been the only holdover from Bowie's glam-rock era. (Garson himself was surprised not to be invited back into the fold, particularly as Bowie had apparently told him, in late 1974, "I want you to be my pianist for the next 20 years."[20] Bowie put it down to the fact that Garson had fallen under the spell of Scientology.)

Bowie's choice of co-producer was also somewhat unexpected. He had in recent years struck up a renewed working relationship with Tony Visconti, who had worked in various capacities on Bowie's last three releases, *Diamond Dogs*, *David Live*, and *Young Americans*, and might have been expecting to produce his next album, too. Instead, Bowie called on Harry Maslin, whom he had enlisted in January to produce the two late additions to *Young Americans*, a cover of The Beatles' 'Across The Universe' and 'Fame', both of which feature John Lennon. This came after Visconti had returned to Britain to mix what he had assumed was a completed album. Not only did Bowie and Maslin tinker with several of Visconti's 'final' mixes, they also removed two of his favourite songs from the sessions, replacing them with their flimsy Lennon-assisted creations. All of this might sound enough to have driven a wedge between Bowie and Visconti, but the good-natured producer denies any hard feelings, recalling in his recent autobiography that Bowie "genuinely felt bad"[21] about the situation.

For his part, Bowie claimed to have opted for Maslin because of the ad hoc nature of the sessions, suggesting that it would have been difficult to call Visconti back from London, where he had been working with groups such as Sparks, at short notice. But there remains a lingering suspicion that Visconti, like Mike Garson, had fallen victim –

albeit temporarily – to Bowie's desire to distance himself from anybody that he had worked with under his MainMan contract (Coco Schwab being the notable exception).

After a couple of weeks of rehearsal and the pulling together of song ideas, Bowie and his band went into Cherokee Studios on Fairfax Avenue, North Hollywood, to formally start work on what ended up as *Station To Station*. In the past, Bowie had become accustomed to recording his albums in a sprightly fashion, often between tours, and spending no more than two or three weeks on them. Now he had the luxury of time, afforded him both because of his previous album's worldwide success and the fact that he was no longer being man-managed by Tony DeFries. Although the momentum of his record-making had ground almost to a halt, Bowie's commercial stock was at its highest, with *Young Americans* his biggest international success to date. One of the late additions to the album, 'Fame', had given him his first US chart-topping single in June, despite a complete lack of promotion by Bowie or Lennon, while a double A-side reissue of 'Space Oddity' and 'Changes' became his first British Number One hit a few months later.

Although he was working to no particular deadline, Bowie was in no mood to take it easy. According to Harry Maslin, the general pattern for the sessions, which lasted until early December, was for Bowie to do three or four days of "very strenuous hours" and then "take a few days off to rest and get charged up for another sprint".[22] In one legendary instance, Bowie had already been working for 26 hours straight when he was asked, at 9am, to vacate Cherokee, as another act was booked in for the morning. Not wanting to lose the momentum, he led his band across town to the Record Plant, where they continued to work until midnight. Needless to say, these 'sprints' were fuelled by a lot more than creative adrenalin. His New Mexican sobriety fast becoming a distant memory, Bowie was back to the old L.A. diet of milk and cocaine. He grew ever more frail, claiming later to have dropped to little more than 80 pounds at several points in 1975. As before, his mental state suffered significantly as a consequence. "I was paranoid, manic depressive," he later told journalist and presenter Dave Fanning, summing up his symptoms as "the usual paraphernalia that comes with abuse of amphetamines and coke".[23]

Bowie was, of course, among the many rather than the few when it came to musicians working through a fog of cocaine during the 1970s. His bandmates, too, were similarly indulgent, a fact that Carlos Alomar later defended by explaining how "the coke use is driven by the inspiration … if there's a line of coke which is going to keep you awake until 8am so that you can do your guitar part, you do that line of coke, because it basically just keeps you up and keeps your mind bright".[24] But such was the level of Bowie's drug use at the time that he now says he recalls next to nothing of the making of *Station To Station*, claiming only to know that the record was cut in Los Angeles because he has subsequently read about it. Of the time spent recording the album, Bowie told Fanning that he remembered only one specific incident: screaming an approximation of the feedback sound he wanted for the beginning of the title track at guitarist Earl Slick, and "telling him to take a Chuck Berry riff and play it all the way through the solo".[25]

Station To Station established the working method that Bowie would employ on all three of his 'Berlin' albums, as well as other subsequent releases. He would arrive at the studio with little more than a couple of song fragments – in this case 'Word On A Wing' and 'Golden Years' – which he then handed over to bandleader Carlos Alomar. Alomar would then figure out several arrangements of each song with Dennis Davis and George Murray, from which Bowie would pick the one he liked best. These rhythm parts would be recorded quickly, while the ideas were still fresh and exciting to the players, before Bowie oversaw the more laborious process of overdubbing (which in the case of this album generally began with Alomar and Slick adding lead-guitar parts).

The fact that this was the first of Bowie's albums to be recorded on 24-track (and with no deadline) was both a blessing and a curse. It meant that numerous multi-tracked instrumental parts could be recorded and then left to tinker with later, where previously they would have had to have been nailed early on, and then mixed down; and Bowie and Maslin could tinker with layers of special effects, such as the rumbling train sounds that open the album.

But it also encouraged a tendency to overindulge the songs. Carlos Alomar was hardly exaggerating when he told Bowie biographer David Buckley, with some relish, that these sessions marked "the height of our experimental time". Bowie has since told of how he would "work at songs for hours and hours and days and days" only to realise later that "I'd only been rewriting the first four bars ... An obsession with detail had taken over."[26]

Bowie's obsessing over the details of what was originally to be called *The Return Of The Thin White Duke* was interrupted briefly in November by three television appearances that confirmed the depths to which he had fallen since returning to Los Angeles. On November 4th he was invited to perform on ABC-TV's *Soul Train*, making him only the second white artist ever to appear on the show (Elton John had beaten him to it by six months). He sang his recent US Number One, 'Fame', and the only completed track (so far) from the Cherokee studios sessions, 'Golden Years'. The song was reportedly first offered to, but rejected by, Elvis Presley, then in a terminal decline and without an American Top 10 hit since 1972's 'Burning Love'. Instead, despite the fact that the accompanying album was nowhere near ready, Bowie's version was rushed out to capitalize on his transatlantic marketability. It duly hit Number Ten on the US chart and Number Eight in Britain.

His performance of 'Golden Years' on *Soul Train* shows neither him nor the song in the greatest of lights. The version that aired was the best of several fluffed takes, in the midst of which the show's host, Don Cornelius, took Bowie to one side and told him to pull himself together, reminding him of how many other musicians would kill to be in his position. Prior to performing his songs, Bowie announced that he would "adore to answer" questions from Cornelius and the audience. He confessed a few weeks later that "I was very nervous so I had a couple of drinks",[27] which might account for his wayward performance and often unintelligible responses during the interview segment (when asked, for example, about his move towards soul music, he rambled disconnectedly about "poppin' 'em" as a teenager and how "we have street corners in London").

Later in November, on the 23rd, Bowie made a less auspicious and rather incongruous appearance on *The Cher Show*, singing 'Fame' and two duets with the show's host: 'Can You Hear Me' and a medley that took in his own 'Young Americans' mixed in with past hits such as 'Blue Moon' and 'Day Tripper'. Five days later, he was interviewed via satellite by the British talk-show host Russell Harty. The interview is perhaps most notable for the backstage shenanigans that preceded it. At the time, satellite link-ups were by no means commonplace, and had to be booked in advance. Bowie was asked to relinquish his slot in order that the Spanish government be able to announce the death of Generalissimo Franco, but refused, apparently deeming himself, and his announcement that he would be touring Europe and America during the first half of 1976, to be of more importance.

Russell Harty gave British audiences their first look at the new Bowie, with his crimson hair slicked sharply back and his extravagant costumes of old replaced by a stark white shirt. It also offered a taster of *The Man Who Fell To Earth*, for which Bowie announced (as he had on *Soul Train*) that he would be providing the soundtrack music. In conversation with Harty, Bowie seemed as frosty and uncomfortable as he had a year earlier on *The Dick Cavett Show* – only this time the discomfort was accentuated by the delay as each waited for the satellite link to relay the other's words. Whether being asked about his live act, image, or spiritual leanings, Bowie was defensive and evasive, answering in riddles about how "this Thursday is nothing like last Thursday but it's just as important. I'd miss it if it wasn't after Wednesday". He chided Harty at one point for not contributing enough to the conversation, and bristled when the subject of the interview turned to his wife and son: "He's a child … he's as bright as any child should be at four-and-a-half. He's not a prodigy of any kind, thank God."

Having completed his media obligations for the year, Bowie returned to Cherokee to put the finishing touches to *Station To Station*. The completed album contains only six songs, one of them a cover, and runs to only 38 minutes. It is not his most influential album, nor his most popular, but is among the most rewarding and engaging of his career. Many would cite *Ziggy Stardust* or *Low* as Bowie's single greatest achievement on LP but, pound for pound, *Station To Station* is at least their equal, if not their better.

Musically, *Station To Station* sits almost exactly between what preceded it, *Young Americans*, and what was to come next, *Low*. If *Young Americans* was Bowie's attempt at making a fairly straight American soul record, *Station To Station* sees him take those influences and make them his own. The rhythm'n'blues rhythms are still present, but are harder and tauter than before, while rock'n'roll theatricality makes its return in the form of razor-sharp guitar riffs and extravagant piano parts. At the top of the mountain sits Bowie himself, introducing the world to the cold, hard Thin White Duke and his disembodied, faux-Sinatra croon.

The opening title track is the longest and most complex song in a 40-year catalogue of repeatedly epic, finely detailed material, its ten minutes telling the listener more about the David Bowie of 1975 than any number of pronouncements by or about the man ever could. The song begins, fittingly, with the sound of approaching locomotives, whistles and all, which Bowie had found on an old sound-effects record and subjected to harsh equalization and phasing effects. (The mix was conceived with the shortlived vogue for quadraphonic sound in mind; even now, reduced back to stereo, the train sounds feel as though they could burst through your speakers.) Earl Slick's pleading feedback glides into view next, gradually augmented by Bowie's tight but emotive rhythm men. Roy Bittan is first up to the plate, his lonely bar-room piano tick-tocking from major to minor before being anchored by George Murray's roomy bass, a sweet, funky Carlos Alomar guitar line, and the rock solid drumming of Dennis Davis.

All five stay locked in the cyclic groove of 'Station To Station' for what seems like an age before Bowie's voice – the same as ever and yet, as always, completely different – arrives on three minutes. The song's relentless rhythm has often been likened to the 'motorik' sound of the leading German groups of the time, of which Kraftwerk were the frontrunners, and which was an undoubted influence on Bowie's latest stylistic shift. But where Kraftwerk aspired towards order and precision, 'Station To Station' has a markedly more human feel, more in common with other less robotic German acts of the time, such as Neu! and Can, or even the jazz-rock fusion of Miles Davis's late-1960s group. Dennis Davis's drumming might be metronomic, but is keenly felt, while Murray's bass is responsive rather than restrictive.

When Bowie himself finally joins the fray, he unfurls perhaps the most convoluted and multi-layered lyric of his career. He has since noted that the title refers to the stations of the cross (and not Kraftwerk's *Trans Europe Express*, as is often wrongly assumed, which actually came out a year later). The bulk of the lyric comprises a somewhat rudimentary, if undeniably poetic, guide to the Kabbalah (a strand of Jewish Gnostic mysticism), focusing on the Tree Of Life, which describes the nature of God, His creation of the world, and the Gnostic myth of the Fall. At one point, Bowie notes a "magical movement" from Kether, the Crown Of Creation, to Malkuth, the Kingdom (or the physical world). Kether and Malkuth mark the opposite ends of the Tree Of Life, a diagram of which Bowie can be seen drawing in the sleeve notes to the 1999 CD reissue of *Station To Station*. Elsewhere in the song, Bowie misquotes Shakespeare – Prospero's line from *The Tempest*, "We are such stuff as dreams are made on" becoming "Such is the stuff from where dreams are woven"

– and renews his acquaintance with Aleister Crowley, first by "throwing darts in lovers eyes" – perhaps a reference to an incident in 1918 in which Crowley's followers killed a young couple by throwing darts at them – and then by name-checking Crowley's book *White Stains*.

Five minutes in, 'Station To Station' shifts gear into what Harry Maslin has said was originally another song altogether, a looser, funkier workout propelled by juddering piano chords that arrive just before the beat. Charles Shaar Murray of the *New Musical Express* later noted that "if Bowie was James Brown he could well have entitled the second, up-tempo half [of the song] 'Diamond Dogs '76'".[28] The key lyric here is Bowie's dubious claim that "It's not the side-effects of the cocaine / I'm thinking that it must be love", which perhaps brings the confused meanderings of the first half of the song into focus. The final four minutes are built around Bowie's almost shrieking, mantra-like cry that "It's too late / To be hateful / The European canon is here." That last line is both an acknowledgment of the return to prominence, in Bowie's eyes at least, of European music, and an indication of his desire to return to the continent. "Towards the end of my stay in America," he told *Melody Maker*'s Allan Jones two years later, "I realised that what I had to do was experiment. To discover new forms of writing. To evolve, in fact, a new musical language. That's what I set out to do. That's why I returned to Europe."[29]

The rest of *Station To Station* is, thankfully, somewhat easier to digest. The warm, slinky 'Golden Years' has certain mystical overtones but is, essentially, a love song to Bowie's "angel": Angela Bowie believed this to be her husband's attempt to repair their crumbling marriage; Ava Cherry, whose relationship with the singer ended just before he began filming *The Man Who Fell To Earth*, thought the song was about her. It doesn't make a lot of difference either way; 'Golden Years' is in essence a final slab of 'plastic soul' in the *Young Americans* vein, and one of Bowie's most naggingly addictive mid-1970s hits. It is followed on the album by something of a curio, 'Word On A Wing', a soft ballad driven by bright piano chords and melodic lead-guitar, on which Bowie seems to have found God: "Lord I kneel and offer you my word on a wing / And I'm trying hard to fit among your scheme of things." How genuine (or not) Bowie is here is unclear – his sentiments certainly jar with his treatise on the Kabbalah two songs earlier, although he could perhaps have been leaving the door ajar, just in case his dabblings with black magic went awry. It's just as probable, coming from an ideological chameleon such as Bowie, that the repentant Christian might just have been another role to play. Even those in the studio with him at the time were unsure: Interviewed shortly after the album's release, Harry Maslin could only offer that he didn't think Bowie was "into any specific kind of religion", while Earl Slick simply wondered, "who knows what he's thinking?"[30]

The second half of *Station To Station* throws up three more contrasting songs. The first, 'TVC15' is the most throwaway, a punch-drunk sing-along clearly inspired by the memorable *Man Who Fell To Earth* scenes in which Bowie, as Thomas Newton, is captivated by a wall of television screens all showing various different programmes at once. It's not the greatest thing Bowie has ever recorded, but not as bad as some might suggest either. ('TVC15' ended up being the second single to be drawn from the album, but wasn't anywhere near as successful, or memorable, as 'Golden Years.') Next up is 'Stay', which makes good on the hints at a disco sound present on *Young Americans*, and features white-hot guitar interplay between Slick and Alomar. Dennis Davis and George Murray are in their element here too, providing a joyous, stop-start backing to what is actually quite a tortured (if unremarkable) vocal. *Station To Station* closes with a reading of 'Wild Is The Wind', a magisterial ballad by Dimitri Tiomkin and Ned Washington that Bowie apparently recorded in homage to Nina Simone's sparser rendition of the song, the title track on one of several albums she made in 1965. Keen, as ever, to show himself to be not just a great singer and songwriter but a fine interpreter of other people's material, Bowie puts in one of the greatest vocal performances of his career, feeling his way cautiously around Tiomkin's tender melody. The instrumental backing has a similarly stately, romantic feel, providing a fitting climax to an album driven by a search for spiritual and emotional fulfilment.

In late 1971 the *New Musical Express* called Sly & The Family Stone's magnum opus *There's A Riot Goin' On* "one of the most drugged-sounding albums yet to be released". Just over four years later, Bowie's *Station To Station* could easily have challenged that title, given the mood in which it was conceived and the length and extravagance of its songs. Instead it stands alongside the great pop, rock, and disco discs of the era, because – even with his mind blistered by chemicals and Gnosticism – Bowie was canny enough to render it in dazzlingly bright Technicolor. It is, as the esteemed music critic Ian MacDonald later wrote, "one of Bowie's most glamorous discs",[31] and a suitably populist successor to his great US breakthrough, *Young Americans*. Bowie himself later suggested that his decision to mix it in such a way was a commercially minded cop-out, and that the cold, dry sound of *Low* is an indicator of how he should have left *Station To Station*. Had it ended up like this, however, the album might have sounded like the wild ravings of a drug-addled megalomaniac. As it is, it just sounds wild.

After signing off on *Station To Station* in early December Bowie turned his full attention to another project, one on which he had already made a tentative start and had been talking up during his recent television appearances: the soundtrack to *The Man Who Fell To Earth*. For this he retained the core rhythm players of his band, but also brought in Paul Buckmaster, who had arranged the string parts for 'Space Oddity' some years earlier. Sessions took place both at Cherokee studios, where J. Peter Robinson (now a composer of music for film and television) came in on Fender Rhodes electric piano, and Buckmaster played cello and synthesizer. Further recordings were made at Bowie's Bel Air home, during which he and Buckmaster, inspired by Kraftwerk's recent *Autobahn* and *Radioactivity*, experimented with more obtuse song structures and electronic instrumentation, including an ARP Odyssey and an early Japanese drum machine. Buckmaster has since described the results as producing a mix of "medium-tempo" instrumental rock, "slow and spacey cues with synth, Rhodes, and cello", and "a couple of weirder, atonal cues using synths and percussion".[32]

Ultimately, however, the music Bowie, Buckmaster, and company created was not used in *The Man Who Fell To Earth*. Reports have since suggested that Bowie wanted more money to complete the project than the film's producers were willing to offer; the singer himself says he pulled out in a rage after being told that his was not the only music being considered for the film, and that his work would be weighed up against other prospective candidates' offerings. It has also been claimed that Nicolas Roeg, the director, simply didn't consider Bowie's efforts suitable for the film. (In the end Roeg hired The Mamas & The Papas' John Phillips, who provided a winning mix of quirky Americana, golden oldies by Bing Crosby and Artie Shaw, and otherworldly instrumentals by the Japanese composer and percussionist Stomu Yamashta.)

There might well be an element of truth in each of these suggestions, but in the end it seems most likely that the music Bowie and Buckmaster made was simply not good enough. Both Michael Lippman and Harry Maslin have suggested that Bowie was in no fit state to be making music by the end of the *Station To Station* sessions – particularly for this kind of project, which involved working to strict cues and time constraints. Paul Buckmaster, meanwhile, has since confessed that his efforts, like Bowie's, were hampered by heavy cocaine use, and that the music they produced was "just not up to the standard of composing and performance needed for a good movie score".[33] Few of the songs were in anything approaching a state of completion when they were played to Roeg and the film's producers in December 1975. Intriguingly, Roeg gave Mike Flood Page of *Street Life* a preview of one track – a simple melodic instrumental based around organ, bass, and drums, according to Page's subsequent article – during an interview about the film conducted around the turn of the year. But this was the closest Bowie's soundtrack got to a public airing; the project was swiftly abandoned, with the official line blaming 'contractual entanglements', and the tapes have never been released.

Bowie's aborted film soundtrack might have ended up as a brief, forgotten footnote were it not that his attempts to record it inaugurated a whole new way of working. His next three albums – *Low*, *"Heroes"*, and *Lodger* – were all made alongside Brian Eno, who is often credited with moving Bowie's music towards wordless soundscapes and electronic instrumentation. But the *Man Who Fell To Earth* soundtrack sessions demonstrate that, rather than being one of Eno's many disciples, Bowie was his peer, having already started working on moody, instrumental, *ambient* textures of his own long before the pair of them began their self-proclaimed 'Berlin Triptych'.

The link between the music recorded by Bowie and Buckmaster and the songs Bowie cut the following year with Eno is sometimes overstated, but at least one *Low* track, 'Subterraneans', started out as an idea for the soundtrack. Bowie clearly saw a parallel between the two projects: he played the unfinished soundtrack tapes to the musicians who worked with him on *Low*, and dressed the sleeve of that album in an altered still for the movie. (A variation of the same image had already been used on the front of a tie-in edition of the Walter Tevis novel that inspired the film; *Station To Station*, too, wears a still from the film on its sleeve.) Even more tellingly, Nicolas Roeg would later receive an advance copy of *Low* alongside a note that said, simply: *This is what I wanted to do for the soundtrack.*

GOING ROUND & ROUND

In general terms, David Bowie's 1976 began in much the same way as had his 1975. On the one hand, he had just completed an album that marked a significant artistic leap forward from its predecessor; on the other, he was on the verge of sacking another manager, and needed desperately to escape from an American megalopolis that threatened to swallow whole a man ravaged by cocaine abuse and borderline anorexia.

Michael Lippman, a former lawyer and close confidant of Bowie's during his two-year stay in the USA, had taken over as the singer's manager during the early months of 1975, following the protracted sacking of Tony DeFries. But by the end of the year Bowie had grown disillusioned with Lippman, too. Bowie had been irritated by what he perceived to be ineffective management during the collapse of the deal for him to score *The Man Who Fell To Earth*, but the final straw came when he arrived in Ocho Rios, Jamaica, at Christmas, to begin rehearsals – in Keith Richards's studio on the island – for the 1976 Station To Station / White Light tour: Lippman, it seems, had forgotten to arrange any accommodation for Bowie and his band in Jamaica, much to the singer's annoyance. Bowie ended up having to stay at Richards's house. He called Lippman from there and informed him that his services were no longer required.

Bowie initiated legal proceedings against Lippman on January 27th 1976, claiming that Lippman had unlawfully withheld almost $500,000 of the singer's earnings; Lippman countersued for lost earnings of $2 million. The case would not be resolved for another nine months, and became another source of unwanted anxiety for Bowie right through the making of *Low*. Lippman eventually won, but he did not receive as much of a settlement as he had hoped. It is difficult, still, to gauge the veracity of either Bowie or Lippman's grievances; what is likely is that Bowie's falling out with his manager had as much to do with his overall feelings of self-loathing and paranoia at the time – just as had been the case with Tony DeFries's sacking – as anything else. Two years later, Lippman told *Crawdaddy* magazine that the singer's "very weak mental state [was] what caused our relationship to break down". He recalled "dramatically erratic behaviour" and noted that the singer was "overworked and under a lot of pressure, and unable to accept the realities of certain facts".[1]

In any event, Michael Lippman ended up being Bowie's final manager, at least in a conventional sense. From then on, the singer trimmed his entourage down to a close-knit foursome: Coco Schwab continued as his personal assistant; former head of payroll Patrick Gibbons took care of day-to-day business management; Barbara Le Witt handled press and publicity; and Tony Mascia – Bowie's driver in real life and in *The Man Who Fell To Earth* – was his bodyguard. The split with Lippman also hastened the departure of Earl Slick from Bowie's band: the guitarist had recently begun to take steps towards a solo career under Lippman's stewardship, prompting questions about his loyalty and commitment. (Slick returned to the fold for the 1983 Serious Moonlight tour, and was reunited with Bowie for a second time in the early 21st century.) For the Station To Station live shows, Slick was replaced by a 21-year-old unknown from Canada, Stacey Heydon. Tony Kaye, a founding member of British prog-rock group Yes, took over on keyboards from Roy Bittan, who had prior commitments in Bruce Springsteen's E-Street Band; Carlos Alomar, Dennis Davis, and

George Murray remained from the album sessions, completing Bowie's smallest and most musically intuitive backing group since The Spiders From Mars.

Immediately after the New Year, the ten-strong David Bowie organisation travelled to New York for the taping of the January 3rd edition of Dinah Shore's CBS chat show, *Dinah!* The band debuted the blistering 'Stay' and performed a show-stopping rendition of 'Five Years' either side of what was, by comparison with other recent media appearances, a fairly unremarkable interview with Bowie, who seemed eager to behave in a polite and respectable manner among his fellow interviewees – actors Nancy Walker and Henry Winkler, and singer Natalie Cole. Most surreally of all, he found himself being given a karate lesson during the show, telling his instructor that his first response to an assailant attempting to strangle him would be to "scream very loudly".

January's only promotional obligation fulfilled, Bowie spent the rest of the month in New York, rehearsing and devising a theme for his upcoming tour.

Just over a week before opening night – February 2nd in Vancouver, British Columbia, Canada – Bowie unveiled *Station To Station*. Its release was delayed by his decision to tone down the original, full-colour sleeve in favour of a starker, monochromatic version of the same image – a treated still from *The Man Who Fell To Earth* of Bowie/Newton entering a soundproofed chamber – better suited to both the music and his forthcoming black-and-white stage production. (Strange, then, that he chose to revert to the colour print for later CD editions.) The album was an even greater success than *Young Americans*: it hit Number Three in America, and Number Five in Britain, and met with acclaim from the majority of critics on both sides of the Atlantic. Most strikingly, *Melody Maker*'s Allan Jones heralded "one of the most significant albums released in the last five years", drawing particular attention to "a commentary on the spiritual malaise of this decade [as] powerful as anything by Thomas Pynchon". Richard

Cromelin of *Circus* magazine applauded "the most challenging leg of [Bowie's] winding journey", while the more pop-orientated *Record Mirror & Disc* enjoyed what was, "very simply, a fine album". *Rolling Stone's* Teri Moris was a little more cautious, commending Bowie's evolving musicality but noting a lack of "the obsessively passionate conviction of his earlier works". Among the detractors, John Rowntree of *Records & Recording* dismissed the album as "a white rocker's bad misunderstanding of black rhythm ... disfigured with portentous solos by mediocre guitarists and unnecessarily overlaid psychedelia". If anything, *Station To Station's* reputation has only grown over the years. In 1999, no less an authority than Brian Eno called it "one of the great records of all time".

The tour that accompanied the album was something of a paradox. It remains among the most acclaimed and artistically successful of Bowie's many world tours, but also contributed further to his physical and emotional decline. There is some doubt as to whether he even wanted to tour at all: less than two weeks in, he was already complaining to *Hit Parader* journalist Lisa Robinson that he was "a little bored" and merely "doing it for the money". He had begun to realise, while in Jamaica, that he needed to get away from Los Angeles and the life he led there. As he recalled in 1996, "I was lucky enough to know somewhere within me that I really was killing myself, and that I had to do something drastic to pull myself out of that."

Fortunately, a plan had been hatched on his behalf in that regard by Stan Diamond, a lawyer colleague of Bowie's soon-to-be ex-manager, Michael Lippman. With a $300,000 tax bill looming, Diamond suggested that Bowie move to Switzerland – a land of significantly lower taxes and, as the singer's wife later noted, a relative lack of "demons and witches and roadies with bags full of cocaine".[2] Angela Bowie went to boarding school in Switzerland, and would now use her connections there to negotiate residency – and a favourable tax rate – for her husband, and find them a home in the small town of Blonay, above Lake Geneva. (In reality, David would spend little time there, but it would serve as his 'official' home until midway through the 1980s.)

The last time David Bowie embarked on a world tour, it had been as part of 1974's extravagant, theatrical Diamond Dogs production, which was so involved that it required weeks of choreographed rehearsals and the construction of a $250,000 backdrop, dubbed Hunger City, based on Robert Wiene's 1919 classic of German expressionist cinema, *The Cabinet Of Doctor Caligari*. By contrast, the Station To Station shows were as stark and slick as Bowie's latest incarnation, The Thin White Duke, a cruel, Aryan crooner whom Bowie later summed up as "a would-be romantic with no emotion at all".[3] (Not coincidentally, such an epithet would also be apt to describe Thomas Jerome Newton, Bowie's character in *The Man Who Fell To Earth* – a clear and present influence on his latest musical role, if not in dress then unarguably in mood.)

Instead of a warm-up act, attendees of the Station To Station shows were treated to a screening of *Un Chien Andalou*, a 1922 art film by Luis Buñuel and Salvador Dali, famed for the sequence in which a razor blade slices through an eyeball, backed by the sounds of Kraftwerk's recent *Radio-Activity* LP. Kraftwerk and Buñuel were rather perverse choices, given that the tour called at such vast venues as the Englewood Forum in Los Angeles and New York's Madison Square Garden, and tore through great swathes of Middle America. But then Bowie always had, and still has, an almost childlike enthusiasm for thrusting his latest discoveries on anyone available to look or listen – an admirable quality most of the time, but one perhaps not best suited to the million hordes in Milwaukee's Mecca Arena.

With his audience sufficiently enlightened by surrealist art and modernist techno, Bowie sent his band out onto a stage bathed in bright white light – "the most imaginative use of lighting at a rock concert I have ever seen," according to *Melody Maker*'s Michael Watts. The backing musicians had played behind a screen on the Diamond Dogs tour, but were now allowed back into view – as were their instruments, amplifiers, and all manner of cables. Each night's performance began with 'Station To Station', which allowed the main man to ramp up audience expectation by delaying his arrival onstage: he gave the band ample time to work up the song's tense, feedback-laden introduction before striding on in neat black trousers and waistcoat and starched white shirt, his red hair slicked back, like a Nietzschean Sinatra. The rest of the Duke's set was made up of tracks from the current album – apart from 'Golden Years', which he struggled to sing in the right key – and an even assortment of past favourites, including 'Changes', 'Five Years', 'The Jean Genie', and 'Fame'. 'Space Oddity' was defiantly left out, with Bowie telling *Hit Parader*'s Lisa Robinson that he'd "rather the energy level came from the eye line [than] an association with any particular piece of theatre". There was room, however, for a pumped-up take on The Velvet Underground's 'Waiting For The Man' and an embryonic 'Sister Midnight', which ended up a year later on Iggy Pop's Bowie-produced solo debut, *The Idiot*.

Bowie's North American jaunt worked its way down the West Coast during the first week of February, stopping at Seattle, Portland, and San Francisco before the singer arrived – for what would be the last time in quite a while – in his adopted home, Los Angeles. His three-night stand at the Englewood Forum on the 8th, 9th, and 11th attracted an impressive roster of celebrity fans and admirers, among them Alice Cooper, Carole King, David Hockney, Elton John, Ray Bradbury, Linda Blair, Patti Smith, and Steven Ford, the son of the incumbent US President. Perhaps the most crucial attendee of these gigs, however, was the writer Christopher Isherwood, to whom Bowie was introduced backstage on the third night by Hockney.

Although he has never been held in as high a regard as some of his friends and peers, among whom were WH Auden, Tennessee Williams, and Truman Capote, Isherwood was an important and influential writer. With a certain degree of serendipity, he found himself in the midst of some of the key times and places of the inter- and post-war years, to such an extent that John Bate of *The Daily Telegraph* recently described his life as "a microcosm of the 20th century".[4] Born into a wealthy, respected family in England in 1904, Isherwood studied at Corpus Christi College, Cambridge, before being reintroduced to an old school friend, the young poet Wystan Hugh Auden, who became his long-term friend, confidant, and sometime lover. In 1928 he and Auden travelled to Berlin, encouraged by the city's Weimar-era decadence and tolerance of homosexuality.

Auden returned to Britain after nine months, but Isherwood remained in Berlin for much of the 1930s, working as an English tutor while writing his most famous, semi-autobiographical works, *Mr Norris Changes Trains* (1935) and the short-story collection *Goodbye To Berlin* (1939), against the backdrop of Hilter's rise to power. *Goodbye To Berlin* was turned into a play, *I Am A Camera*, by John Van Druten in 1951, which itself then inspired *Cabaret*, the Broadway musical and Oscar-winning film.

Isherwood spent less time in Germany as the decade progressed, travelling to Denmark, Portugal, and China at various points while collaborating with Auden on a book about the Sino-Japanese War and three plays. On the eve of World War II, he and Auden, having briefly returned to Britain, emigrated to the United States, sailing to New York in January 1939 to the consternation of many back home, who saw the move as decidedly unpatriotic. (Auden was later questioned by both MI5 and the FBI about his links with Guy Burgess, a Soviet spy during the early years of the Cold War.) After a few months, Isherwood moved again, to Hollywood, leaving Auden on the East Coast and effectively ending their relationship. In California, Isherwood fell into a new creative circle that included Aldous Huxley and the philosophers Bertrand Russell and Gerald Heard; he also befriended Ray Bradbury and Igor Stravinsky.

Like Bowie, Isherwood went on a journey of spiritual discovery in California, having been introduced by Heard to Swami Prabhavananda, one of the senior monks at the Hindu Vedanta Society. This religious conversion inspired a series of lesser works such as *An Approach To Vedanta* and *Ramakrishna And His Disciples*. Isherwood, like Auden, is generally considered to have produced his best work during the first half of his life, but was still well thought of in the 1970s, by which time he had been living for two decades in Santa Monica with Don Bachardy, an artist 30 years his junior, with whom he would remain until his death in 1986. Shortly before he came to meet David Bowie, a compilation of his Berlin stories had been reissued as *The Berlin Of Sally Bowles* (Bowles being one of the principal characters in *Goodbye To Berlin*).

By all accounts, Bowie and Isherwood spoke at some length after the February 11th gig at the Englewood Forum. For the most part, this involved Bowie probing the writer with questions about Berlin, principally in relation to its atmosphere of decadence and artistic liberty, which, by way of *Cabaret*, had already informed the mood of the Station To Station tour. Berlin already sat at the top of Bowie's list of potential new homes, so it's not hard to see why he was so keen to meet the original 'Englishman abroad'. Although Isherwood reportedly told Bowie that Berlin was by no means as exciting a place as his writings from the 1930s suggested, the singer seemed sold on the idea of moving there. By the end of the year, he would be living within a mile of where Isherwood had lived in Berlin; the city would have much the same effect on Bowie as it did on Isherwood, driving him to produce the greatest and most influential work of his career.

Bowie cleared out his Bel Air home prior to leaving Los Angeles, symbolically drawing a line under his time there. Fittingly, the day he left L.A., February 12th, also marked the publication of Cameron Crowe's *Rolling Stone* interview – the most detailed and revealing contemporary portrait of Bowie's dark days in Southern California. But this was by no means a clean break. Although he had decided to leave Los Angeles, he was still hooked on cocaine and still living on the edge of psychosis. And it was not as though Bowie could leap straight into the new life of isolation, anonymity, and creative fulfilment that he so craved: there was still the matter of the four-month, 65-date tour he had just begun – hardly an environment conducive to physical and emotional recovery.

Even so, the American leg of the Station To Station tour was a great artistic and commercial success, and passed almost without incident. Almost, that is, because in the early hours of March 21st, Bowie and three friends – including Iggy Pop, who had been part of the Bowie entourage since the L.A. stopover and was easing himself back into musical life as a backing singer on the tour – were arrested at the Flagship Americana hotel in Rochester, New York, after being found to be in possession of eight ounces of marijuana. The arrest was somewhat ironic, and more than a little fortunate, given the kind of substances Bowie was actually into at the time. Bowie, Iggy, and two others – named in police reports as Dwaine Vaughs, a member of Bowie's touring entourage, and Chiwah Soo, a young woman from Rochester – spent a few hours in Monroe County Jail, before Bowie paid the $2,000 bail for each of them to be released. (Bowie told the Rochester police that he was David Jones of 89 Oakley St., London, England.) The singer immediately protested his innocence and, at the same time, pointed the finger elsewhere. "Rest assured the stuff was not mine," he told Cameron Crowe. "I can't say very much more, but it did belong to the others in the room that we were busted in. Bloody potheads."[5] While sensationalist local press reports claimed that Bowie faced "a minimum of 15 years' imprisonment"[6] after his date in court on March 25th, the case was in fact adjourned, and then quietly dropped. The night after his appearance at Rochester City Court, Bowie concluded his US tour with a sold-out performance at New York City's Madison Square Garden, after which he held a small party at a club in the city and set sail for Europe.

Three days before the Rochester drugs bust, on the other side of the Atlantic, *The Man Who Fell To Earth* had its world premiere in Leicester Square, London. Bowie's touring commitments meant that he was unable to attend, but most of the rest of the cast and crew were there (as was his wife). The film was generally well received by critics, particularly in Britain, where billboards appeared later in the spring that announced Bowie as the renaissance-man star of the cinema, the record player, and the concert hall. In the USA, the film's widespread appeal was stunted by the decision of the American distributor, Cinema 5, to cut 20 minutes from its runtime – both to bring it down to a more palatable two hours and to rid it of most of the sexual content which, while graphic, is largely key to the story. The original version of *The Man Who Fell To Earth*, which director Nicolas Roeg and editor Graeme Clifford had spent nine months piecing together, is hardly the most linear of films to begin with; by lopping great chunks of it out with little consideration for mood or plot, Cinema 5 rendered it even less intelligible (which is perhaps why the distinguished critic Roger Ebert lamented its "gaps of logic and credibility"). Candy Clark bailed out of promoting the streamlined version of the film after a couple of days, later claiming that the butchery of Roeg's cut made her sick; Bowie too later complained that the rough editing brought the film "to its knees".

If the film itself received a somewhat mixed response, its principal star was heralded pretty much unanimously as having made a highly successful transition from singing to acting. *The New Yorker*'s Pauline Kael led the charge, hailing Bowie as "the most romantic figure in recent pictures". He was immediately linked to roles in other films, including a proposed Frank Sinatra biopic and *The Eagle Has Landed*, John Sturges's well-liked World War II drama, which Bowie would have starred in had the shooting of it not clashed with his current tour. Ultimately, however, his film career since has been somewhat erratic. Thomas Jerome Newton remains as his greatest acting role, mostly because Bowie was so well suited to play Newton that he barely had to act at all. He starred next in David Hemmings's *Schöner Gigolo, Armer Gigolo* (*Just A Gigolo*) as a Prussian soldier returning to Berlin after the First World War; the film was so poorly received that Bowie later dismissed it as a significant misstep. Since then he has appeared in around two dozen other films, taking both leading roles and brief cameos that range from the Goblin King in Jim Henson's fantastical *Labyrinth* (1988) to a convincing Andy Warhol in *Basquiat* (1995). *The Man Who Fell To Earth*, meanwhile, has grown in reputation in the three decades since its cinematic release. It is now considered to be one of the most inventive science fiction films of its time, and an important forerunner to other big-screen fables of aliens and alienation, among them *E.T. The Extra Terrestrial*, which is often thought, like *The Man Who Fell To Earth*, to reflect the life of Christ.

The European leg of the Station To Station tour was much more eventful than the US trek that preceded it. It began with six dates in Germany, which gave Bowie a good opportunity to explore more fully his latest prospective homeland. After two further shows in Switzerland, there were no gigs for a week, so Bowie decided to travel by train to the next date – in Helsinki – via Warsaw and Moscow with Iggy Pop, Coco Schwab, and a few others in tow. On the way up to Russia, the Bowie party was detained at the border town of Brest whilst their luggage was searched by Russian customs officials, who were reported to have confiscated Bowie's latest controversial reading material: books about Joseph Goebbels, the Nazi Minister For Public Enlightenment And Propaganda, and by Albert Speer, the so-called 'first architect' of the Third Reich. (Speer was also the only prominent Nazi to later admit guilt and express remorse.)

Bowie subsequently claimed that he had been carrying these books with him as they were key reference materials for a film he was planning about Goebbels. That may have been the case – like many of his 'film projects' of the time, it never came to fruition – but what is clear is that this was the first of several inflammatory incidents over the course of the next few weeks that would raise serious questions about Bowie's moral and political leanings (not to mention his mental state). This was not the first time Bowie's interest in Hitler and Nazism had come to light: he had gone off on several coke-fuelled tangents in interviews the year before about how Hitler was a "marvellous morale-booster"[7], and how the *Young Americans* track 'Somebody Up There Likes Me' is about how "Hitler's on his way back"[8]. But now he was about to move beyond merely showing an interest in this particular area of German history to seemingly declaring a sympathy and affinity for its key players.

Just over a week after the incident on the Russian-Polish border, Bowie was pursued by a dogged interviewer after performing in Stockholm, Sweden, on April 26th. Responding to a battery of questions about his political leanings, Bowie reportedly answered: "As I see it, I am the only alternative for the premier in England. I believe Britain could benefit from a fascist leader. After all, fascism is really nationalism." A week later, Bowie backtracked, weakly, in an interview with Jean Rook of the UK's *Daily Express* newspaper, not quite able to confirm that he had definitely said such a thing, and offering in response only that he is "not sinister" and "not a great force – well not that sort of force". By then, however, a much greater controversy had been set into motion.

On the afternoon of Sunday, May 2nd, 1976, David Bowie returned to Britain, for the first time in two years, on a chartered hovercraft from Ostend. He was met at Victoria Station in London by a large gathering of fans and press for what was intended to be a victorious homecoming, on the eve of a six-night stand at the Wembley Empire Pool, which would see him play to 50,000 fans – his first full-scale UK gigs since Ziggy Stardust's 'retirement' in July 1973. The singer's record label hoped for him to make a speech on arrival, but the PA system malfunctioned, so Bowie was unable to address the crowd, and ended up staying and waving to fans for less than a minute. Before he left, however, he was captured by a photographer in the middle of an apparently stiff-armed wave from the back of his open-topped car.

Nobody present at the time seems to have felt there to have been anything sinister (to use Bowie's term) about the wave – not even the many non-music journalists who had gathered at Victoria specifically because of Bowie's pronouncements in Sweden. None of them saw fit, either, to report anything as reprehensible as a Nazi salute in their respective newspapers the following day. The controversy only came when the *New Musical Express* printed an image of Bowie mid-'salute' beneath the headline 'Heil And Farewell' in its May 8th edition – albeit without any suggestion of anything untoward in the accompanying article by Tony Stewart, who seemed more irritated that Bowie had "buggered off without so much as saying hello". A week later, Max Bell in the same publication noted that Bowie's political ideas were "unformulated and simplistic", and that he simply seemed to enjoy "giving dumb reporters controversial answers to leading questions".

The rest of the British music press seem to have ignored the incident entirely (at least for the time being), leaving it to the tabloids to debate Bowie's supposed fascist tendencies, their fires stoked by recycled quotes from the past few years, not least the singer's declaration to Cameron Crowe that "Adolf Hitler was one of the first rock stars".[9] Reviews of the Wembley gigs, which were among the finest and most rapturously received of Bowie's career, began to note "Nuremberg overtones".[10] The UK's far-right National Front organisation's *Bulldog* newspaper gleefully adopted Bowie, despite the fact that, when given the chance to fully expound upon his admittedly ill-judged political views, he declared that a fascist uprising in Britain would be useful only if it swept the cobwebs away before promptly being removed. (Ironically, Bowie's views, coupled with a racist pronouncement by a drunken Eric Clapton a few months later, prompted the founding of the Rock Against Racism campaign during the winter of 1976.)

Much ink has been spent on Bowie's alleged fascist sympathies in the 30 years since his untimely wave at Victoria Station. Undoubtedly scarred by the way he had been dealt with in the fallout of that incident, the singer himself did not speak to the British press for close to a year and a half. When he was eventually interviewed by Allan Jones of *Melody Maker* in October 1977 he flatly and furiously denied having given a Nazi salute. "That did not happen," he said. "On the life of my child, I waved. And the bastard caught me. In mid-wave, man. ... I died when I saw that photo." On the subject of his alleged far-right sympathies, he was similarly adamant, claiming only to have made "two or three glib, theatrical observations on English society … I am NOT a fascist. I'm apolitical." Even so, the issue was not one that would just die down at the end of a news-cycle. Bowie has found himself having to explain and apologise time and again in the years since, always with grace and courtesy.

That David Bowie became unhealthily interested in Nazi ideology during the mid 1970s is undeniable, as is the fact that a number of his drug-fuelled pronouncements of the time crossed well beyond the bounds of good taste. There is no excuse for his deeply misguided behaviour during 1975–6, particularly if it is true, as has been alleged, that he gave a genuine Nazi salute at the site of Hitler's wartime bunker in Berlin. But the suggestion that he felt a real sympathy or affinity for far-right politics is misguided too. Fascism remains, quite rightly, among the modern world's greatest taboos, for reasons that are patently obvious. The flipside of that is a tendency for anything approaching – however obliquely – a far-right point of view to be leapt upon and condemned in a manner that is often disproportionate to (and ignorant of the context of) the original offence.

Bowie's interest in fascism is symptomatic of the very aspect of his character that is most often praised: his near-constant desire to grow and change, from wide-eyed Brixton boy to Ziggy, the Actor, the Thin White Duke, the anonymous Berliner, the 1980s pop heavyweight, the everyman leader of Tin Machine, the dapper junglist, and beyond. "My whole professional life is an act," he told *People* magazine in 1976. "I slip from one guise to another very easily."[11] He had left school at 16 with almost no qualifications (a solitary O-level in art), but after that became something of an autodidact, never far from a book on some obscure subject or other, about which he would soon be spouting half-formed ideas to anyone who'd listen. As bandleader Carlos Alomar put it some years later, "He's a pseudo-intellectual. He is what he reads, and at that time in his life, he was reading so much bullshit."[12] Bowie's flirtations with fascism need to be taken, then, in the context of a man who, at other points in his life, has had a pronounced and seemingly all-encompassing interest in everything from Kabuki theatre to Maoist China to black magic and beyond – all of which then fed into the characters he played on stage, on record, and in interviews. He seemed to delight too in making contentious statements, just as the press delighted in dutifully writing them up. Tellingly, when asked by Cameron Crowe if he stood by everything he said, he replied: "Everything but the inflammatory remarks."[13]

Bowie's proclamations about Hitler and Britain's need for an iron-fisted ruler also need to be assessed in the context of his state of mind at the time. His drug use during the mid 1970s led him on a dark and confused path, leaving him so addled that, he later claimed, he simply didn't think to equate what fascinated him about the Nazis – principally their supposed Arthurian pursuit of the Holy Grail, and their ability to control the media – with anti-Semitism, concentration camps, and other such atrocities. Such a suggestion might seem a little dubious until you recall the incidents of burning black candles to ward off evil spirits and being terrified of Jimmy Page's mystical powers. He was not of sound mind.

Bowie had already left Britain, again, by the time the controversy surrounding his supposed fascism hit its peak. He had five more concert dates left to play in mainland Europe – one in Brussels, and two each in Rotterdam and Paris – after which he celebrated the end of the tour at the Alcazar club in the French capital in the company of Romy Haag, a semi-famous transsexual singer and nightclub owner straight out of Isherwood. From there Bowie travelled to Switzerland, where his wife Angela had set up a new family home, but he would not stay there long. The point of his return to Europe, as he had decided six months earlier, was "to experiment; to discover new forms of writing; to evolve, in fact, a new musical language"[14] – not something he could achieve while living in tax-exile luxury beside Lake Geneva. For that, he would need to lead an anonymous existence in a poor, rough part of a city ravaged by war and split into two distinct halves by occupying forces.

PART 2
NEW MUSIC:
NIGHT AND DAY

DUM DUM DAYS

At the end of the 1976 European tour, Bowie was officially set to move into the new family residence of Clos des Mésanges in Blonay, Switzerland, but in fact he barely lived there at all. According to his then wife, Angela, "Whenever I was [there], he wasn't, and vice versa". (She spent a lot of her time in London, while he tended to book into a nearby hotel whenever his wife came back to Switzerland.) A life of quiet contemplation on the outskirts of Lake Geneva held no appeal. Even before he made it 'home', Bowie had already booked time for later in the summer at Château d'Hérouville, a recording studio in Pontoise, 40 miles north of Paris, where he planned to write and produce an album for a certain James Newell Osterberg Jr., better known to the world at large as Iggy Pop.

Before they first met, five years earlier, Bowie had been a keen admirer of Iggy's seminal group, The Stooges, who during the late 1960s and early 1970s made three albums of visceral and hugely influential proto-punk rock. Their paths eventually crossed in September 1971, at Max's Kansas City in New York. The Stooges had recently been dropped by Elektra Records (following the release, a year earlier, of their magnificent second album, *Fun House*) and were fast falling apart and into the depths of drug addiction. Nonetheless,

Bowie urged his then manager, Tony DeFries, to take Iggy on as a client. DeFries hooked the newly renamed Iggy & The Stooges up with CBS, for whom they recorded *Raw Power* (1973). Bowie ended up mixing the album (having already offered to produce it) after CBS called him in to salvage Iggy's initial effort, which by all accounts used only three of the available 24 tracks. Iggy later described Bowie's mix as an act of sabotage, and took the opportunity to remix it himself for a 1997 reissue. His version is heavier and more aggressive than Bowie's, but not really any better.

Prior to mixing *Raw Power*, Bowie had produced *Transformer* for Lou Reed, kick-starting the former Velvet Underground frontman's solo career. He was unable to repeat the feat this time, however, for while *Raw Power* was well received by critics it limped in at Number 182 on the *Billboard* album chart. By the time of its release, in May 1973, The Stooges were on the verge of disbanding again, with their leader slumping back into a drug-addled, low-life existence in Los Angeles. The *New Musical Express* journalist Nick Kent – no stranger to rock'n'roll excess himself – visited the singer there and found that he "had a nervous system that had been shot, and he'd never taken the time to mend it".

While in L.A., Iggy made several failed attempts at beginning a post-Stooges career, including forming a shortlived band with Ray Manzarek, formerly the keyboard player in The Doors. But by the middle of 1974, Iggy had become sufficiently desperate that he briefly considered auditioning to join Kiss. (Iggy and Manzarek first met a few years earlier, when Iggy was briefly considered as a replacement for Jim Morrison in The Doors, before the band opted – at least for the time being – not to continue without their original frontman.)

In September, Iggy tried on two occasions to reunite with the one-time Ziggy during the Californian leg of his *Diamond Dogs* tour, but – in a mark of exactly how far his stock had fallen – was unable to gain access to either the gig or Bowie's hotel. A month later, he was picked up (not for the first time) by L.A. County police while behaving badly under the influence of heroin. Given the choice of jail or therapy, Iggy wisely chose to check into the Neuropsychiatric Institute at the University of California, Los Angeles, whereupon, after being weaned off drugs, he was diagnosed with hypomania, a symptom of bipolar disorder. Fortunately for Iggy, his mother had continued to pay his medical insurance premiums.[1]

Perhaps the most commonly told anecdote about Iggy's time at UCLA is that, during his stay, he only had one visitor: David Bowie. This isn't completely accurate. Bowie, for one, was not alone: he turned up with the actor Dean Stockwell; both were let in by star-struck staff against the facility's visitor policy. Several other friends of Iggy had already been turned away for fear that they might supply him with drugs, which makes Bowie's admittance all the more ironically unfortunate, since his first act was allegedly to offer Iggy some cocaine. Bowie, of course, was now well on his way to a state of drug-induced mania himself, although he, unlike Iggy, still managed to keep his wits about him enough to maintain a relentless and successful schedule of record making, touring, and now acting.

For the next year, Iggy lived a nomadic, shambolic lifestyle, largely reliant on the kindness of friends and acquaintances who put him up and put up with him as he continued to fight a seemingly endless battle with heroin addiction. His next encounter with Bowie came in May 1975, in an almost exact echo of a moment that lives in rock'n'roll legend. In early 1966, Neil Young happened by complete coincidence upon Stephen Stills and Richie Furay while stuck in traffic on Sunset Boulevard; within weeks the three of them had formed Buffalo Springfield. Nine years later, David Bowie was being driven down the same street when he caught sight of his old friend Jim. This fortuitous meeting led Bowie to book some time at Oz Studios in Hollywood with the intention of making a solo album for Iggy. The time was not quite right, however, for a Bowie-produced Iggy Pop record. Iggy failed to turn up for the second day of recording on the morning after a night of overindulgence, leading a furious Bowie to scrap the project altogether.

And so their paths separated once again. For the rest of the year, Bowie managed to hold himself together enough to film *The Man Who Fell To Earth* and record *Station To Station*; Iggy merely stumbled further into drug dependency and another spell at UCLA.

As 1976 faded into view, Iggy Pop had reached his lowest point – desperate to change his lifestyle and environment, but unable to ask for help in doing so. Luckily for him, the Station To Station tour rolled into town during the second week of February. Bowie had by this point already begun to realise that his own lifestyle was causing him severe physical and psychological damage, and that he needed to make abrupt changes to it if he wanted to see out the 1970s. He must have been aware that the same was true of his friend, too, for after the second of three dates at the Englewood Forum, he asked Iggy to join the rest of the tour, ostensibly as a backing singer, but more importantly as an ally against a world fast closing in. Once again, there was talk of Bowie producing an Iggy Pop solo record, with a loose plan to begin work on it after the tour, using 'Sister Midnight', a song Bowie had recently written with Carlos Alomar, as a starting point. What was even more important for these two men fast approaching their 30th birthdays, however, was to leave America – and more specifically Los Angeles – and embark on a new life, at a better pace, in Europe.

On the face of it, the friendship between David Bowie and Iggy Pop – the foppish English autodidact with a taste for German expressionism and gender-bending, and the uber-masculine American punk perhaps best known for carving into his body with shards of glass onstage – might have seemed an unlikely one. In fact, both had strayed far enough from the stereotypes draped upon them that they met somewhere in the middle, with Iggy now likely to be found quietly immersed in financial newspapers during stops on the Station To Station tour. The real James Osterberg, Bowie later recalled, was "a rather lonely and quiet guy with a drug problem, horn-rimmed glasses, and a huge appetite for reading"[2] – not unlike Bowie himself, except for the glasses. Iggy was greatly impressed and inspired by the professionalism of the Bowie operation: rolling into towns across America and Europe without a hitch, playing to crowds of thousands night after night, and making a tidy profit along the way, all while maintaining a steady stream of high-quality recorded output.

Bowie is often accused of adopting characters such as Iggy Pop (and, before him, Lou Reed) simply to improve his own standing outside the musical mainstream. This seems more than a little unfair, however, given the number of occasions on which he tried to dig the former Stooge out of a hole. Even after living in such close proximity for the majority of 1976–77 drove a wedge between the two, Bowie remained Iggy's greatest supporter. During the 1980s, he reprised a number of their mid-1970s collaborations in bright, colourful pop settings, most notably 'China Girl', partly in an effort to help Iggy escape the clutches of the tax authorities, and then produced his 1986 *Blah Blah Blah* LP.

Moreover, to suggest that Bowie got nothing more out of the relationship than the cachet of cool that came with being associated with the newly crowned 'Godfather Of Punk' does a disservice to Iggy, too. Iggy was, first and foremost, as close a friend as Bowie had had for years. He offered considerable moral support – as did Bowie in return – when both began their respective attempts to clean up, and became a vital creative foil. "I gave him an outlet for an overflow of talent and ideas," Iggy told *Rolling Stone* magazine recently, noting that, when Bowie "had a new idea and wasn't sure how to approach it, he would write or arrange something in a similar manner for one of my projects".[3] (Within a year, this arrangement had mutated into a professional rivalry that drove both to ever-greater songwriting heights, and resulted in the recording of two seminal albums each.)

At the end of the Station To Station tour, Bowie and Iggy had intended to stay on for a little while in Paris, where the final dates had taken place, but soon sought an escape from the many fans buzzing around the city. After some typically quick-witted arranging by Coco Schwab, the pair relocated to the Château d'Hérouville, where Bowie had recorded *Pin-Ups* in 1973. Bowie had originally planned to record Iggy's first album for three years at Musicland in Munich, but was greatly impressed by the Château, which was much more technically advanced than its name might suggest. He also quickly bonded with the studio's new owner, Laurent Thibault, formerly the bassist in Magma, the Parisian prog-rock group about whom Bowie was – to Thibault's surprise and delight – rather knowledgeable. After two nights at the Château, Bowie decided that Iggy's album should be recorded there, and that Thibault should engineer and play bass.

After booking two months of studio time for later in the summer, Bowie returned to Clos Des Mésanges, and spent his only extended period there, reading, painting, and making preliminary plans for his own next record. Then, at the end of June, he arrived at the Château with Iggy, whereupon he instructed Thibault to find a suitable drummer to complete a close-knit playing and recording team. Thibault chose Michel Santangeli, who up to then had worked predominantly with the Celtic-folk revivalist Alan Stivell, and as such was more than a little daunted to find himself in the studio with David Bowie.

Working at home, Bowie had already made rough sketches on keyboard and guitar of some of the songs that ended up on *The Idiot*. As soon as Santangeli arrived, Bowie sat down behind his Baldwin electric piano and led the star-struck drummer through a series of vague arrangements, which both Frenchmen assumed must only be demos. Work continued in this way for two days, with Bowie offering little in the way of direction, but merely working on each song until they arrived at a version that he liked, and then moving on to the next one. Dismissed at the end of the second day, Santangeli assumed that his drumming had been substandard, and that he would not appear on the album. In fact, his contributions were emblematic of the working methods Bowie would adopt throughout his record-making of the next few years. (All of the rhythm parts on *Low*, *"Heroes"*, and *Lodger* were captured at a similar speed.)

With most of the drums on tape, Bowie began adding guitar parts, for which he had brought along his Dan Armstrong/Ampeg Perspex. Although he did subsequently call on a young Phil Palmer to rerecord and develop some of these parts, Bowie still plays more guitar on this album than on any of his previous efforts. On his own recent albums, Bowie had focused his energies almost entirely on being a singer. Here, however, he reasserts himself as a musician, contributing guitar, electric piano, synthesizer, saxophone, and drum machine, as well as the occasional backing vocal.

After building up a basic framework of guitar and keyboard, Bowie invited Thibault to add bass to the songs so far recorded. This again was done without much in the way of supervision or direction, with Bowie happy, for the most part, to let the former Magma bassist find his own way around the songs. Later in July, Bowie brought in his own crack rhythm team, George Murray and Dennis Davis, to give a couple of the songs a little bit more flair and sparkle. This is most obviously apparent on the opening 'Sister Midnight', which both musicians had already played, with Bowie, on the Station To Station tour. As a result, it has a looser, funkier confidence to it than anything else on *The Idiot*, resulting in something akin to a darker, more disturbed 'Golden Years'. Murray and Davis also crop up on the edgy, dissonant closer, 'Mass Production', but elsewhere Bowie stuck with Thibault and Santangeli's simple, intuitive playing. (Exactly who played what is still up for debate to some extent, as there are no instrumental credits on the album, partly as a result of a falling out between Bowie and Thibault during the *Low* sessions – of which more later.)

Where was Iggy Pop while all of this was going on? This was, after all, *his* album, in name at least, although virtually all of the music on it was Bowie's. During the initial phase of recording, Iggy could often be found in the control room, scribbling down fragmentary lyrics in response to the music Bowie was making. These were rarely too close to being fully formed, as Iggy seemed to prefer to improvise most of what he sang while at the mike – something that fascinated and inspired Bowie, who adopted a similar practice a year later during the making of *"Heroes"*.

While Iggy wrote almost all of the words he sings on *The Idiot* himself, the initial spark for some of the lyrics came from the album's musical director. The oblique, comical 'Dum Dum Boys', for example, came about as a result of Bowie suggesting that Iggy chronicle his time with The Stooges ("I was impressed / No one else was impressed"). The most famous lyric on the album, however, stemmed from the weeks during which the record was made. As well as being a top-notch recording studio, the Château d'Hérouville also served as a hideaway for celebrities eager to avoid the glare of the media. While work continued on *The Idiot*, the French actor and singer Jacques Higelin was one such visitor. One day Iggy ran into Higelin's girlfriend, Kuelan Nguyen, in one of the expansive Château's many hidden-away rooms. Despite a complete lack of common language, the pair felt an instant rapport and fell into a brief but passionate affair. Feeling compelled to stay with Higelin and their young son, Nguyen soon ended the relationship, but not before she had inspired in Iggy the doomy, romantic lyric for a song that would soon receive the title 'China Girl'. [4]

At the end of July, Bowie and Iggy moved out of the Château d'Hérouville, which had already been booked by the British hard-rock group Bad Company (whose members included former Mott The Hoople guitarist Mick Ralphs). They relocated to Musicland, a bunker-like basement studio in Munich owned by Giorgio Moroder, the electronic-music producer then in the midst of widening the pop spectrum with such songs as 'Love To Love You Baby' by Donna Summer. The focus here was on recording vocals and guitar overdubs, although it seems likely that more structural work was done on the drum machine-driven, somnambulant 'Nightclubbing' and the industrial 'Mass Production', for which Laurent Thibault built a giant, room-sized tape loop to set off great surges of sound that evoke a dying factory siren. It was here, too, that the fledgling session-player Phil Palmer turned up with his guitar, having taken a call from a certain Mr. Bowie at his mum's house. Much like Michel Santangeli at the Château, Palmer spent a few awestruck days at Musicland translating Bowie's abstract, spoken ideas onto six strings, re-recording some of the original guitar lines (Bowie having deemed his own playing substandard), and not quite believing he was where he was or with whom.

Bowie's original choice of guitarist had been Robert Fripp, but the King Crimson frontman had declined the call-up, having decided, temporarily, to take a break from music. Bowie had hoped that both Fripp and his on-off collaborator, Brian Eno, would contribute to *The Idiot*. But in August 1976 Eno told Allan Jones of *Melody Maker* that, while he had been invited to contribute to the debut album by 'Iggy Stooge', "all kinds of disruptions in the Bowie camp" had led to the project being postponed. Both Fripp and Eno would, of course, drop back into Bowie's orbit soon enough.

With recording of *The Idiot* completed to their satisfaction, Bowie and Iggy travelled a few hundred miles north from the Bavarian capital to mix the album at Hansa Studios in Berlin, the city that was about to become their new home.

"I hold the same opinion as Günter Grass," Bowie told *Vogue* in 1978, "that Berlin is [at] the centre of everything that is happening and will happen in Europe over the next few years." (Grass, the Nobel Prize-winning author of *The Tin Drum*, had called Berlin "the city closest to the realities of the modern age" in an interview with the *New York Times* a decade earlier.) Politically, too, Berlin was at the apex of the modern world. The end of the Second World War had created, in Berlin, a city like no other. It was decided that Germany would be divided into four separate regions, to be governed by the country's principal occupiers: Britain, the United States, the Soviet Union, and France. Berlin, despite being located deep in what became Soviet territory, was subjected to the same subdivisions.

The four occupying nations intended initially to work together in governing Germany, but rising Cold War tensions rendered this plan unworkable. By the end of the 1940s, the British, French, and American parts of the country had merged into the Federal Republic Of Germany, while the Soviet region became the German Democratic Republic. West Berlin remained under Allied control, but became detached from the rest of West Germany. It was accessible only by a 110-mile strip of road and rail out to the border, and while considered from a legal perspective to be a part of West Germany was not under the jurisdiction of the Federal Republic but instead run by an elected city government. The situation was intensified when, in response to the growing flight of East Germans to the West via Berlin, the GDR built the Berlin Wall, first with barbed wire and then with bricks and mortar, leaving West Berlin an inland island at odds with everything that surrounded it – a symbolic centre-point for the remainder of the Cold War, and a place that would feel the East-West tensions more acutely than any other.

What this left, as Bowie put it in 1977, was "a city cut off from its world, art, and culture, dying with no hope of retribution".[5] This was not the city of flamboyant, carefree decadence that Isherwood had written about four decades earlier, but eerie echoes of that time lingered – as did the remnants of Albert Speer's grand designs to rebuild the city as Welthauptstadt Germania (World Capital Germania), a focal point for Hitler's empire. "It's such an ambiguous place," Bowie told *Vogue*. "It's hard to distinguish between the ghosts and the living." The pervading air of faded glamour, economic anxiety, and ideological dislocation gave Berlin a distinctly melancholic feel, but there remained, too, a defiant, renegade spirit.

As the art historian Michael Kimmelman notes, many artists thrive in times of personal struggle. Of Frank Hurley, the photographer who documented Sir Ernest Shackleton's perilous explorations of Antarctica, Kimmelman concludes that "wearing the same clothes, eating the same seal pemmican, staying in the same place, day in and day out, he was better able to concentrate on making the most with what he had at hand".[6] Bowie, it seems, was of the same mind. His stated intention was to "find some people you don't understand and a place you don't want to be and just put yourself into it", and to "force yourself to buy your own groceries".[7] Berlin was, as Tony Visconti put it, "a haven for everyone to be as anonymous as they wished to be"[8] – somewhere to rebuild and recharge, away from prying eyes.

"Nobody gives a shit about you in Berlin," said Bowie. The city's vague aggregation of social misfits, draft dodgers, and struggling artists had more than enough problems of their own to be worrying about an ex-pat British pop star. This suited him perfectly: he could drift in and out of roadside cafes and restaurants, visit galleries, drink himself into oblivion in working men's clubs and transvestite cabaret bars, all the while keeping the requisite low profile, easing himself slowly back from the near self-destruction brought about in Los Angeles – "the most vile piss-pot in the world".[9]

There were of course numerous other places around the globe where someone such as Bowie could disappear into anonymity, but Berlin had other things going for it as well. "Since my teenage years," Bowie later said, "I had obsessed on the angst-ridden, emotional work of the expressionists" – the Die Brücke school in particular, notably Erich Heckel, whose *Roquairol* inspired *The Idiot*'s cover shot – "and Berlin had been their spiritual home."[10] No longer in thrall to the occult and fascism ("I really had to face up to [that]," he later admitted. "Suddenly I was in a situation where I was meeting young men of my age whose fathers had actually been SS men."[11]), Bowie now read and enthused – in typically vociferous fashion – about art, literature, and classical music; painting, previously an intermittent distraction, became a full-time hobby. Many of his own artworks – which included a giant expressionist portrait of the Japanese author and nihilist Yukio Mishima – hung from the walls of his Berlin apartment.

Finally, of course, there was the lure of the contemporary German music scene. Kraftwerk are the most regularly cited group of the era, and were indeed an acknowledged favourite of Bowie's, particularly their *Radio-Activity* LP, an airing of which took the place of a support act on his Station To Station tour. But while Kraftwerk certainly did have an effect on the music Bowie was to make during his Berlin period, particularly in terms of instrumental melodies and chord progressions, the two acts' overall approach to recording and performance were, as Bowie later put it, "poles apart … One had the feeling that Florian [Schneider] and Ralf [Hütter] were completely in charge of their environment, and that their compositions were well prepared and honed before entering the studio".[12] Bowie, on the other hand, preferred to work in a much more spontaneous fashion. In that respect, he seemed to take more from Kraftwerk's less mechanical contemporaries, among them Can, Faust, and Neu!; each specialised in some form or other of organic, subtly shifting, post-psychedelic music, later dubbed (to their dismay) krautrock or, to use their own term, kosmische musik. Of all of these groups, Neu! were the most influential on Bowie's new musical direction. Their *Neu! 75* is, like Bowie's *Low* and *"Heroes"*, very much an album of two sides, the first gentle, ambient, and largely instrumental, the second more visceral, vocal, and song-based. There's even a song on it called 'Hero'.

Many of the finest kosmische records – including *Neu! 75*, Kraftwerk's *Autobahn*, and *Zuckerzeit* by Cluster – were overseen by Konrad 'Conny' Plank, and recorded at his studio in Köln. While the kosmische scene – if indeed there even was such a thing – was rooted in communality and collaboration, if any one figure could have claimed to stand at the heart of it, it was Plank. He certainly had as much as anyone else to do with establishing the hallmarks of the kosmische sound – the shifting textures, radical use of effects processing and tape editing, and avoidance of the rigidity and compression favoured by most rock producers of the 1970s. Had Bowie merely wanted to reproduce the sound that was coming out of Köln, he probably would have headed straight for Plank's studio – just as a number of other British acts would do later in the 1970s, including Ultravox, Eurythmics, and even Brian Eno. Bowie, however, decided to plough his own furrow in Berlin.

There is a certain irony about Bowie's choice of destination, and the route of his escape, particularly given the whirlwind of controversy he had just whipped up in Britain. After Hitler assumed power in 1933, many of the finest creative minds of the Weimar years, fearful for both their artistic freedom and their very lives, fled Germany for more liberal climes. Some of the most distinguished among them – including the dramatist Bertolt Brecht, the filmmaker Fritz Lang, the composer Arnold Schoenberg, and the writer Thomas Mann – chose to seek refuge in Los Angeles. (Three of the four eventually became naturalised US citizens, but Brecht – a longstanding influence on Bowie – returned to East Berlin soon after the war following investigations by the House Un-American Activities Committee into his alleged communist sympathies.) Bowie, of course, made the opposite journey, having reached his lowest ebb on America's west coast (to which he had moved just a few months after Fritz Lang died at his Beverly Hills home).

Forty years on, Berlin – or at least West Berlin – was a place to escape to, not from, not just for convalescent rock stars but also for East Germans slumped, in more than one sense, in depression on the other side of the Wall. The Wall itself, which for three decades kept friends and families apart and served as the very epicentre of the Cold War, still cast a long and unavoidable shadow over the city. But by the mid 1970s, when most of its inhabitants had if not accepted then at least come to terms with the existence of the Wall, West Berlin had become, according to the historian Christopher Hilton, a bustling, cosmopolitan hub of "draft-dodgers, revolutionary students, and solid citizens making a lot of money".[13]

This, then, was the city that would inform Bowie's record-making for the next couple of years, and would, for much of that time, be his home. First of all, however, he had to oversee the mixing of *The Idiot*, for which he called on the technical expertise of Tony Visconti. The pair had not shared a studio since November 1974, but with Visconti already booked in to produce the next Bowie album, it made perfect sense for him to familiarise himself with the singer's new way of working by mixing Iggy Pop's record.

Visconti's recollections of *The Idiot* in his recent autobiography are a little confused; he claims to have mixed the album only after completing work on *Low*, but most other accounts suggest that *The Idiot* was done and dusted before serious work on the Bowie album commenced, which would seem more logical. What probably is true, however, given the somewhat chaotic and spontaneous nature of the recording sessions, is that the resulting tracks "were a mess ... a clash of clean German [actually French] engineering and British grit". In particular, he notes that Iggy's vocals often began softly and "gradually built up to a scream".[14] This led to problems with distortion and over-modulation that would nonetheless give *The Idiot* its signature vocal sound – and inspire the effect Visconti later captured on Bowie's "'Heroes'", albeit with a lot more technical know-how.

The resulting album is often described, rather backhandedly, as some kind of prototype for *Low*, or a stopgap between 'proper' Bowie records. There is an element of truth in that. As Iggy suspected, he was to some extent being used, as Bowie later admitted, as "a guinea pig for what I wanted to do with sound".[15] But *The Idiot* is, also, a great album in its own right and, to repeat a cliché so often overused in relation to records such as this, a very underrated one at that, simultaneously darker and more human than the Bowie albums that followed it. If *Low* is the sound of Bowie edging his way out from cocaine psychosis into a cleaner but much more vulnerable insularity, *The Idiot* is still suffused with a drunken, druggy haze, but a little harder and more confident for it. It is also a record that neither of its principal creators would or could have made without the other: Iggy's attempts at recording in the last few years had floundered almost as soon as they had begun, while Bowie "didn't have the material" to record an album such as this of his own yet, and "didn't feel like writing at all".[16]

The Idiot also dispels the myth that Brian Eno led Bowie away from conventional rock and pop music and down the garden path of experimentation, offering as it does proof that Bowie was already formulating his own ideas for a bleak, proto-electronica sound. The album inaugurated a new style of writing and recording for Bowie, too, partly of his own design and partly as a result of Iggy's own methodology.

By the time *The Idiot* went on sale (which was not until March 1977), it would have been almost four years since anyone had heard Iggy on record, his last act having been to bring The Stooges' third album to a raucous, fuzz-drenched close with 'Death Trip'. Listen to that song and then 'Sister Midnight' and it's hard to imagine that they were both made by the same man. It is often said that *The Idiot* is the least recognisably 'Iggy' of all of his albums, so covered is it with Bowie's musical fingerprints. Indeed, if The Stooges were all about raw power, Iggy's first album is a work of tension and control, the proto-punk guitars of old replaced by rumbling bass, motorik drums, and icy synths. Vocally, at Bowie's behest, Iggy keeps the balls-out screaming under wraps for much of the record, instead affecting a deep, almost crooner-like baritone not a million miles from the Bowie of 'Golden Years'.

Iggy had made a tentative stab at this sort of singing during his Stooges days, most notably on the *Fun House* track 'Dirt', but Bowie pushed him to take it further, encouraging him to try on different voices for different songs. (Most famously, he instructed Iggy to sing 'China Girl' "like Mae West".) That said, *The Idiot* is still very much an Iggy Pop record. It's highly unlikely Bowie would have put out (or even conceived of on his own) something as raw and dissonant as 'Funtime', nor has he ever recorded a song so bleak and primal as 'Mass Production'.

The Idiot was finished well before the end of August, but would not be released for a little while yet. Canny as ever, Bowie wanted to make sure that he had a new record of his own on the shelves before *The Idiot* came out, wary of letting anyone think he was simply following Iggy's lead. That might have felt like a daunting prospect a few months earlier, but now, reinvigorated by his collaborations with Iggy and with the foundations of a new working method in place, it was time to make *Low*.

IGGY POP: THE IDIOT

Produced and arranged by David Bowie. Mixed by Tony Visconti. Engineered by Laurent Thibault. Recorded at Château d'Hérouville, Pontoise, France (June–July 1976) and Musicland, Munich, Germany (August 1976); mixed at Hansa Tonstudio 2 (August 1976).

SISTER MIDNIGHT 4:19
(Bowie/Pop/Alomar)
Iggy Pop: vocals; **David Bowie**: guitar, synthesizer, backing vocals; **George Murray**: bass; **Dennis Davis**: drums.

■ Of *The Idiot's* eight songs, the opening 'Sister Midnight' is the most evocative of pre-Berlin Bowie, largely because of the fact that it was co-written on the Station To Station tour by Bowie, Iggy, and Carlos Alomar, and features the distinctive kraut-funk rhythm playing of bandmates Dennis Davis and George Murray.

Alomar and Bowie had already come up with the basic framework of the song and its opening lines before Iggy joined the tour and finished off the lyric. Iggy's contribution changed the mood of the song entirely: while it mostly likely started out in the pleading, quasi-religious vein of 'Stay' and 'Golden Years', the final version is a snarling, oedipal nightmare. Bowie had merely asked the Sister Midnight of the title if she could hear him; Iggy wanted to know if she could do anything about his dreams of a mother "in my bed" and a father who "hunted me with his gun".

Bowie performed 'Sister Midnight' with Iggy on the US chat show *Dinah!* in April 1977 and, two years later, reused the melody (and one line of the lyric) for the *Lodger* track 'Red Money', which has a similarly doomy, narcoleptic feel.

NIGHTCLUBBING 4:14
(Bowie/Pop)
Iggy Pop: vocals; **David Bowie**: drum machine, synthesizer, piano; **Laurent Thibault**: bass; **Phil Palmer**: guitar.

■ 'Nightclubbing' is, in a way, the most forward-thinking of the songs on *The Idiot*. It marked the first time that Bowie (or Iggy, for that matter) had used a drum machine as the rhythmic foundation of any recording. This most likely came about as a result of he and Iggy relocating midway through the *Idiot* sessions to Giorgio Moroder's Musicland studio in Munich, although Bowie has stated that, by 1976, he regularly used one as a writing aid. 'Nightclubbing' is about as straightforwardly autobiographical as it gets, even if much of it is written in a vague, fragmented style. It is, in that respect, one of the most influential of Iggy's lyrics on Bowie's shift (on *Low* and beyond) toward a starker, more direct songwriting style.

'Nightclubbing' was subsequently covered by The Human League – whose entire musical output owes a huge debt to Bowie – in 1980, and then a year later, more memorably, by Grace Jones. (Trent Reznor of Nine Inch Nails later used a backwards sample of the kick drum for his 'Closer'.)

FUNTIME 2:54
(Bowie/Pop)
Iggy Pop: vocals; **David Bowie**: guitar, synthesizer, vocals;
Laurent Thibault: bass; **Michel Santangeli**: drums.
■ 'Funtime' is as close as *The Idiot* gets to the hypothetical sound of a Stooges song put through the Berlin-era Bowie production wringer, combining brash guitar chords and taut, cymbal-heavy drumming with otherworldly processing and compression effects. Bowie's 'backing' vocal is mixed almost as high as Iggy's, while the song's use of the first-person plural makes clear that *The Idiot* was the work of two minds travelling in virtually the same direction.

Lyrically, 'Funtime' evokes Bowie and Iggy's final dark days in Los Angeles ("Talkin' to Dracula and his crew"), while the music – somehow murky and insistent at the same time – seems to predate the mood of 'Fashion', from Bowie's 1980 album *Scary Monsters (And Super Creeps)*.

BABY 3:24
(Bowie/Pop)
Iggy Pop: vocals; **David Bowie**: guitar, synthesizer, backing vocals;
Laurent Thibault: bass; **Michel Santangeli**: drums.

■ Of all the songs on *The Idiot*, 'Baby' comes closest to the bleak soundscapes of *Low*, particularly in the way that it arrives out of nowhere and then, having said all that it wants to say, drifts off into the distance. The mood is decidedly Germanic, but more *Cabaret* than Kraftwerk. Drums play an important, up-front role in all of the other seven songs on the album, but here they are allowed to drift in and out of the mix, leaving the job of anchoring the song to its two-beat bassline and a three-note synthesizer riff. While the guitars are restricted to a few stray licks here and there, the synths are more prominent here than on any other *Idiot* track, building into a discordant wall of noise for the blink-and-you'll-miss-it chorus.

Like a lot of Iggy's songs of the time, 'Baby' is about a relationship that seems doomed to fail. But where he warns a prospective lover of his own bad influence on 'China Girl', here he takes the role of protector, pleading with his subject to "stay young" and "stay clean" and to heed the temptations on "the street of chance" ("There's nothing to see / I've already been").

CHINA GIRL 5:08
(Bowie/Pop)
Iggy Pop: vocals; **David Bowie**: guitar, synthesizer, saxophone;
Phil Palmer: guitar; **Laurent Thibault**: bass;
Michel Santangeli: drums.

■ Thanks to Bowie's disco-pop reworking of it six years later, 'China Girl' is by some distance the most famous song on *The Idiot*. Even here, however, without the cooing backing vocals and Nile Rodgers' effortlessly funky, faux-oriental guitar line, 'China Girl' sticks out like the proverbial sore thumb. It seems typical of Bowie and his often contrary nature that one of his most deftly crafted musical creations should be found slap-bang in the middle of what is essentially a noisy, dissonant side-project.

Originally known as 'Borderline', before Iggy came up with the engaging, cinematic lyric, 'China Girl' still has the ability to catch the listener by surprise, however many times it's played. The insistent, two-pronged attack of upbeat guitar and synthesizer jump out of nowhere in marked contrast to the distortion and discord of the four songs that precede it. Iggy, however, is at his most sinister. He begins by trying to convince both himself and his "little China girl" – in reality Jacques Higelin's girlfriend, who as noted elsewhere was staying at the Château d'Hérouville while Bowie and Iggy worked on *The Idiot* – that life could be so much easier if only they were together, until, later in the song, he realises that his decadent western ways would have a corrupting effect on her. Most notoriously, he sings of "visions of swastikas" and "plans for everyone", echoing the kind of taboo imagery Bowie had been flirting with in the press in the months before they wrote 'China Girl' together. (The lines jar in Bowie's 1983 version, which for all of its pop savvy is about as unnerving as a Walt Disney cartoon.)

Bowie has described the song as being about "invasion and exploitation",[17] which seems about right, while also expressing his amazement on several occasions at the way Iggy could come up with lyrics such as these, pretty much spontaneously, whilst standing at the mic. Iggy's version was released as a single to coincide with the release of *The Idiot*, but failed to chart. Bowie then reprised the song – partly to earn Iggy some substantial royalty cheques – in what was the first of several acts of benevolence on behalf of his friend during the mid 1980s: a year later, he included five Iggy Pop co-writes on *Tonight* and another on 1987's *Never Let Me Down*, and in between times lent several songs and his production expertise to Iggy's *Blah Blah Blah* LP. Iggy himself has also got further mileage out of 'China Girl' over the years, including versions of it on a pair of live albums, *Heroin Hates You* (recorded at the Stardust Ballroom in Los Angeles in 1979) and *Live At The Ritz NYC* (1986).

DUM DUM BOYS 7:12
(Bowie/Pop)
Iggy Pop: vocals, piano; **David Bowie**: guitar, synthesizer;
Phil Palmer: guitar; **Laurent Thibault**: bass;
Michel Santangeli: drums.

■ A seven-minute epic of beat poetry and marauding guitars, 'Dum Dum Boys' came about as a result of Bowie's simple suggestion to Iggy (who it seems had made a tentative start on the song at the piano in the Château d'Hérouville): why not tell the story of The Stooges? Iggy being Iggy, of course, this isn't a straightforward narrative, but rather a series of stark and disconnected reminiscences, beginning with a darkly humorous spoken meditation on the present whereabouts of his former bandmates. Iggy notes early on that life has been difficult since the band's split, concluding that "I can't seem to speak / The language" – which seems somewhat ironic, with the benefit of hindsight, given that, by the time *The Idiot* went on sale, he had taken on a new role as a founding father of the punk rock scenes on both sides of the Atlantic.

Musically, 'Dum Dum Boys' (originally 'Dum Dum Days') isn't far from *Fun House* at its most expansive, although there is also a strange whiff, in the slow, deliberate guitar-arpeggios, of classic rock about it, too. Bowie recorded all of the guitar parts himself initially, but later had Phil Palmer re-do some of them, virtually note-for-note, because he didn't feel that his own six-string playing was up to the task.

TINY GIRLS 2:59
(Bowie/Pop)
Iggy Pop: vocals; **David Bowie**: guitar, synthesizer, saxophone;
Phil Palmer: guitar; **Laurent Thibault**: bass;
Michel Santangeli: drums.

■ Like 'China Girl', 'Tiny Girls' feels somewhat incongruous in the context of the rest of *The Idiot* – particularly given that it is located between the album's two longest tracks. As with 'Baby', there's a hint of cabaret to the swinging, three-beat rhythm, and a suggestion, too, of both doo-wop and French pop in the arrangement. The first minute of the song is a showcase for David Bowie the saxophonist, and in fact is probably his best recorded performance on the instrument. Then Iggy takes over with another of his romantic laments, this time deciding that the best thing for him would be a "tiny girl" with "no past" and "no tricks".

MASS PRODUCTION 8:25
(Bowie/Pop)
Iggy Pop: vocals; **David Bowie**: guitar, synthesizer;
Laurent Thibault: tape loops; **George Murray**: bass;
Dennis Davis: drums.

■ *The Idiot's* final song is a rival, in length and scope, to some of the great epics in its authors' back catalogues – The Stooges' 'Dirt', for example, and Bowie's 'Station To Station'. There's a suggestion, too, of Iggy's old Elektra labelmate Jim Morrison, in terms not just of the vocal delivery, but also of the song's sweeping structure and the almost dystopian imagery it deploys (burial, burning, "smokestacks belching").

The song begins and ends with around a minute of proto-industrial noise – the harsh, atonal loop that Bowie had Laurent Thibault play all around the room (literally, given the length of tape involved) for almost an hour until the sound was right. In between, out of the darkness, come George Murray and Dennis Davis, somehow managing to be both funky and funereal, while Bowie doubles up the song's central, circular riff on guitar and synthesizer. The synths gradually overwhelm the other instruments around them, rising in volume while simultaneously slipping out of time and tune as Iggy pleads for one last favour: "Give me that number … get me that girl".

'Mass Production' is often heralded as a key influence on Joy Division, who formed in the months between the release of *Low* and *The Idiot* (and originally called themselves Warsaw in reference – and reverence – to a track on the Bowie album). It's not hard to make the connection between the song and such Joy Division tracks as 'I

Remember Nothing': the slow but seemingly unassailable pace, the icy guitars, the doomy, portentous vocals are but three points of comparison. Beyond Joy Division, however, the mood of 'Mass Production' seems to preempt modern alternative rock at its most expansive, as played by bands such as Smashing Pumpkins and Radiohead.

WHAT IN THE WORLD

Low starts, and ends, with a fade. This in itself is not a particularly remarkable concept (it wasn't even the first David Bowie album to do so), but it couldn't be more fitting. *Low* is a snapshot; or, rather, a sequence of disparate, fragmentary glimpses of a life in the midst of being hauled back from the brink. It makes complete sense, then, that we are thrown in at what could very well be somewhere in the middle of 'Speed Of Life', and bidden farewell at a point by which 'Subterraneans' has not yet conclusively or satisfactorily resolved anything. Of the 11 tracks, only 'Always Crashing In The Same Car' reaches a proper conclusion; each of the others pops up, says its piece, and slinks off into the distance.

Work on the album officially began on September 1st, 1976, but some of its songs date back further than that. 'What In The World' was once a contender for *The Idiot* (and as a consequence of that features backing vocals from Iggy Pop), while the album closer, 'Subterraneans', was written with the soundtrack to *The Man Who Fell To Earth* in mind. Bowie started making plans for what became *Low* almost as soon as the Station To Station tour arrived in Paris on May 18th. After visiting the Château d'Hérouville with Iggy and booking studio time for later in the summer, he went back to his new home in Blonay,

Switzerland, where he spent a few weeks reading, painting, and working on ideas for new songs. During that time he was also visited by the man who would help shape the sound and mood of his next three albums: a glam rocker turned ambient-music pioneer by the name of Brian Eno.

Although they did not become much more than acquaintances until 1976, Bowie and Eno's paths had crossed on a handful of occasions in years past. Eno's former group Roxy Music had supported Bowie and his Spiders From Mars at the Rainbow in London in August 1972; late the following year, they found themselves working in adjoining rooms at Olympic Studios in Barnes, near London, where Bowie was recording *Diamond Dogs* (the last of his albums to be made in Britain) at the same time as Eno was cutting his solo debut, *Here Come The Warm Jets*. Then, in May 1976, Eno met up with Bowie after the fifth of six Station To Station shows at the Empire Pool, Wembley, London. The pair talked into the early hours, during which time the idea of collaborating was first mooted. The original plan, according to Eno, was for him and erstwhile King Crimson guitarist Robert Fripp to contribute to Iggy's album. But then, Eno told *Melody Maker*, "I was told that there were all kinds of disruptions in the Bowie camp so everything's been cancelled for the moment."

While Bowie's association with Iggy Pop seemed somewhat ill-fitting to some, his decision to work with Eno made more sense. Both had risen to prominence as extravagant key players in the UK's glam-rock scene, but were bookish and intellectual at heart and defiant in their desire never to take the same musical turn twice. This was much more obviously a meeting of equals. If any musician of the 1970s could claim to have made as many interesting, intelligent, and influential records as Bowie, it was Eno. In Roxy Music he provided deft, avant-garde flourishes to Bryan Ferry's classic pop structures, thereby helping to establish a whole new modus operandi for rock groups. Unable to reconcile the tensions between himself and the dour, dapper Ferry, he left the group after completing work on its second album, *For Your*

Pleasure (released around the same time as Bowie's glam-pop peak, *Aladdin Sane*).

From there Eno embarked on a run of engaging and innovative solo and collaborative works. His first move as a free agent was to make *No Pussyfooting*, an album of improvisation and tape loops, with Robert Fripp. Then came a pair of song-based solo LPs, *Here Come The Warm Jets* and *Taking Tiger Mountain By Strategy*, that further developed the experimental themes of his work with Roxy Music. By then Bowie had begun to sink into his Californian abyss, but Eno was only just hitting his stride. In 1975, having already cut *Evening Star*, the second and best of the Fripp/Eno records, he made his two strongest and most important albums yet: *Another Green World*, a masterful blend of pop, art, and minimalism, and *Discreet Music*, his (and the world's) first fully realised ambient album.

Bowie spoke highly of these albums when he met up with Eno in May 1976, impressing and endearing himself to their creator in much the same way as he soon would Laurent Thibault by displaying a working knowledge of Magma. *Discreet Music* was, as Eno later recalled, "a very out-there record", which suggested that, if Bowie appreciated it, "he must be so smart!"[1] Eno has since suggested that Bowie "used *Discreet Music* as the soundtrack of his recovery"[2] as he emerged from his exile in Los Angeles. This seems fairly plausible, and provides a neat link to the album's genesis. Eno first arrived himself at the idea of 'ambient' music during a period of convalescence. The concept of music designed purely to be played in the background came to him while temporarily bedridden after a road accident, and unable to get up to turn up the volume of a record that he couldn't quite hear over the sound of heavy rainfall.

As deep a chord as *Discreet Music* might have struck in Bowie, it is *Another Green World* that most strongly foreshadows his work with Eno. The third of four song-based solo albums Eno made during the 1970s, it is widely considered to be his masterpiece. The most striking link to Eno's work with Bowie is that it combines relatively conventionally structured art-rock songs with minimalist instrumentals, although these are scattered throughout the 14-song tracklist, not grouped together on the album's B-side, as is the case on *Low*. There are other similarities, too. The overall mood is fairly withdrawn and ethereal, and, from a lyrical perspective, sparse, fragmented, and impressionistic. Most of the more 'pop' moments, while accessible enough, drift in and out, avoiding the big choruses and strident hooks of the era. (More specifically, the opening 'Sky Saw' is a dead ringer for 'Beauty And The Beast', the first song on Bowie's *"Heroes"*.)

Whether Bowie would have arrived at all of these themes and ideas on his own, without Eno's input, is still up for debate. Both have since claimed that their musical careers were on similar, almost parallel trajectories prior to their working together. A few weeks after *Low* came out, Eno told *Melody Maker* that Bowie "got in touch with me because he recognised that I was in a similar position. When you find someone with the same problem you tend to become friendly with them".[3] It does certainly seem that Bowie had been making his way towards the sound of *Low* in his previous musical projects. 'Station To Station' points the way; his soundtrack to *The Man Who Fell To Earth* was certainly intended to be more minimalist and synthesizer-based; and *The Idiot* shares much of the same mood, and was recorded in a similar fashion. What is undeniable, however, is that Eno, with *Another Green World*, got there first.

One area in which Bowie seemed definitely to be following Eno was in the way that he presented himself from mid 1976 onwards. During his days with Roxy Music, Eno had dressed in satin and boa feathers and made himself up just as flamboyantly as Ziggy Stardust, but after that made an effort to distance himself from his former celebrity. He was among the first pop figures to let his music do the talking, as the well-worn expression has it; to present his work as everyman, not as a rock'n'roll star. After six years of turbulence and excess, Bowie was ready to do the same; as Eno memorably put it in an interview with Paul Gambaccini some years later, he was "trying [to] duck the momentum of a successful career" – by losing himself in Berlin and making a new, fragmentary, and decidedly European music. "You know I've been into all of that for a while," Bowie told the *New Musical Express* shortly after *Low*'s release. "It's influenced by the new wave – not the American new wave bands, the European new wave"[4] – Neu!, Faust, Tangerine Dream, and, yes, Kraftwerk.

With Eno on board, Bowie's next crucial move was to bring Tony Visconti back into the fold. Throughout the 1970s, Visconti had drifted in and out of Bowie's musical orbit. He was called upon when needed, but often cast aside without warning, and sometimes even without notification (as was the case the last time they had worked together, on *Young Americans*). Perhaps surprisingly, given that he is generally considered to be the pre-eminent producer of Bowie records, he hadn't actually been involved in the making of one from start to finish since *The Man Who Sold The World* – which was barely a Bowie album at all, as the singer conspired to miss most of the sessions, leaving Visconti and Mick Ronson to piece the songs together in his absence. In between times, Visconti had missed out on *Hunky Dory*, *Ziggy Stardust*, *Aladdin Sane*, *Pin-Ups*, and *Station To Station*, and was only partially involved with *Diamond Dogs* and *Young Americans*.

Even so, Visconti – like many record producers of the time, one would assume – had learnt not to take the transience and flightiness of rock stars too personally, and was pleasantly surprised to be called up – out of the blue, as ever – by Bowie in June. With Eno also on the line, Bowie invited Visconti to join them at the Château d'Hérouville in September to work on something that "might be incredible or a complete waste of time", as the producer later recalled being told.[5] Bowie spoke excitedly of his and Eno's intention to combine raw rock songs (in the vein of *The Idiot*) with the kind of ambient experiments Eno had begun making already. He then asked Visconti what he might be able to contribute to the sessions. Here it was the producer's turn to impress, describing how his newly bought Eventide Harmonizer "fucks with the fabric of time".[6] (More prosaically, the Harmonizer was a kind of proto-sampler, the first effects processor capable of capturing and repeating sounds – instantly, or with a delay – at an altered pitch without changing tempo. It was originally designed, in the days before AutoTune, to correct wobbly vocal performances, but Visconti ended up using it for much more devious – and influential – purposes.)

Visconti's role in the making of *Low*, *"Heroes"*, and *Lodger* continues to be underappreciated. Many still labour under the misapprehension that Eno produced all three – perhaps because he subsequently took that role on landmark albums by Talking Heads, U2, and others, or perhaps simply because he *is* Brian Eno. In actual fact, Eno's contributions to Bowie's 1977–9 output, while undoubtedly important, were rather sporadic. By the time he arrived at the *Low* sessions, much of what became the album's first side had already been recorded, and he had packed up and left before many of the songs had vocals. He was present from the start for *"Heroes"* and *Lodger*, but long gone before either was finished. Visconti, on the other hand, was there from the initial 'demo' phase of *Low* to the final mix of *Lodger* – and, indeed, beyond.

The *Low* sessions began almost immediately after *The Idiot* was completed. Although Bowie was now very much ready to drop anchor in Berlin, he had already booked another month at the Château d'Hérouville, so returned there to start work on the album. While the method of recording followed, for the most part, the pattern established for *The Idiot*, the circumstances were quite different. For one thing, with Tony Visconti back at the desk, the sessions were rather more organised, even if they did retain an air of informality and an openness towards chance and improvisation. This time around, there would be no problem with slapdash, muffled recordings: knowing how Bowie tended to operate, Visconti had everything – instruments, amplifiers, microphones, and so on – set up exactly as it needed to be from the outset, and made sure the tapes were rolling at all times. As he later wrote, he knew "full well" that what the singer might initially consider to be demos "could end up as masters, and they did".[7]

As well as serving as a dry run for some of the musical ideas later developed on *Low*, the making of *The Idiot* also gave Bowie an opportunity to hone the three-stage pattern of recording (used, to some extent, on past albums such as *The Man Who Sold The World* and *Station To Station*), to which he has stuck rigidly for every one of his albums since. The process is as follows. For the first few days, Bowie and a nucleus of three or four musicians (often plucked from his current touring band) race through the rhythm tracks, trying to capture them as quickly and instinctively as possible. Then Bowie, his current musical director (Carlos Alomar, in the case of *Low*), and one or more guest musicians work on overdubs, generally at a much more leisurely, cerebral pace. Finally, and usually after everyone but the producer has been sent home, Bowie adds his vocals (often at roughly the same time as the record is being mixed). Prior to this, he tends to have little idea as to what the lyrics or vocal melodies will entail; sometimes there is a vague guide vocal, but the rest of the time nothing at all. This goes against the grain of most popular music, in which the various instrumental embellishments tend to be added in response to the lead vocal melody or the mood of the lyric. For Bowie, however, it clearly works; it is, moreover, quite likely as a result of this that so many of his songs contain such startling, intuitive melodic interaction between voices and lead instruments.

As with *The Idiot*, the first few days at the Château were spent on the rhythm tracks of the songs that eventually made up *Low*'s first side. The rhythm players worked quickly, beginning in the early evening and continuing right through the night, which seemed to suit the mood of the music. At some point early on in the sessions, Bowie played his band the rejected/abandoned soundtrack to *The Man Who Fell To Earth*, the sound of which he hoped to build on for the new album. (Guitarist Ricky Gardiner later described the material as "excellent" and "quite unlike anything else he's done".) He also had a few fragments of songs left over from the *Idiot* sessions, notably 'What In The World', and a handful of other sketches of ideas that he'd taped at home in Switzerland at the start of the summer. But while Bowie generally had a fair idea of how he wanted the *Low* songs to sound, he often left it to Alomar – as he had done in the past, and would again in the future – to come up with appropriate arrangements for the guitarist himself, for Dennis Davis, and for George Murray.

It was during the initial phase of recording (before half of the musicians had arrived, in fact) that Tony Visconti laid the groundwork for his most important contribution to the *Low* sessions – and, perhaps, his most important contribution to popular music in general. On the first evening, he fed Dennis Davis's snare drum into his much-trumpeted Eventide Harmonizer, and set it to feed back into itself, at an almost imperceptible delay, with the pitch gradually lowering each time, resulting in a strange, weightless thump that sounds as if it might carry on indefinitely even after it fades out of earshot – a sound, as Davis later put it, "as big as a house".[8] Intuitive as ever, Davis quickly realised that the timbre and velocity of his playing affected the sound the Harmonizer created, so adjusted his drumming style accordingly.

Not everybody was too keen on the sound to begin with. Bowie told Visconti that he didn't think it quite right for what he was trying to achieve on *Low*, but the producer persevered, engaging in a spot of musical subterfuge by turning the effect off in the main studio monitors but leaving it on in Davis's headphones, so that the drummer could continue to work the sound into his playing. As the sessions continued, Visconti gradually turned the effect back up; fortunately, Bowie and the others eventually warmed to it, and the sound went on to become one of the record's key ingredients. The Harmonizer might not quite have been powerful enough to cause a rift in the space-time continuum, but it did result in what *Rolling Stone* magazine later called "one of rock's all-time most imitated drum sounds".[9] (Wary of copycats, Visconti withheld the secret of the drum sound for some years, instead inviting guesses from his awed peers in the production world as to how he might have achieved it. Most of them assumed it required a much more elaborate setup.)

Whereas much of *The Idiot* had been made by the close-knit team of Bowie, Iggy, and Laurent Thibault, there were a lot more musicians in and out of the studio this time around. One direct result of this was that Bowie relinquished the role of principal guitarist, which he had taken a couple of months earlier. He did play a bit on *Low*, but most of the guitar work was handled by the returning Carlos Alomar, who, unlike his rhythmic sidekicks, had not featured on *The Idiot*, and Ricky Gardiner, one of three new additions to the team.

During the same conversation in which he had wowed Bowie and Eno with the concept of messing with time, Visconti had suggested Gardiner as a suitable lead guitarist for the project. Earl Slick, who had played on *Station To Station*, had long since fallen out of favour, and his last-minute replacement for the subsequent tour, Stacey Heydon, was no longer in the running either. Bowie had hoped to recruit Klaus Dinger of Neu!, but received a polite but firm 'thanks but no thanks'. Gardiner might not have been so well known, but he had the right credentials, having played for several years in the avant-garde prog-rock quintet Beggars Opera. Visconti had been working with Gardiner's wife, Virginia Scott, on "an opera she had written, with Colin McFarlane [also of Beggars Opera], called *The Immortal Show*."[10] During these sessions, Gardiner recalls, "it transpired that Visconti was recording his own solo album (*Visconti's Inventory*) at the same time, so I put down a guitar line or two".[11] According to Visconti, Gardiner was "totally leftfield and completely savvy with special effects"[12] – just right, then, for *Low*. He also ended up touring and recording with Bowie and Iggy Pop in 1977, during which time he contributed the infectious guitar riff that drives one of Iggy's finest and best known songs, 'The Passenger'.

By the time Gardiner arrived, a few days into the sessions, "over half of the tracks were already recorded";[13] by the end of the first week, basic structural work on side one of *Low* was complete but for vocals and overdubs. (Dennis Davis, George Murray, and Roy Young were all dismissed at this point, their work deemed to be complete.) In what was becoming the general pattern for lead guitarists invited to play on Bowie records, Gardiner "was given no instructions whatsoever" as to what he should play, except for "one solo where [Bowie] sang the first three notes [most likely 'Always Crashing In The Same Car']. I took it from there".[14] Gardiner played through a small, tinny Fender amp that he later described as sounding like a "transistor radio" – not what he would have chosen to use, but he "wasn't about to put my head above the parapet, as the new boy," and hadn't wanted to risk putting his own custom-built Romano Lombardi amplifier on a plane. In the end, however, the sound the Fender amp produced lent his guitar "a rather plaintive quality",[15] which suited the songs he was playing on perfectly.

Another new recruit for *Low* was Roy Young, an expatriate Londoner who had been resident in Hamburg since playing with The Beatles there in the early 1960s. He had initially been invited to lend his piano-playing skills to *Young Americans*, but had prior commitments. Of all the musicians on *Low*, Young is probably the least visible, but his contributions are by no means superfluous. His piano and organ playing are integral to the foundations of several of the songs on side one, notably 'Always Crashing In The Same Car' and 'Be My Wife'.

The most important of the new arrivals was, of course, Brian Eno. Eno had spent some time brainstorming with Bowie before work officially began on the album, but missed most of the first week at the Château. He had spent the end of August and the first three days of September playing with 801, a loose-fitting collective led by his former Roxy Music bandmate, Phil Manzanera. (The album *801 Live* was cut at their third and final gig, on September 3rd.) The result was that his effect on the songs on the first side of *Low* was often more theoretical than practical, his actual contributions largely restricted to adding shape and texture to what was already on tape or offering sage advice. His main tool was his current calling card, the EMS Synthi A, a 'synthesizer in a briefcase' comprising three oscillators and a patchbay system, all controlled by a joystick rather than a keyboard, which he used both to add colourful flourishes of his own and to manipulate the sound of parts played by the other musicians – not, however, to the extent that he would on *"Heroes"*. "He isn't really a musician as much as he is a technician and an ideas man," recalled George Murray.[16] Robert Fripp, meanwhile, would later note that Eno's approach to record-making is "not governed by musical thinking", and driven instead by "break[ing] up the associations which a musician would [normally] use".[17]

With the dependable rhythm trio of Alomar, Davis, and Murray back on board alongside three further highly skilled instrumentalists, one might be forgiven for assuming that Bowie himself would return to his *Station To Station* role: that of singer, rather than musician. But whereas many of his previous albums had seen Bowie adopting various characters – Ziggy, Aladdin, The Thin White Duke – and focusing his energies on telling song-stories through them, his object on *Low* was to find a new world of sound, and to involve himself fully in that, as more than just the general overseer of the band. Having asserted a three-stage plan for the recording of the album, it would have been more than a little odd for Bowie to remain on the periphery until the final (vocal) stage. In fact, he plays more on *Low* than on almost any of his other albums. A quick scan of the sleeve-notes reveals that he played over a dozen different instruments on *Low*, from piano, harmonica, and xylophone to the more idiosyncratic "pump bass" and "brass-synthetic strings". These unusually named sounds came from his Chamberlin M1, a pre-sampling keyboard similar in mechanism to the Mellotron (which was based on the earlier Chamberlin Music Master). The Chamberlin, of which only a few hundred were made, is particularly prevalent on side two of the album, where Bowie and Eno both play it.

To begin with at least, the pervading mood of the *Low* sessions was upbeat and relaxed. The process was so informal, in fact, that when interviewed by *Melody Maker*'s Allan Jones towards the end of August, Brian Eno had "no real idea about the nature of the project", or, indeed, what his contribution to it would entail. With neither a deadline to speak of, nor any rigid scheme for how the music might turn out – or even if it would be released – the musicians involved were free to experiment, and simply enjoy the process of making music; even Carlos Alomar, the most reluctant of the bunch when it came to Bowie and Eno's avant-garde "bullshit",[18] warmed to the new way of working. Bowie had originally assumed that the sessions would result merely in a collection of demos to use as a starting point for a 'proper' new record. But when Visconti made him a tape of what they'd done during the first two weeks, Bowie realised that, to his surprise and amazement, they were well on the way to making an album.

Hidden away from the world in the French countryside, the musicians developed a strong sense of camaraderie. They would all eat together, and spend their off hours watching tapes of the British comedy series *Fawlty Towers* or talking around the communal dining table. "We had some good conversations about music, astrology – the world," said Ricky Gardiner. Dennis Davis would entertain the others with tall stories from his past, chief among them his oft-repeated anecdote about stumbling upon a crashed UFO after wandering into a high security US Air Force hanger. "I was on my way to Vietnam," he later added. "We saw something moving really fast in the sky and sent fighter jets to chase it."[19] According to Tony Visconti, he would also "do a mime act on the closed-circuit-TV camera and have us in stitches".[20] As Davis himself put it, "I was the comedian there."[21]

Although he only makes a fleeting appearance as a backing vocalist on 'What In The World', Iggy Pop was present throughout the making of *Low*, too. Gardiner remembered him being "fit, healthy, and positive".[22] He, like Davis, helped engender a cheery atmosphere by regaling his cohorts with his daft and often depraved memories of life in The Stooges. Bowie and Visconti enjoyed these so much that they set the tapes rolling one night with the intention of turning Iggy's reminiscences into a spoken-world album; sadly, it was never completed, and remains unreleased.

As idyllic as the surroundings might have been, however, the Château d'Hérouville was not without its problems. These seemed mostly to stem from the fact that, it being the end of summer, most of the studio's staff were on holiday, leaving only a very junior assistant engineer barely able to operate the tape machines and kitchen staff who served nothing but rabbit for days. "We found the studio totally useless," recalled Visconti, some months later. "The people who own it now don't seem to care. We all came down with dysentery."[23] (By contrast, when Bowie recorded *Pin-Ups* at the Château in 1973, his weekly column in *Mirabelle* magazine – ghostwritten, in fact, by publicist Cherry Vanilla – made mention of "fresh and lush" fruit and vegetables, and "that famous Paris bread, [with which] everything tastes great".[24] Ricky Gardiner, meanwhile, recalled that the "apparent food problem had been resolved before I arrived",[25] which suggests it only lasted a few days.)

There was also the small matter of the Château apparently being haunted. It had, in the middle of the previous century, been home to the Polish composer Frédéric Chopin. His ghost, and that of his lover, the novelist, playwright, and proto-feminist George Sand, are said to haunt the Château's master bedroom, which Bowie refused to sleep in on account of the dark, deathly cold atmosphere in one of its corners. Eno took the room instead, and has since recalled on numerous occasions that he was woken in the early hours of the morning by a hand on his shoulder, but upon opening his eyes always found the room to be empty. According to Ricky Gardiner, it was also felt that the fact that Chopin died there of consumption "resulted in Eno developing a cough".[26]

Ghosts and rabbits aside, the Château d'Hérouville sessions were also interrupted by a series of personal clashes and upheavals (including Bowie and Visconti contracting food poisoning after eating cheese that had been left out all night). Having engineered and then assisted with the mixing of *The Idiot*, Laurent Thibault found himself usurped by the full-time return of Tony Visconti for the making of *Low*.

He also had a run-in with Bowie after the publication of an article in
Rock Et Folk magazine that listed the musicians set to appear on *The
Idiot*. Thibault has since claimed that Bowie gave him permission to
talk to *Rock Et Folk* earlier in the summer, but when the article came
out Bowie was reportedly furious, branding the engineer a 'traitor'.
(This incident may be what Visconti is referring to when he writes, in
his autobiography, of being "infiltrated" by the French music press.)

Bowie himself was in a fragile state throughout. The dark days of
cocaine psychosis and borderline schizophrenia were still a very recent
memory. "I was at the end of my tether, physically and emotionally," he
later recalled, "and had serious doubts about my sanity."[27] It would take
several years of recovery (and regularly spaced relapses) before Bowie
came close to regaining his equilibrium. Until then, he was a fragile
shell of the indestructible rock'n'roll star of years past – weak,
depressed, and often barely able to see a way back from the depths to
which he had sunk.

After the incident with Thibault, Bowie's next run-in came when his
wife, Angela, turned up at the studio to introduce her new boyfriend,
Roy Martin. The two men reportedly ended up brawling, and had to be
separated by Visconti. Bowie's marriage had been far from stable in
recent years – he would later conclude that it "didn't work out even
remotely"[28] – but now it was heading, finally and irrevocably, towards
divorce. Separating from his wife would not be too much of an issue,
since they had not been living together for some time, but what Bowie
now dreaded was the seemingly inevitable battle for custody of their
young son, Joey (formerly Zowie). More imminently, Bowie faced a
second legal battle, this time with his former manager Michael
Lippman, who was suing his former charge for around $2 million worth
of lost earnings. This understandably cast a long and anxious shadow
over Bowie during the *Low* sessions, particularly as he had to leave
them, in mid September, to meet his lawyers to discuss the case.

Somewhat ironically, it was this – at least in part – that allowed Eno
to really make his presence felt on the second side of *Low*. Visconti

travelled with Bowie to Paris for two days, leaving Eno alone at the Château (the other musicians had by this stage all gone home). Not wanting to let good studio time go to waste, Eno carried on working on the understanding that "if [Bowie] didn't like it, I'd use it myself".[29] As it happens, Bowie liked very much indeed what Eno did – which was to spend two days building up the majority of the instrumental parts for 'Warszawa' and 'Art Decade' – and ended up placing the two songs together at the start of the second side of *Low*.

In what Eno later described as "a very clear division of labour",[30] Bowie took the lead in the recording of the other two songs on side two of *Low*, 'Weeping Wall' and 'Subterraneans'. Eno claimed in 1978 that these both originated from *The Man Who Fell To Earth*, and that they "worked on top of"[31] the unfinished 1975 recordings, but according to Bowie, "the only holdover from the proposed soundtrack that I actually used was the reverse bass part in 'Subterraneans'. Everything else was written for *Low*".[32]

Although the four songs on *Low*'s second side are arranged mostly for synthesizers, each does also feature some form of acoustic instrumentation: 'Warszawa' is underpinned by stark, processed piano, while 'Art Decade' is bulked out by gently bowed cello; 'Weeping Wall' is dominated by Bowie's kinetic xylophone and vibraphone playing, before he brings 'Subterraneans' (and the album itself) to a close with a mournful saxophone refrain. The most striking aspect of this material is not so much its largely instrumental nature, or its synthetic sheen, so much as its refusal to resort to conventional song structures. This came about as a direct result of the way it was recorded. The first seven songs on *Low* were conceived in a much more 'normal' way: Bowie played or sang an idea to his band, who jammed it out until they hit upon the right arrangement, which was then quickly recorded. In the case of the 'ambient' pieces, however, Eno would record a metronomic framework, counting out the required number of bars onto tape, onto which he and Bowie could then build up layers of sound. The upshot of this was that, rather than have to stick to the kind of four and eight-bar chord progressions – and regular time signatures – around which most rock music is built, they could work much more freely, allowing melodies and sequences to build and then resolve themselves in their own time in a manner closer to the work of the avant-garde classical composers of the time than Bowie's 'pop' peers.

By the time Bowie reached the third recording phase of *Low* – lyrics and vocals – he and Visconti had left the Château in search of a better working atmosphere. Bowie had not been in the best frame of mind there, having agreed while in Paris to pay a fairly hefty settlement to Michael Lippman. In his final days at the Château, Bowie found himself too physically and emotionally drained to record (the wordless vocal for 'Warszawa' being the only notable exception). Visconti, meanwhile, had grown increasingly irritated at the facilities on offer to him, and the lack of hired help. So after three weeks in France, Bowie, Visconti, Iggy Pop, and Coco Schwab headed back to Berlin to complete the album at Hansa Tonstudios.

Founded in 1964, Hansa was an offshoot of the record label of the same name; both enterprises were, in 1976, entering a period of increased visibility and international prominence. The label had just released the debut album by Boney M, *Take The Heat Off Me*, featuring 'Daddy Cool', the first of several pan-European hit singles; the studio, meanwhile, was about to benefit significantly from the patronage of Bowie, Iggy, Eno, and co. Initially, Bowie used one of Hansa's smaller studios (not the famous room By The Wall, which served as both recording location and prime inspiration for *"Heroes"*). Here he spent a few days making his final instrumental contributions to the songs on the second side of *Low* – specifically 'Weeping Wall', on which he plays everything – before turning his attention to creating vocal parts for the album's first seven songs.

From a lyrical perspective, *Low* marks quite a change in Bowie's style of writing. Gone are the flamboyant, character-based tales of old; in their place is a series of short, often rather oblique phrases about the state of David Bowie in 1976. Initially, he put this down to the influence of his new home, telling Phillip Manoeuvre and Jonathan Farren of *Rock Et Folk* magazine, in one of his first post-*Low* interviews, that "Berlin has the strange ability to make you write only the important things – anything else you don't mention". By 1978, however, he had come clean on the Eno effect: "He got me off narration, which I was so intolerably bored with. … Brian really opened my eyes to the idea of processing, to the abstract of communication."[33]

Bowie's other close musical friend of the time, Iggy Pop, had a similar effect. Bowie had been greatly impressed by the spontaneity of Iggy's lyric-writing while they were making *The Idiot*, and while he might not have considered himself able to 'write on the mic' as Iggy had done (at least not yet), he did clearly take inspiration from the former Stooge's stark, direct style. *Low*'s short, snappy couplets – "What in the world can you do? / I'm in the mood for your love", for example, or "You're such a wonderful person / But you got problems" – could easily have found a home on one of Iggy's records.

Iggy also had an audible impact on Bowie's vocal delivery, which is less mannered and emotive than on previous albums. The last time Bowie's listeners had heard him on record, he had draped 'Wild Is The Wind' in all the romantic anguish he could muster. By marked contrast, when he first opens his mouth on *Low* (on 'Breaking Glass'), he sings in a low monotone, almost without affectation. 'Sound And Vision' is as close as he gets to the faux-crooning of old, but by the next track, 'Always Crashing In The Same Car', his delivery is for the most part so gentle that he barely sings the words at all.

Bowie didn't find the process of writing the lyrics for *Low* easy. "He couldn't come up with more than one verse for some things," recalled Tony Visconti, "which is why a lot of the tracks fade out."[34] Bowie intended each of the seven songs on side one to have words, but in the end failed to write anything suitable for the first and last of them, 'Speed Of Life' and 'A New Career In A New Town'. As a result, both are instrumental, but it's clear from listening to them that they were originally intended to have a vocal element to them: each is structured, like the rest of the material on the album's first side, in a familiar way, with verse, chorus, and bridge – unlike, say, 'Warszawa', which is another type of music entirely.

In the end, *Low*'s lyrical brevity is such that it would be possible to write the entire album on the back of a postcard, but what little Bowie does say reveals a lot. Perhaps surprisingly, the songs are reflective more of his time in Los Angeles than this new European home. "When I left [L.A.]," Bowie later revealed, "I tried to find out more about the world. I discovered how little I knew, how little I have to say. The lack of lyrics on *Low* reflects that I was literally stuck for words."[35] The first three lyrical pieces, 'Breaking Glass', 'What In The World', and 'Sound And Vision', are all, essentially, about the same thing. In each one, the setting is simply a room – sometimes "your room" and sometimes "my room" – into which Bowie has retreated from the world outside. There are no geographical signifiers, but then they are not needed: the paranoid, psychotic stench of Doheny Drive is unmistakable. In 'Breaking Glass', Bowie is at pains that the subject of the song not see the "something awful" that he has drawn onto the carpet, which we can safely ascertain to be some form or other of Kabbalistic symbol designed to ward off demons. By the time of 'Sound And Vision', he has the blinds pulled, the world shut away, and is sitting in his empty, anaesthetised room, "waiting for the gift"; longing to be released from his Californian prison, and reunited with what drives him: sound and vision.

The last two sung songs on side one offer a slight change of perspective, in that they find Bowie to be back on the move, but are cloaked in a similarly despairing air. 'Always Crashing In The Same Car' is the closest the album gets to presenting a coherent narrative, and it's not a particularly joyous one. Bowie might have left his sterile, electric-blue room, but is still trying to escape the world at large – just as he is on the album's sixth track, 'Be My Wife', on which he announces, clear as day, that for all the globe-trotting he might have done in the preceding decade, he's still a long way from the comfort and security he craves.

The songs on side two of *Low* are generally thought of as being instrumental in nature, but in fact Bowie does sing on two of the four – just not in English, or, indeed, in any recognisable language whatsoever. The dislocated syllables that make up the words to 'Warszawa' and 'Subterraneans' were chosen purely for their phonetic resonance, in order, according to Eno, "to get rid of the language element. ... As soon as there's language it creates a focus, and it's very very difficult not to accept that as the central point of the piece, with the other instruments ranked, or arranged, around it, supporting it." This, Eno noted, is something Bowie took from the current wave of kosmische bands, whose music is "very unfocal – it has a lot of drift in it, if you like, whereas rock music has a lot of anchorage".[36]

But while 'Warszawa' and 'Subterraneans' have no literal meaning, Bowie's delivery of them is very much in keeping with the album's overall narrative thread. By the end of side one, having realised that he must leave behind his destructive lifestyle and environment in Los Angeles, Bowie is actively seeking a new career in a new town. On the second side of the album, he begins a tentative exploration of his new world. Even if we can't understand the words on 'Warszawa', we might assume that this is Bowie repenting, casting out the demons that have hung around his neck for the past couple of years. By the time of 'Subterraneans', even if the general mood is still one of unease and foreboding, he sounds as though he could be singing a lullaby, albeit one from another planet – perhaps the one Thomas Newton fell from in *The Man Who Fell To Earth*, the film for which the song was originally written.

Side two of *Low* is much more evocative of Berlin and the New Europe than the first half of the record. Its four songs form a series of auditory sketches of places Bowie had recently visited or passed through. *Record Mirror*'s teen reporter Tim Lott achieved something of a coup in the autumn of 1977 when he found himself on a train back from Manchester with Bowie (and, indeed, Eddie & The Hotrods, who had, like Bowie, just taped an appearance on Marc Bolan's TV show), and coaxed him into speaking in detail to the British press about *Low* for the first time. 'Warszawa', Bowie explained, was a reflection on the "very bleak atmosphere" of the Polish capital, while three other songs focus on Berlin: 'Art Decade' concerns the artistic dislocation felt by West Berliners in a city that was formerly one of Europe's cultural centres; 'Subterraneans' is "about the people who got caught in East Berlin after the separation", with its "faint jazz saxophones" intended as an echo of what once was; and 'Weeping Wall' is, of course, the Berlin Wall itself – "the misery of it," as Bowie put it.[37]

Despite being conceived from the start as an album of two halves – the title was initially set, fittingly, to be *New Music: Night And Day* – *Low* forms a very strong whole. The music on side one is frenetic and often unresolved, each song fading out inconclusively before the record lurches back into life with the next one. Most of the songs start with some kind of drum fill, but these rarely give the impression of heralding a conventional starting point, instead sounding as though they've just brought to an end another part of a song that we weren't privy to. On side two, the pace drops as Bowie begins to settle into a fitter, healthier speed of life, but the music is no less insistent. Unlike Eno's *Discreet Music*, the very point of which was that it was designed to merge into the background, the 'ambient' songs on *Low* demand to be listened to. 'Weeping Wall' in particular could never be classed as dinner party music.

The greatest of Bowie's leaps into the future, *Low* was met if not by deaf ears then certainly by mild panic when he handed it in to his record label, RCA. In fairness, what they heard did represent a marked change in direction from its predecessors, the big-selling *Young Americans* and *Station To Station*. Those albums had given Bowie a significant commercial footing in the United States, which the label was understandably keen to preserve; one executive famously declared that he would buy Bowie a house in Philadelphia if he would, *please*, make another *Young Americans*. Tony DeFries did his best to have the record shelved; although he no longer had any direct involvement in Bowie's career, DeFries still earned a percentage on any records sold as a result on his settlement with Bowie the previous year, and as such was anxious for anything his former charge released to do well.

Bowie, of course, flatly refused to make any changes to *Low*. He was, as Tony Visconti later put it, "absolutely tired of being RCA's sure thing, and he also felt he was losing his pioneer spirit".[38] For Bowie, *Low* and its successors were about "examining what I want to do" and seeing "if I should go any further with music or not".[39] So determined was he to follow this new path that he "didn't care if RCA sued me". RCA didn't, of course, but did intervene to the extent that *Low* was the third Bowie album in a row to miss its original release date. It had initially been set for release in November 1976, but was put back until the New Year by RCA executives who considered it to be distinctly unpalatable for the Christmas market.

The delay suited Bowie. He had made the decision to 'clean up' some months earlier, but had not yet given himself the kind of time and space required to do so. Since bringing the Station To Station tour to a close in Paris in May, he had written, recorded, and mixed two albums, and relocated twice – briefly, and half-heartedly, to Clos des Mésanges, in Switzerland, and then to Berlin. What he needed now was a period of proper recuperation. Carlos Alomar later recalled that, as he left the Château d'Hérouville towards the end of the *Low* sessions, Bowie told him "he wanted to take some time off the road to take care of his family situation".[40] Finally acknowledging his responsibility to his son played a key role in Bowie's decision to try to straighten himself out. "At first it frightened me, and I tried not to consider the implications," he told *Melody Maker* in 1977. "Now it is his future that concerns me. My own future slips by."

By the time *Low* was completed, Bowie had moved, with Iggy, from his original, temporary Berlin base (the largely unremarkable Hotel Gehrus) into a relatively modest flat above an auto-parts store in the Schöneberg district. The flat, at 155 Hauptstrasse, a mere ten minutes on foot from where Christopher Isherwood had lived, was found for

Bowie and Iggy by Coco Schwab, who lived there with them. So too did Joey, who had turned five in May and was promptly enrolled in an English-speaking school in the city. The location – among the poorest parts of West Berlin, and mostly populated by Turkish immigrants – and living quarters – decidedly spartan by comparison to Doheny Drive or Clos des Mésanges – suited Bowie's new outlook and desire to live a simple, anonymous life, and his current financial situation; with the terms of the MainMan deal still hanging over him and the Michael Lippman settlement to pay, his bank balance was not looking too healthy. There was also the fact that the flat put Bowie within walking distance of Hansa and, by extension, the Wall (and all that lay behind it).

Despite their stated intention to clean up, Bowie and Iggy's initial time spent in Berlin was very much a period of transition – of binging and purging, relapse and recovery. They might have escaped the clutches of Los Angeles, a city seemingly built on cocaine, but they now found themselves in what Bowie later called "the heroin capital of the world",[41] which made life particularly difficult for Iggy. Reminiscing on VH1's *Behind The Music* two decades later, Iggy described the pattern of their first weeks in Berlin thus: "There's seven days in a week: two days for bingeing for old time's sake; two more days for recovery; and that left three days to do any other activity." The city "hadn't changed since 1910," according to Iggy. There were "organ grinders who still had monkeys; quality transvestite shows. A different world. By evening, I'd go have dinner with Bowie, see a film or watch *Starsky And Hutch* – that was our big thing, me and Bowie. If there wasn't enough to do, I knew some bad people, and I'd get stoned or drunk. Sometimes I'd do the bad stuff with Bowie, and the good stuff with the bad people."[42]

Each of these recovering dum dum boys had, in fairness, managed to reduce his drug intake significantly, but both now drank heavily instead, and would continue to do so through 1976 and into 1977. "Virtually every time I saw him in Berlin," writes Angela Bowie of this period, "he was drunk, or working on *getting* drunk."[43] Berlin seemed the perfect place for living in an alcoholic haze; in Bowie's view, as he told Allan Jones around the time of *"Heroes"*, it was "a city made up of bars for sad people to get drunk in". Bowie and Iggy would drift in and out of these anonymous watering holes, both in their own Schöneberg area and beyond (Iggy often being sent to scout out new venues in advance for his more famous, more reserved friend). Among their regular haunts was the Exile restaurant in the Kreuzberg district, which Bowie later recalled having "this smoky room" at the back that was "like another living room, except the company was always changing".[44]

In more sober periods, they did what any other intellectually curious young men might do in an unfamiliar, cosmopolitan city: explore the streets on foot or on bike, go to market, visit record shops and galleries, sip coffee in quiet cafes, idly watching the locals live their lives. They also took regular (sometimes covert) trips across the border into East Berlin and beyond, often with Iggy's girlfriend of the time, Esther Friedmann, the daughter of a Berlin-based diplomat.

In November, another chapter of Bowie's life came to a close when his estranged wife paid him a visit for what would amount, ultimately, to a final fling. In the midst of this, Bowie suffered a suspected coronary, leading his wife to drive him to the British military hospital in Berlin. A hospital spokesman later revealed, however, that "he'd just overdone things, and was suffering from too much drink".

Angela Bowie's undoing came a few days later, as a result of her serving her husband with an unwise ultimatum, which effectively boiled down to this: Coco Schwab – "the gatekeeper and the assassin … [who] did his dirty work for him and took all the consequences"[45] – or me. He responded by asking for a divorce. Before she left, Angela went into Schwab's bedroom, "gathered up her clothes", and "threw them out of the window into the street. … And for David and me, that was the end."[46]

DAVID BOWIE: LOW

Produced by David Bowie and Tony Visconti. Engineered by Tony
Visconti, Laurent Thibault, and Eduard Meyer. Recorded, unless
otherwise noted, at Château d'Hérouville, Pontoise, France, and
Hansa Tonstudio 2, Berlin, Germany (September–October 1976) and
mixed at Hansa (October 1976).

SPEED OF LIFE 2:46
(Bowie)
David Bowie: ARP 2600, Chamberlin; **Carlos Alomar**: guitar;
Roy Young: piano; **George Murray**: bass; **Dennis Davis**: drums.
■ *Low*'s opening track is a fitting introduction to the new Bowie sound,
a kind of overture to what follows. Most (if not all) of the sonic signifiers
of the album are here: the stark, processed drums; the effortlessly
funky yet unobtrusive bass; intricate, duelling guitar and synthesizer
lines that vie for attention in a manner oddly reminiscent of The Velvet
Underground's 'Sister Ray'. For a man known principally for his
character-based songs and shape-shifting singing, starting the album off
with an instrumental track (the first of Bowie's recorded career) was not
just a bold move, but also an act of defiance.

'Speed Of Life' starts with a fade-in, but it is so abrupt that, rather
than easing the listener gently into this brave new world, it gives the
impression instead that we have wandered into something already in
full flow. Straight away, we are presented with a tumbling, dissonant
synthesizer line and given an instant introduction to Tony Visconti's
revolutionary reinterpretation of Dennis Davis's drum kit.

It's often the case, on an album opener, that instruments join in
gradually, one by one, but here all the constituent parts are in place
from the outset. The bass, guitar, and synthesizers all follow an
insistent, descending chord progression; Visconti's Harmonizer gives
the drums a similar downward momentum.

The structure of the song is disconcertingly cyclical, never once
anchoring itself to any fixed point. It starts with what might be the

chorus, which runs into a 'verse' and a 'bridge' before beginning the whole thing again. The fade at the end of the third chorus gives the impression that, even though we can no longer hear them, the musicians will play on for some time yet, until they can find a way out of the song's seemingly never-ending, circular construction. Of all the songs on *Low*, 'Speed Of Life' is perhaps the one that most betrays the (often overstated) influence of Kraftwerk. The similarity is most striking in the bridge, where a pair of call-and-response synthesizer lines introduces a strict but upbeat melody over a militaristic two-beat rhythm. But while there is a clear surface link to something like 'Ohm Sweet Ohm' (from 1975's *Radio-Activity*), 'Speed Of Life' sounds much more spontaneous than anything Kraftwerk might have produced, which is perhaps why it simply fades out at the end of its third minute: the musicians were making it up as they went along, and didn't know how to bring the song to a close.

BREAKING GLASS 1:51
(Bowie/Murray/Davis)
David Bowie: vocals; **Brian Eno**: Minimoog; **Ricky Gardiner**: guitar;
Carlos Alomar: lead guitar; **George Murray**: bass;
Dennis Davis: drums.
■ The shortest song on *Low*, 'Breaking Glass' is also the most outwardly straightforward. It is unique on side one as being the only song not instigated by Bowie itself: as its rhythm-heavy arrangement suggests, the song arose from a jam led by drummer Dennis Davis, who wanted to inject more fun and looseness into the *Low* material. He and George Murray, whose bassline echoes the staccato rhythm of the drums, were duly given co-authorship of the song with Bowie, although it is Carlos Alomar's wailing lead-guitar line that first catches the listener's ear.

Like 'Speed Of Life', 'Breaking Glass' doesn't come to any kind of satisfactory conclusion. After the spacious, open-ended intro, Bowie tears through two short verses in his new, Iggy-inspired monotone, neatly divided by a single chorus (a reprise of the intro). Then, long before the song can become familiar, it fades out, apparently as a result of Bowie's inability to come up with any more words. As brief and fragmented as his lyrics are, they pack in enough detail to make the setting clear: Doheny Drive during the dark days of 1975 (also the theme of the next two songs, 'What In The World' and 'Sound And Vision'). When he sings "You're such a wonderful person / But you got problems" during the song's lone chorus, it's hard not to assume that Bowie is talking to himself, bringing to the forefront *Low*'s underlying themes of psychosis and (borderline) schizophrenia. The gaps in the story, meanwhile, are filled by sporadic, shock-like bursts – at 0:32, 0:52, and 1:31 – from Eno's Minimoog.

WHAT IN THE WORLD 2:23
(Bowie)
David Bowie: vocals; **Iggy Pop**: vocals; **Brian Eno**: ARP, EMS Synthi; **Ricky Gardiner**: guitar; **Carlos Alomar**: guitar; **Roy Young**: Farfisa organ; **George Murray**: bass; **Dennis Davis**: drums.

■ If *The Idiot* was full of distinctly Bowie-esque songs, then 'What In The World' is *Low*'s Iggy Pop moment. The one-time Stooge sings on a song that, at one stage, was in line to appear on his album instead. The lyric certainly would have fitted the bill: still ruminating on his American exile, Bowie sings about a "little girl with grey eyes" (the kind, one might assume, that Iggy seemed so wary of corrupting on *The Idiot*) whose love he is "in the mood for". The affair seems doomed before it has even started, despite Bowie's attempts to present "the real me" – a common, self-reverential, and almost rap-like theme of his lyrics throughout his career. In "talking through the gloom", meanwhile, Bowie refers back to one of the touchstones of his early songwriting career, Syd Barrett, by way of James Joyce, whose poem 'Golden Hair' (featuring the line "For I heard you singing through the gloom") Barrett set to music on *The Madcap Laughs*.

Structurally, 'What In The World' is about as conventional as *Low* gets: three verses, two choruses, no messing – but the arrangement is complex and contradictory. Murray and Davis provide a jerky, stop-start rhythm not dissimilar to the one they came up with for 'Breaking Glass'; Alomar and Gardiner trade slick, circular guitar licks; Bowie and Iggy vie for the title of lead vocalist; and while Roy Young hammers out a Farfisa organ part reminiscent of mid-1960s garage, Eno hauls the song back into the future with a show-stealing, arrhythmic synthesizer part that has the effect of an electronic frog chorus. Once again, the song ends in a fade, but in a more traditional fashion than elsewhere on *Low*: whereas 'Speed Of Life' and 'Sound And Vision' suggest that the players are stuck in some kind of musical moebius loop, here they just sound like they're enjoying bashing out an extended final verse.

SOUND AND VISION 3:03

(Bowie)

David Bowie: vocals, ARP, saxophone; **Brian Eno**: backing vocals; **Mary Hopkin**: backing vocals; **Ricky Gardiner**: guitar; **Carlos Alomar**: guitar; **Roy Young**: piano; **George Murray**: bass; **Dennis Davis**: drums.

■ The unlikely pop moment on *Low* – Bowie's biggest hit single in the UK for four years – sounds, at first, like an instrumental jam, with no serious thought given to verses, choruses, and suchlike. Guitars, bass, drums, and piano feel their way jauntily around yet another circular riff, augmented at one stage by an ethereal synthesized-string motif played by Bowie. Then, at 1:14, comes what is in many respects the most incongruous sound on *Low*: a cooing backing vocal, echoing the main guitar line, sung by Brian Eno and Mary Hopkin (Tony Visconti's wife at the time). Before the listener has a chance to fully process this strange development – a pastiche, perhaps, of 1960s girl-group pop – Bowie darkens the mood considerably with a quick blast of sax, heralding the start, finally, of the 'song' part.

Eno and Hopkin's contribution to 'Sound And Vision' highlights just how unusual Bowie's three-stage method of recording was (and is). The backing vocals were recorded some time before Bowie had even conceived of what the main vocal melody might be – just as were virtually all of the lead guitar and keyboard parts on the album. The song also demonstrates the extent to which Bowie, Visconti, and Eno used pre- and post-production effects on the most basic of sounds and musical figures. Virtually everything on 'Sound And Vision' is played through some sort of processor. The drums, of course, have an indestructible, futuristic sheen, but are also joined here, at the start of every other bar, by a gated, whip-like snare sound. The bass is heavily compressed, the piano has been subjected to some kind of phasing effect, and the descending synth-string line is drenched in delay and sustain, merging the first seven notes together before being abruptly supplanted by the eighth. Even the saxophone, which bends in and out of phase, sounds as though it might have been subjected to Visconti's Harmonizer.

Bowie's half-spoken, half-sung vocal carries on the themes of the first two sung songs on the album, its low, reflective tone at odds with the upbeat, almost parodic sensibilities of the music that surrounds it. He's still stuck in his bedroom, but has at least managed to replace the one in Los Angeles with "awful" things scrawled on the floor with a blue-walled sanctuary in Berlin. His pervading attitude, however, remains to "pull down the blinds and fuck 'em all"[47], as he later put it – not the healthiest of signs, and a clear demonstration of the fact that it would take him some time to feel his way back into the real world. The main chorus lyric, if there is such a thing here, echoes Bowie's exhortations in 'Breaking Glass' to "Listen!" and "See!" By the end of the song, he's back where he started, still wondering and waiting, not yet ready to face whatever might be outside.

'Sound And Vision' confounded all expectations – not least those of RCA, who considered the *Low* material to be distinctly uncommercial – by hitting Number Three on the UK singles chart when released, in February 1977, backed, fittingly, by 'A New Career In A New Town'. In the USA, however, it fared rather less well, stalling at Number 69

(Bowie's last two major singles, 'Fame' and 'Golden Years', had reached Numbers One and Three respectively). Surprisingly, given its status as *Low*'s lead single, 'Sound And Vision' was played only once on Bowie's 1978 tour – surprisingly, that is, until you learn that he struggled to sing it (just as had been the case with his last big single, 'Golden Years').

ALWAYS CRASHING IN THE SAME CAR 3:29
(Bowie)
David Bowie: vocals, Chamberlin; **Brian Eno**: EMS Synthi; **Ricky Gardiner**: guitar; **Carlos Alomar**: guitar; **Roy Young**: piano; **George Murray**: bass; **Dennis Davis**: drums.

■ 'Always Crashing In The Same Car' is the only song on side one of *Low* that starts properly *and* reaches a recognisable end-point; it is also the first of a pair of songs that feature guitar solos (at the height of punk, no less). But, as with the earlier 'What In The World', any concessions to regularity in terms of structure are counterbalanced by a rich, involved arrangement, built up from multiple guitar and synthesizer parts, bass, and drums.

Once again, the first sound heard is a drum. But whereas the previous three tracks on *Low* were all jolted into life by a swift, hard hit, 'Always Crashing' opens with a snare drum rattling so gently as to barely be audible, paving the way for the general air of somnambulence that dominates the first verse. Most of the instruments are put through an effects processor of some kind, but with the aim of masking rather than highlighting them. Alomar plays a single note on his guitar every two bars that rolls in and out of phase; Bowie answers it with a lonely, repeating horn riff on his Chamberlin; Young's broken piano chords echo into the distance; Eno lets a Theremin-like oscillator rise and fall in the distance. Davis's drums are still played through the Harmonizer, but are lower in the mix than elsewhere on the album, while Murray refrains from his usual funky embellishments on the bass, restricting his playing to a slow, unfussy pulse. Bowie's vocal, drenched in reverb, confirms the overall mood of despairing inertia. The lyrics clearly find him in the midst of a great crisis (as discussed in more detail elsewhere in this book), but the fact that they are presented in the past tense – unlike the rest of *Low* – offer a slight ray of hope, suggesting that Bowie might now be on the way back up out of the abyss.

After the bleak first verse, 'Always Crashing' is roused from its slumbers by the arrival of Ricky Gardiner, who interrupts proceedings with a show-stealing lead-guitar line that climbs several octaves and dominates the largely vocal-free choruses. The bass and drums join in, giving the piece a renewed momentum through its second verse and chorus, which peaks when Bowie lets out a wordless cry at 2:18. Gardiner then unleashes an extraordinarily lyrical guitar solo, which effectively takes the place of a third verse, before the song ends in the album's only big 'rock' crescendo of distorted chords and cymbal crashes. (One might assume that Eno played a part in creating the molten-lava sheen of the guitar lines, but not according to Gardiner himself, who "can't hear any evidence"[48] of any post-production Enosification.)

BE MY WIFE 2:55
(Bowie)
David Bowie: vocals; **Ricky Gardiner**: guitar; **Carlos Alomar**: guitar; **Roy Young**: piano, Farfisa organ; **George Murray**: bass; **Dennis Davis**: drums.

■ After the careful, considered 'Always Crashing In The Same Car', 'Be My Wife' is the most direct, throwaway song on *Low*. Like 'TVC15' on the previous year's *Station To Station*, it sounds somewhat incongruous, giving the impression that the musicians needed to let their hair down a little after all the 'serious' work they'd been doing on the other songs. Roy Young, in his big *Low* moment, leads the way with jovial, music-hall piano (which he later augments with brash organ chords); Davis is back on full throttle; and Murray returns to his sinuous, funky best, notably in the chorus, which sounds like slowed-down disco played by a garage band. Bowie holds down the root guitar chords, freeing Alomar and Gardiner to trade lead licks; towards the end, the latter is given the opportunity to solo, and doesn't disappoint, using the main riff as a starting point and then launching off into the stratosphere at the song's close (which is, inevitably, another fade out).

Bowie's vocal delivery, like the music behind it, bears the influence of Syd Barrett, whose "impact on my thinking was enormous", he revealed after the original Pink Floyd frontman's death in 2006. But beneath the general air of joviality is one of *Low*'s most stark and despairing lyrics. Despite having "lived all over the world", he has "left every place", and now simply longs for someone to "be mine". Some commentators have suggested that this song marks Bowie's last attempt at saving his marriage, but the singer himself, while agreeing that the lyric is "genuinely anguished", told *Melody Maker* in 1978 that it "could have been [about] anybody".

'Be My Wife' is the last song on *Low* to feature any form of intelligible lyric. As such it marks the end of a suite of five songs about the life Bowie was so desperate to leave. Overall, the mood of these songs is undeniably bleak, but there is a hint of optimism in them, too, particularly in this track and (oddly) 'Always Crashing'; a suggestion that, as 'low' a point as Bowie might have reached, he's determined to get better. ('Be My Wife' was the second and final single to be drawn from *Low*. Despite being the most straightforward song on the album, it didn't fare well on its own, suffering the indignity of being the first Bowie single since 1971 to fail to chart.)

A NEW CAREER IN A NEW TOWN 2:51
(Bowie)
David Bowie: synthesizer, harmonica; **Brian Eno**: "synthetics", sequencer; **Ricky Gardiner**: guitar; **Carlos Alomar**: guitar;
Roy Young: piano; **George Murray**: bass; **Dennis Davis**: drums.
■ 'A New Career In A New Town' is, in effect, *Low*'s tipping point: the instrumental bridge between the pop sensibilities of side one and the ambient textures of side two, and also the point at which Eno begins to assert control over the sound of the record. As on 'Speed Of Life', the

other instrumental track on side one, the influence of German synth-pop looms large. But 'A New Career' is much more than just Bowie-does-Kraftwerk, as is often suggested. Bowie's own attitude to this is that his aim for *Low* (and beyond) was to create a hybrid of European electronic-music techniques and US rhythm and blues – something far more visceral (and, by extension, more human), therefore, than the records Kraftwerk were making.

'A New Career In A New Town' is a perfect demonstration of this. In what might be termed the verse – for this was, like 'Speed Of Life', clearly intended to be a 'song', not just a piece of music – a pair of synthesizers with very different timbres take it in turns to play a six-note sequenced figure over a bed of ambient Enosound and a metronomic pulse that again recalls *Radio-Activity* (but which in fact is probably a 'real' kick drum fed through one of Eno's filters). Then, at 0:35, the false dawn of tranquillity is shattered as the rest of the band pile in en masse. Dennis Davis lays down a strident two-beat rhythm; George Murray punches out a great walking bassline; pretty, busy synthesizers flit in and out; and, atop a wall of guitars and piano, Bowie lets loose with a cathartic burst of harmonica – a distinctly American embellishment to counterbalance the European feel of what preceded it.

Almost a minute of raucous abandon passes before the calm opening section returns, the abrupt transition between the two recalling the way Brian Wilson built his 'pocket symphonies' a decade earlier. Then, after the briefest of reprieves, bass, drums, and the rest jump back in as if they'd never been away. As the song reaches its close, Bowie and Eno's primary motivation becomes clear: the 'real' instruments are joined by a rush of synthesizers, merging the song's two distinct halves into a marvellous, electro-organic whole.

WARSZAWA 6:20
(Bowie/Eno)
David Bowie: vocals; **Brian Eno**: piano, Minimoog, EMS Synthi, Chamberlin.

■ The opening track on the second side of *Low*, 'Warszawa' is where Bowie and Eno left pop music behind and embarked on an entirely new direction. It is also the moment, above all others, where Eno took charge of the project. Eno's role in the making of *Low* (as well as *"Heroes"* and *Lodger*) is regularly overstated to the detriment of Bowie – who, lest we forget, had done his fair share of innovating on his own already – and Tony Visconti, the album's producer. In the case of 'Warszawa', however, Eno deserves all the credit he can get, since he effectively wrote and recorded the entire piece himself, but for Bowie's surprising, freeform vocal.

Somewhat surprisingly, given its decidedly synthesized final form, 'Warszawa' (and the similarly electronic 'Art Decade', which follows it) started life on piano. Bowie had to leave the Château d'Hérouville to go to Paris for a few days, to meet his lawyers and discuss the Michael Lippman case. Eno remained at the Château, where one morning he heard Visconti's son, Morgan, pick out a tentative, three-note figure – comprising the notes A, B, and C – on the studio grand piano. Eno joined the boy at the piano to complete the motif that became the defining melody of 'Warszawa', applying it to an instruction Bowie had earlier given him to compose "a really slow piece of music" with a "very emotive, almost religious feel to it".

Shortly after the release of *"Heroes"*, Bowie described the material on *Low*'s second side as being about things "I couldn't express in words. Rather it required textures, and of all the people that I've heard write textures, Brian's always appealed to me the most".[49] This explanation seems particularly fitting for 'Warszawa'. Apart from the vocal element that Bowie introduces, four minutes in, there is not much in the way of melodic progression. The tempo, too, dictated by Eno's pre-recorded click-track, remains the same throughout. What changes Eno makes are, in the grand tradition of his ambient music, much more subtle.

The only rhythmic element to speak of on 'Warszawa' is a funereal pulse that sounds every three seconds or so, played simultaneously on piano and several synthesizers. Eno gradually alters the texture of it by altering synthesizer filters and applying gentle treatments to the piano, the combined result of which is that it seems constantly to be in a state of growing or receding in the mix, echoing the way that various other sounds in the 'sonic bed' rise and fall around it. Eno employs a similar trick for the graceful melodic parts, which are arranged principally for a woodwind-like Chamberlin sound, but often joined by a wall of harmonically sympathetic synthesizer layers.

The end result is a disarmingly emotive piece of music. While there are clear links to the ideas Eno had been pursuing (and would continue to pursue) in his solo work, 'Warszawa' is too powerful to be deployed as ambient, 'background' music. Despite the lack of any words to which the listener might relate, it is by some distance the most affecting track on *Low*. On his return from Paris, Bowie himself was sufficiently inspired by what Eno had created to add a wordless vocal to it, the delivery of which drew on a record he had recently been bought of a Bulgarian boys choir. Bowie's vocal is a multi-tracked assortment of syllables chosen for the sound they make rather than their meaning. One of Bowie's vocal parts is sung in a disconcertingly high register, which was achieved by Visconti slowing down the tape, recording Bowie's voice at that slower rate, and then speeding it back up again, thereby raising the pitch and mimicking the sound of a choirboy.

ART DECADE 3:43
(Bowie)
David Bowie: piano, Chamberlin, guitar, ARP; **Brian Eno**: piano, Minimoog, EMS Synthi, Chamberlin; **Eduard Meyer**: cello.
■ The second of the two songs Eno worked on in Bowie's absence, 'Art Decade' started out earlier in the sessions as an unconventional piano piece that required four hands – Bowie's and Eno's – to play. Bowie "didn't like it very much, and sort of forgot about it",[50] according to Eno, but Eno persevered with the idea, building up layers of ambient sound and discord around the slow, central riff.

It is apparent just from listening to it that 'Art Decade' was much more of a collaborative effort than 'Warszawa'. Although there is still a strong harmonic resonance to 'Art Decade', there is also a sense of competition and conflict between the various melodic and textural elements, a result, surely, of the fact that, on this song, Bowie added several layers of his own to what Eno had already recorded, including a track of "pre-prepared percussion", which he generated on his Chamberlin.

While 'Art Decade' is in some respects more dynamic than 'Warszawa', the overall mood is darker. The title, of course, is a play on words that reflects both Bowie's own fear of diminishing artistic returns and the idea of art in Berlin having 'decayed' in the years since the War and the building of the Wall. This is reflected in the music, which opens, atonally, with what feels like a last-gasp reach for former glories before settling into melancholy. In amongst the various synthetic elements is a gentle reminder of the value of 'real' instruments: an aching cello, used more for texture than harmony, which was scored by Tony Visconti but played by the in-house engineer at Hansa, Eduard Meyer.

WEEPING WALL 3:26
(Bowie)
David Bowie: vibraphone, xylophone, piano, Minimoog, Chamberlin, guitar, vocal.

■ While Eno's fingerprints are all over 'Warszawa' and 'Art Decade', Bowie played everything on 'Weeping Wall' himself. Eno once suggested that this piece, along with the initially unreleased 'Some Are', was a relic from Bowie's attempt at scoring *The Man Who Fell To Earth*; Bowie, however, is adamant that only 'Subterraneans' was recycled from that time.

Bowie's first (completed) attempt at creating a textural and largely instrumental piece on his own, 'Weeping Wall' was also the only track on *Low* to be recorded entirely at Hansa. Driven by insistent malleted percussion and a nagging synthesizer pulse, this track is much more dynamic and kinetic than the rest of the material on side two. It recalls the repetitive minimalism of Philip Glass and Steve Reich, notably Reich's 'Music For Mallet Instruments, Voices, And Organ'. (His *Music For 18 Musicians* adopts a similar theme, but it's unlikely that Bowie would have heard it yet; although it premiered in New York in April 1976, Bowie had already set sail for Europe, while the recorded version wasn't released until 1978.) Intended, according to its author, to evoke the misery of the Berlin Wall itself and those trapped on the wrong side of it, 'Weeping Wall' is, like the majority of the songs on *Low*, a fittingly unresolved snapshot, peppered with abrupt synthesizer melodies and frustrated, wordless vocals, and ending, as ever, with a fade.

SUBTERRANEANS 5:39
(Bowie)
Some instrumental parts recorded at Cherokee Studios, Los Angeles, USA (December 1975). **David Bowie**: electric piano, guitar, saxophone, vocal; **Brian Eno**: piano, ARP; **Carlos Alomar**: guitar; **George Murray**: bass.

■ *Low*'s closing track, 'Subterraneans' is, like virtually everything else on the album, fragmentary and inconclusive. It arrives mid-thought, just as did 'Speed Of Life' 35 minutes earlier, and, after five lugubrious minutes, simply drifts off into the ether. The only confirmed remnant of the *Man Who Fell To Earth* soundtrack, it was subsequently moulded by Bowie and Eno into a sound-painting about the forgotten residents of East Berlin, complete with a mournful, free-jazz saxophone solo. Carlos Alomar makes his only appearance on side two of the album, his formless, backwards guitar-lines floating in and out of the mix. George Murray is also credited on the original LP sleeve, but there's no evidence of anything other than a slow, synthesized bassline on the song. The sleeve notes also credit "Peter and Paul" with additional ARP and piano. The Paul may well be a nod to Paul Buckmaster, who worked with Bowie at Cherokee Studios in late 1975 on the aborted movie soundtrack; the identity of Peter remains a mystery.

'Subterraneans' rides in on a wave of moody synthesizer textures, slowly descending bass, synthetic strings, and various backwards-recorded sounds. As well as the guitar parts, there are also backwards flourishes of Rhodes Electric Piano. These are most likely what Bowie recycled from the unfinished soundtrack recordings; when played in reverse (or, rather, forwards), they certainly have a clear cinematic quality that evokes the feel of Miles Davis's landmark album, *In A Silent Way*. On top of this moody, atmospheric backdrop, Bowie alternates between a downbeat saxophone refrain (which, as noted elsewhere, was conceived as an echo of the East Berlin jazz scene) and a repeating vocal chant, sung, like 'Warszawa', in a made-up language of fractured syllables.

SOME ARE 3:24 / **ALL SAINTS** 3:35
(Bowie/Eno)
Mixed at Mountain Studios, Montreux, Switzerland (1991). **David Bowie**: piano, Chamberlin, guitar, vocal; **Brian Eno**: piano, ARP, Minimoog, EMS Synthi.
■ In 1991, as part of a two-year programme of CD/LP reissues of Bowie's back catalogue, Rykodisc/EMI released a version of *Low* with three bonus tracks: a fairly pointless remix of 'Sound And Vision', and these two previously unheard songs, both of which had been left unfinished at the end of the *Low* sessions. They were mixed 15 years later by Bowie and David Richards, whose association with Bowie began when he served as assistant engineer on *"Heroes"*. (Richards was subsequently promoted to 'engineer' on *Lodger*, and has since worked in various capacities on a number of other Bowie albums, including *Never Let Me Down*, *The Buddha Of Suburbia*, and *1. Outside*.)
    'Some Are' is very much in the same vein as the material of side two of *Low*. It is driven by virtually the same single-note pulse of piano that underpins 'Warszawa', and draped in a similar shroud of icy synthesizers. What sets it apart, however, from the rest of the ambient material on *Low*, is that Bowie deigns to sing on it in English (albeit rather foggily). The brief, sparse lyric – only four syllables longer than

a haiku – avoids the personal themes that dominate *Low*, with Bowie choosing instead to write, in a similarly bleak fashion, about "sleigh-bells and snow". This has led some to speculate that it was written for the scene in *The Man Who Fell To Earth*, in which Mary Lou watches Father Christmas pass down the street in his sleigh[51]; Bowie, however, maintains that this is not the case, and that he conceived of the idea during the *Low* sessions.

Even if it wasn't designed with the film in mind, 'Some Are' would have made a fitting addition to the proposed soundtrack, as might 'All Saints', were it to have been finished. While 'Some Are' has the feel of a complete entity, 'All Saints' seems very much a work-in-progress: an insistent, sequenced bassline over which Bowie and Eno let loose slabs of discordant guitar, synthesizer, and feedback. Much more ragged than its fellow bonus-track, it is closer in sound to the more aggressive, dissonant instrumental tracks on *"Heroes"*. Left untitled at the time of recording, it was named in 1991 after co-author Brian Eno's record label at the time.

Subsequent CD issues of *Low* do not include either track, but 'All Saints' can be found on the 2001 compilation of Bowie instrumentals to which it lent its name, alongside Philip Glass's orchestral reworking of 'Some Are' (more on that later).

NEIGHBOURHOOD THREAT

D espite RCA's misgivings, *Low* was unveiled to the record-buying public at the end of the second week of January 1977. Bowie had originally intended to call the album *New Music: Night And Day*, but changed his mind at the last minute. The new title was chosen partly as a kind of reference to the singer's new 'low profile' when seen in conjunction with the cover art, an orange-hued, heavily treated still from *The Man Who Fell To Earth*, showing Thomas Newton in profile, the collar of his duffle coat pulled up to his ears.

Bowie had turned 30 the previous Saturday, and had celebrated his birthday in Berlin with Iggy Pop and Romy Haag, the nightclub owner and cabaret singer with whom he enjoyed a brief relationship. The timing of *Low*'s release, a week after its author bade farewell to his twenties, couldn't have been more fitting. Bowie's days of adopting a new character with each passing season had passed, and he was determined now to make a new, more serious music that didn't need to hide behind a Ziggy Stardust or Thin White Duke. Working with Eno, it seems, had begun to instil a newfound confidence in the brittle, uncertain Bowie, so that he "really didn't need to adopt characters to sing my songs".[1] He was determined, too, to let the record speak for itself. The man who had, in years past, revelled in giving extravagant, controversial copy to interviewers now had nothing to say to them at all. Virtually his only dialogue with the press, in fact, for the first six months of 1977, was a terse letter to *Melody Maker*, in February, to "correct the misconception that Iggy Pop is managed by myself".

What this meant, first and foremost, was that journalists who had been used to being spoon-fed Bowie's own rationale for each of his new records now had to make sense of *Low* on their own. It's perhaps not so surprising, then – even when, today, *Low* is regarded not just as one of Bowie's finest works, but as one of the most innovative albums of its era – that the initial critical response was both confused and distinctly divided. This was reflected particularly in the *New Musical Express*, where, unusually, two separate reviews were published, side-by-side. Ian MacDonald, having reminded his readers that Bowie had already adopted "more creative idioms than the average artist could name", declares *Low* to be "the ONLY contemporary rock album", and one on which its author "achieves the ultimate image-illusion available to an individual working within the existing cultural forms of the West. He vanishes". A few inches to the right, however, Charles Shaar Murray, a long-term Bowie fan and later co-author of one of the first and best book-length appraisals of the singer, could hardly have been more vitriolic. "Who needs this shit?" he asks – this shit being "the sound of nothing"; "a bunch of intros that fade out while you're waiting for something to happen", the result of Bowie's "profoundly selfish and egotistical" descent into a sound-world of "purest hatred and destructiveness".[2] (While the writers' opinions were poles apart, readers of the *NME* appeared to take a unified pro-Bowie stance. The letters page for the next few weeks was awash with praise for *Low*, and claims that Murray had "lost all credibility" for writing the record off.)

Elsewhere, the response was largely one of mild bafflement. *Records And Recording* decided that *Low* was "weird as anything".[3] In *Melody Maker*, Michael Watts seemed to conclude that Bowie had only partly achieved a "successful marrying [of] pop music with electronic concepts", and that the material on side two "doesn't seem as interesting or experimental as most of the works on Eno's own Obscure label, let alone Reich, Berio, Stockhausen, and all the rest".[4] A week later, however, Watts called *Low* "remarkable" and "deeply relevant".[5] *Rolling Stone* finally got around to reviewing the album in its April 21st issue. Like many of his peers, the reviewer, John Milward, found more to praise on the album's first side, notably the band's "squeaky performances" and Bowie's "lyrical playfulness". On side two, Bowie's "mask begins to slip … [he] lacks the self-assured humour to pull off his avant-garde aspirations". Milward did at least consider *Low* to be a "moderately interesting conduit through which a wider audience will be exposed to Bowie's latest [musical] heroes"; the editors of *Trouser Press* magazine, by contrast, summed up their feelings with a two-part feature entitled 'The Man Who Fell From Grace'.

It didn't help, of course, that RCA weren't quite sure what to make of *Low* either. A contemporary report in *Circus* magazine quotes an unnamed label operative as suggesting of side two of the album that, "frankly, it needs more work"[6] – and this from an RCA employee who, one would hope, was supposed to be talking up Bowie's new sound. (As if to render the party line even more damning, the same reviewer was then told that Iggy Pop's forthcoming LP, *The Idiot*, is "a great album … Everybody's gonna find out where all the punk bands that are making it did their homework. Iggy's so far ahead of everybody".)

Bowie was in no mood to face his accusers, but then he didn't really need to: by the time most of the reviews had hit the presses, however, *Low* was already a success in commercial terms. It peaked at Number Two on the UK albums chart – three spots higher than *Station To Station* – and came in at an impressive 11 on the other side of the Atlantic. Then, despite the fact that Bowie had made none of the usual promotional efforts, such as filming a promo video or appearing on *Top Of The Pops*, 'Sound And Vision' gave him his 12th British Top 10 hit single. Instead of promoting *Low*, he spent the early weeks of 1977 enjoying a life that was as close as his ever came to normal: painting, writing, visiting art galleries, and propping up Berlin's bars and nightclubs.

RCA had (understandably) hoped that there might be a *Low* tour. The British music press was similarly optimistic, *Melody Maker* even going so far as to predict a live band featuring Tony Visconti on bass and Brian Eno on synthesizer.[7] Bowie, of course, had other ideas. Instead of going out in support of his own album, he returned to his continued efforts to resuscitate the career of Iggy Pop. With *The Idiot* set for release in mid March, Bowie assembled a band to take Iggy's album out on the road. Ricky Gardiner, having impressed with his work on *Low*, was called up to play guitar, while Bowie himself took the keyboard player's role. The rhythm section, meanwhile, played host to the madcap genius of Hunt and Tony Sales. The sons of the legendary American comedian and disc jockey Soupy Sales, bassist Hunt and drummer Tony had met Bowie in New York in 1972 and apparently made a lasting impression. Prior to that, they had played together in the mid-1960s Detroit combo Tony & The Tigers, with whom they scored a local hit entitled 'Turn It On Girl', and appeared on *Runt: The Ballad Of Todd Rundgren* in 1971.

Rehearsals began in mid February on the outskirts of Berlin. Bowie hired out an old screening-room at the rather dilapidated UFA building, which was once one of Europe's most prominent film studios (Fritz Lang's *Metropolis* was one of numerous classics of early cinema to have been made there), but which since the war had struggled to shake off a reputation for having produced Nazi propaganda films during the 1930s and 1940s. "They still had all these wonderful German Expressionist films just sitting in cans rotting," recalled Iggy. "You could smell the film slowly going bad."[8] The rehearsals, according to Ricky Gardiner, "went productively and smoothly with little apparent disturbance".[9] Bowie, it seems, was happy to restrict his involvement, for the most part, to just playing the keyboards. "David played a very diplomatic role," says Gardiner, "and did not appear to undermine Iggy at all", while the presence of the Sales brothers, who had "inherited a good sense of humour from their father",[10] helped maintain a light, convivial atmosphere.

Iggy's first tour without The Stooges began on Tuesday, March 1st, with a relatively low-key appearance at the Friars Club in Aylesbury, a small town around 40 miles to the northwest of London. (Bowie had warmed up for his very first Ziggy Stardust tour at the same venue in 1972.) Support was provided, for this and the six subsequent UK dates, by The Vibrators, who had released one of the first British punk singles, 'We Vibrate', the previous November, and had previously shared stages with both The Stranglers and The Sex Pistols. Frontman Ian 'Knox' Carnochan concurs with Gardiner about the generally relaxed atmosphere, recalling that both Bowie and Iggy would hang around backstage and chat to the other musicians. Bowie, says Carnochan, really was "just the keyboard player. I think he very much liked not being the centre of attention – it was like he was on holiday".[11]

More than anything, Bowie seemed to enjoy watching Iggy. "I'd never seen him onstage up until then," he later admitted. "I couldn't get over his energy and commitment to savage realism."[12] Bowie, on the other hand, remained in the seat behind his keyboard throughout, lit only by a row of fairy lights, but some observers were still convinced that he was calling the shots. Writing in the *New Musical Express*, Nick Kent felt that the "totally workmanlike" Bowie was "very much in charge here",[13] at least from a musical perspective. He was certainly a big draw for the audience, too, with the number of Bowie fans in attendance generally matching those who had come just to see Iggy. Knox Carnochan recalls a "50/50 split" between the two, and the presence of large numbers of "kids dressed as Aladdin Sane"[14] – this despite the fact that Bowie's membership of Iggy's band was not officially confirmed until the musicians took to the stage; even after the first night, at Aylesbury, many assumed that Bowie's appearance might have been a one-off.

Throughout the UK tour, which continued with three dates in the north of England and three more at the Rainbow in London, the band's set was split fairly evenly between new tracks from *The Idiot* and old Stooges numbers, including 'TV Eye', 'Raw Power', and 'Dirt'. One as yet unrecorded new song, 'Turn Blue', was also played regularly. Six months earlier, a ragged bootleg of two late-period Stooges shows at Detroit's Michigan Palace had been issued to widespread acclaim in Europe and America. *Metallic KO* might have captured a band in disarray, at a time when most of their gigs tended to degenerate into a conflict between singer and audience, but its release, in September 1976, came at a time when The Stooges were the band every punk on either side of the Atlantic wanted to be. Everyone from The Ramones to The Damned put Iggy atop the punk-rock pedestal; appropriately, as a document of his band at their most destructive, *Metallic KO* drew rave reviews across the board, even if the music it contained was ramshackle and at times barely listenable. (Lester Bangs later recalled a show from The Stooges' dying days in which, responding to hecklers, the band played a 45-minute version of 'Louie, Louie' complete with improvised lyrics about the "biker faggot sissies" in the audience.[15])

Iggy, naturally, was repeatedly asked around this time about his impact on and reaction to the nascent punk scene. His responses – usually along the lines of "I caused it,"[16] or "it sound[s] like me"[17] – suggest that his return was a celebratory homecoming of sorts. The reality was rather more complex. For a lot of contemporary reviewers, the sense of joy that Iggy had returned to the stage, at a time when, according to Nick Kent, the rest of the world had finally caught up with his "hell-fire rhetoric", was tempered by a feeling that this was "all too damn well-rehearsed"[18] – and just not *punk*. Mark P., editor of the influential fanzine *Sniffin' Glue*, was given the opportunity to air his views in *Melody Maker*, and was even less impressed. "Watching Iggy Pop in 1977 is like watching a film," he wrote. "He's not real any more, he's like a puppet. His songs, new and old, need furious movement, but from this band there was nothing."

The makeup of Iggy's band seemed to be a particular concern – as though, by bringing in Bowie on keyboards and giving a platform to the thoughtful, experimental guitar-style of Ricky Gardiner, Iggy had sacrificed the raw power that had seen him installed as punk's 'godfather' in order to play a new music that lacked the visceral energy and general unpredictability of a Stooges show. This misses the point on several levels. For one, Iggy – under Bowie's tutelage – had moved far ahead of the sound of The Stooges, so for him to then go out on a Greatest Non-Hits tour would have made little artistic sense; to call him punk's godfather, too, is faintly ridiculous – he was not an aged overseer, but somebody who, having sat out the past few years, was clearly eager to prove that he could still cut it, onstage and on record. (And, as Knox Carnochan notes, the 'Godfather Of Punk' tag "makes him out to be really old, [but] I'm a couple of years older than him".[19])

Bowie, too, would repeatedly be asked for his take on the punk scene by journalists keen for a pithy soundbite. As ever, Bowie obliged, declaring punk to be "absolutely necessary [as] a sort of musical enema"[20], but expressing his disappointment that so many musicians had "[put] a boundary on their writing scope"[21] by allowing themselves to be pigeonholed almost as soon as they'd formed. While there is some truth in both statements, they reflect Bowie's ability to keep his ear to the ground, even from afar, rather than any deep interest in or involvement with the punk scene in the UK or abroad. The Iggy Pop tour marked pretty much the only time Bowie came into contact with punk in any tangible sense (most notably, backstage at the Rainbow, where he and Iggy were introduced, in a kind of changing of the punk guard, to Johnny Rotten and Sid Vicious). In Britain at least, punk was at its most prominent, broadly speaking, during 1976–7. Bowie spent the balance of that period in a vacuum, first at the Château d'Hérouville and then in Berlin, where his focus was twofold: rebuilding his fractured psyche, and furthering his own musical creativity. Punk didn't get much of a look-in, and what little of it that did seep into his orbit merely struck him as being derivative of what Iggy had been doing almost a decade earlier.

One common supposition is that Bowie decided to tour with Iggy, rather than go out and promote *Low*, for fear that, on his own, he might have been rejected in a musical climate dominated by punk rock. This is, at best, a simplistic reading of the situation. Playing in Iggy's band allowed him to stay out of – or at least to the right of – the spotlight, but Bowie's reasons for doing so had little to do with any fear of rejection by a younger, angrier music scene, and much more to do with the fact that it gave him a chance to ease back into performing and being a musician after a messy and dispiriting couple of years. "I never enjoyed a tour so much," he recalled, "because I had no responsibilities ... I just had to sit there, drink a bit, have a cigarette, wink at the band ..."[22] Just as importantly, the British music scene during 1976–7 was never quite so starkly revolutionary as is now so often assumed. Popular wisdom would have it that, within mere moments of The Clash, The Damned, and their ilk arriving on the scene, each and every member of the old guard of rock music was cast out, never to return; and that Bowie, aged 30, was one of a very small minority of these old fogies to gain acceptance following punk's Year Zero.

There was, certainly, a sea change of some description, and it is true that rock in some of its most bloated and self-indulgent forms was shown the door, but the situation was not quite so cut and dried. The British weekly music press might have given punk top billing at this time, but it certainly wasn't the only thing going on. While 1977 might have been the year of The Sex Pistols, it was also the year of Abba and *Rumours* by Fleetwood Mac. And even the *NME* acknowledged this: it might have announced, in a January 1977 headline, that "Bryan [Ferry], Cheri, the *NME* it say you are so passé", but a month later gave Single Of The Week to Gene Vincent, and called *Animals* by Pink Floyd – perhaps *the* anti-punk band – "great, generous, healing music". The April 16th edition, meanwhile, featured The Kinks' Ray Davies, The Beach Boys, and Genesis on the cover.

In any case, Bowie was not the only rock'n'roll fogey to join forces with the new wave. Three days after the completion of the UK leg of the Idiot tour, Bowie's old glam-rock pal Marc Bolan took a reformed T. Rex out on the road with The Damned as the opening act. This, perhaps, was a more calculated attempt at wooing a younger audience by a musician who, unlike Bowie, had clung to the glam-rock sound throughout the 1970s. "I think I got a lot of respect for having a punk band on my tour,"[23] as Bolan put it a month later. Nonetheless, while glam itself was certainly a thing of the past by 1977, its progenitors – Bowie and Bolan chief among them – could rightly lay claim to having influenced the mindset of what followed. Although punk was much less showy and, by extension, more democratic (at least in theory) than glam, there is a clear link both in terms of sound – brash guitar chords, short, sharp songs – image, and identity, notably the adoption of comical pseudonyms (Aladdin Sane paving the way for Sid Vicious, Poly Styrene, and so on). This is hardly surprising when you consider that many of the current wave of safety-pinned punk rockers would have grown up with glam serving as the soundtrack to their adolescent years. "You don't get much originality in punk," admits Vibrators frontman Knox Carnochan. "I got the idea for the Vibrators song 'Wrecked On You' from [Bowie's] 'Hang On To Yourself', so there's obviously an influence. You have to remember that [good music] was a bit thin on the ground before punk started."[24]

After the last UK date of the Iggy Pop tour, at the Rainbow on March 7th, Bowie spent a few days holed up at Bolan's flat plotting a multi-media collaboration. A month later, the T. Rex frontman told *Record Mirror* that this would entail a film about "a future society [that] reflects our own feelings", and an album for which each singer would record one side. "What a combination it's going to be," said Bolan, in typically boastful fashion. "The two greatest musical influences of the Seventies joined together!"[25] Whether this audio-visual extravaganza would ever have made it off the ground is questionable; as prodigious as Bowie's work rate was during the 1970s, for every project that did see the light of day, there were numerous others – most of them announced, prematurely and enthusiastically, to the press – that never made it over the first hurdle. In this instance, of course, tragic circumstances intervened. Six months later, shortly after Bowie had taped an appearance on the *Marc* TV show, Bolan died in a road accident, two weeks short of his 30th birthday.

On March 10th, the day that T. Rex began their final tour, Bowie travelled to the USA with Iggy to play a month-long engagement there and in Canada. Somewhat surprisingly, for the first time in six years, he flew, from Heathrow, having belated decided that "the aeroplane is a really wonderful invention".[26] Upon arrival in New York, Bowie and Iggy dipped their toes into the American punk scene, attending a performance by Patti Smith at the Lower Manhattan Ocean Club, during which Iggy took to the stage to duet with Smith on a cover of the garage-punk classic '96 Tears'. Bowie also spent time with another proto-punk associate, David Johannsen of The New York Dolls.

Iggy's US tour began at Le Plateau Theatre in Montreal before heading down the East Coast, across through the northern states, and down the West Coast, finishing in Los Angeles in mid April. The fourth show, at the New York Palladium, coincided with the release, on March 18th, of *The Idiot*, Iggy's first album in four years. Like *Low*, it seemed to confuse some reviewers, but the response was largely positive, and certainly much more so than to the tour that accompanied it.

In the *NME*, Nick Kent noted that, while *Low* "lacked any real tension", *The Idiot* is "totally riveted and fettered to a thoroughly unhealthy aroma of evil and twilight zone zombie-time unease". Kent was one of a number of critics to view parts of the album as a continuation of Jim Morrison's work with The Doors. In conclusion, he found *The Idiot* to be "damn unhealthy, perverse, harrowing, and … strangely addictive", and "the next logical step [to] keep the Pop's demon-in-residence biting back on vinyl".[27] (In an unrelated article in the same issue, another writer, Max Bell, summed up his feelings on the current punk scene by announcing, "When the new wave puts *Fun House* in the shade, come back and tell me.") In *Melody Maker*, Allan Jones rather uncharitably described *The Idiot* as "my second favourite David Bowie album", but made amends later on by calling it "a disturbingly pertinent expression of modern music".[28] *Rolling Stone*, meanwhile, summed the album up as "the most savage indictment of rock posturing ever recorded"[29] – in a good way, of course.

Almost as striking as the music is the cover art, a stark, monochromatic shot of an unhinged-looking Iggy, wearing a jacket belonging to his on-off girlfriend Esther Friedmann. The original plan was for the album cover to feature a reproduction of *Roquairol*, a portrait of the artist and printmaker Ernst Kirchner by one of his associates in the Die Brücke movement, Erich Heckel. Bowie had already paid for the rights to reuse the image, but then decided to have Iggy strike the same pose for photographer Andrew Kent, who had documented Bowie and Iggy's infamous train-ride to Moscow a year earlier. Several months later, Bowie would base the sleeve of his *"Heroes"* on the same Heckel portrait (and not, as is often assumed, a self-portrait by another German expressionist, Walter Gramatté), further entwining *The Idiot* and his own recorded works of the era.

The release of *The Idiot* and the accompanying tour brought Iggy more fame and success than he had ever had with The Stooges. He made two notable television appearances during the North American leg of the tour. First, on March 11th, was a memorable interview with Peter Gzowski on the Canadian television show *90 Minutes Live*, during which Iggy was asked to clarify the concept of 'punk rock'. "I'll tell you about punk rock," he began, before launching into a measured but forceful defence of a music that, in his mind, had been denigrated by "dilettantes" and "heartless manipulators". "I don't know Johnny Rotten," Iggy continued, "but I'm sure he puts as much blood and sweat into what he does as Sigmund Freud did." (A sample of his speech later formed the basis of a song entitled 'Punk Rock' by the Scottish group Mogwai.) A month later, Iggy appeared on *Dinah!*, and seemed to revel in regaling Dinah Shore, the show's ladylike host, with tales of cutting himself onstage and other decadent behaviour. "I've had treatment for that sort of thing since," he declared, cheerily, in between Bowie-assisted performances of 'Sister Midnight' and 'Funtime'.

The Idiot itself peaked at a solid if unspectacular Number 30 on the UK albums chart (none of the Stooges albums had even made the charts), while the tour, which took in venues much bigger than any Iggy had played at before, drew celebrity fans ranging from The Sex Pistols to The Rolling Stones (Jagger and Richards having been at the New York City date). This kind of turnaround, from washed out junkie to rock'n'roll royalty in barely a year, would have satisfied a lot of musicians, but not Iggy. Everywhere he went, it seemed, he was followed by a single word that echoed into infinity behind him: Bowie, Bowie, Bowie.

"How's David?" asked *Melody Maker* in February. "I think I've had enough [of this interview]," was Iggy's short-tempered reply. "It's *my* noise and *my* choice of musical instruments."[30] "Iggy is under Bowie's control, I think," reported Harald Inhülsen, president of The Stooges' European fan club around the same time. "He would like to break away. Get his own apartment."[31] "I saw David entertaining *and* running his own life," Iggy told *Rolling Stone* a couple of months later. "I thought, 'I can do [that] too.'"[32] The next phase of Iggy's career, then, was about nothing so much as taking control. While he didn't necessarily dislike Bowie as a person, he hated the idea of being perceived as Bowie's underling – and it was becoming increasingly clear that that was exactly how the music press now saw him.

The first step, as suggested by Inhülsen, was for Iggy to move out of the apartment he shared with Bowie and Coco Schwab into a smaller one of his own (albeit one at the back of the same building). After that, it was time to reassert his authority over his musical career. Of course, this didn't mean ditching the man who had pulled him back from the brink, co-written and produced his comeback, and put together his new band. Not yet, anyway. At the end of the American tour, Bowie and Iggy returned to Berlin to write some songs for their next collaborative album. They already had one in mind, 'Turn Blue', which the Iggy band had played regularly throughout March and April. Bowie had written the music to the song with Warren Peace, one of his *Young Americans*-era backing singers, in 1975, and made a very cursory attempt at recording it with Iggy during their aborted collaborative session that

May. Iggy had added new lyrics to it during rehearsals for the Idiot tour, on which they also road-tested 'Some Weird Sin' and 'Tonight'.

Bowie and Iggy's (mostly) friendly rivalry resulted in a flurry of songwriting. They were joined in May at Iggy's flat by Ricky Gardiner, who recalled that "quite a few ideas were already present".[33] The trio spent a few more weeks adding to the pool of ideas, devising such songs as 'The Passenger', for which Gardiner provided the memorable riff, and 'Lust For Life', which Bowie reportedly wrote on a ukulele in response to "the army forces network TV theme, which was a guy tapping that beat on a Morse code key".[34] Then, at the end of May, they headed across to Hansa Tonstudio 2, a much larger workspace than the Château d'Hérouville, where they were joined by Hunt and Tony Sales, and Carlos Alomar, whom Bowie had brought in as musical director (perhaps as a way of avoiding a power struggle with Iggy).

The main constituent parts of what became *Lust For Life* went down onto tape fairly quickly. "We were already a tour-hardened band," said Gardiner, and this is reflected in the fact that the album has much more of a live feel than *The Idiot*, on which there were never more than two musicians playing at the same time. The presence of Hunt and Tony Sales made a difference, too. "Hunt and Tony were really a double act," said Gardiner. "Their humour was a great contribution, [and] they sang backing vocals as well. Tony was, I believe, a guitarist who took up bass for the Iggy project. Now, speaking as a guitarist who enjoys playing the bass, it has been my experience that there is a greater freedom available playing the second instrument. I think Tony made the most of this, [which] blended with Hunt's delightful tendency to insert a fill as the mood took him."[35]

The Sales brothers are very much the driving force on these songs, their loosely synchronistic bass-and-drum assault taking hold of each one and not letting go until the end. Generally speaking, the arrangements are simple and direct, in a manner reminiscent at times of contemporary groups such as Richard Hell & The Voidoids, with each instrument sounding as though it has been plugged straight into an amp, unfettered by complex special effects. On *The Idiot*, Bowie spent a fair amount of time piling overdubs onto the rhythm tracks, but to do the same to the *Lust For Life* material would have been unnecessary – unhelpful even. Fittingly, given that this was the first of Bowie or Iggy's albums to have been fully realised in Berlin (the previous pair having both been instigated in France), the overall effect is that of a bunch of New York punks let loose in a Weimar-era cabaret club. There's a looseness not present on any of the other records either of its principal authors made at the time, best exemplified by 'Success', which arose from a jam in which Ricky Gardiner found himself on the drums, Tony Sales switched to guitar, and his brother played the bass.

If *The Idiot* was a Bowie/Iggy record, then *Lust For Life* is very much Iggy/Bowie. In terms of songwriting and providing a musical foundation, Bowie still had a key role to play as author or co-author of seven of the nine tracks. But while on *The Idiot* he then played guitar, saxophone, and various keyboards and synthesizers on the album, and sang the majority of the backing vocals, at Tonstudio 2 his instrumental contribution was significantly reduced: he's simply the keyboard player, just as he had been on the recent tour. Iggy, meanwhile, had been little more than an observer at times during the making of *The Idiot*, spending long periods simply watching as Bowie and his collaborators pieced the songs together, and waiting until he was prompted to "sing like Mae West" or write a song about his old band. This time around, he made sure his contributions were more prominent. "Bowie's a hell of a fast guy," Iggy later recalled. "I realised I had to be quicker than him, or whose album was it gonna be?" This resulted in a lot of early starts and late finishes at Hansa for Iggy, and time spent, when Bowie wasn't around, remodelling the songs in his own image. This is reflected in the production credits on the album sleeve, which are attributed to 'Bewlay Bros.' – a reference, yes, to a song from Bowie's *Hunky Dory*, but intended, nonetheless, as an aggregation of Bowie, Iggy, and producer-engineer Colin Thurston, who had been drafted in for this album and also worked on *"Heroes"*.

As with *The Idiot*, Iggy came up with a lot of the lyrics and vocal melodies on the spot, his best ideas seemingly emerging suddenly in response to what the musicians were playing around him. But this time, there's less of the faux-Sinatra croon, and more looseness, and roughness around the edges. While there are suggestions of age and wisdom in Iggy's delivery, *Lust For Life* seems to be more closely linked to *Funhouse* and *Raw Power* than its predecessor. This, in a way, is much more of the kind of record one might have expected Iggy to produce in 1977: whereas *The Idiot* was often withdrawn and contemplative, *Lust For Life* is more visceral, more active, more eager to engage with the world. It's not as musically inventive as its predecessor, but that's not really the point. This is the sound of Iggy shaking off the shackles, making the record that *he* wanted to make, priming himself for the success that *he* so deserved.

The clearest sense of this comes with the lyrics. On *The Idiot*, a lot of the songs feel as though they have emerged from a collective Bowie-Iggy mindset; 'Nightclubbing', in particular, written entirely in the first person plural, is clearly about the pair of them, a couple of dum dum boys out on the town. There's a little bit of that on *Lust For Life*, but not much. Most of the time, it's Iggy and Iggy alone who is worth a million in prizes, who rides and rides, and sees the stars come out of the sky – and also Iggy alone who reflects, rather more bleakly, on his battles with heroin abuse on darker tracks such as 'Tonight' and 'Turn Blue'.

On the evidence of *The Idiot* and *Low*, *Lust For Life* is a much more straightforward record than one might have expected Bowie to be involved with at this point in his career. The whole thing, mixing and all, was completed in just over two weeks, and without much in the way of conflict between its principal authors. But although Bowie told several interviewers of his plans to record a third album with Iggy towards the end of 1978, *Lust For Life* ended up being their last proper collaboration until the mid 1980s. There were, as ever, a multitude of reasons for this, but they can mostly be united under the banner of diverging intentions.

Lust For Life was released to little fanfare by RCA Records on September 9th, 1977. The timing was rather unfortunate: the label's biggest star, Elvis Presley, had died three weeks earlier; promoting the new album by that guy from The Stooges suddenly became a matter of diminished importance. (RCA might also have been more concerned with gearing up for the new release by its second biggest star, a certain Mr. Bowie.) The press response was similarly muted. When *The Idiot* was released in March, both the *New Musical Express* and *Melody Maker* issued what amounted to Iggy specials, each containing both a lengthy interview and a glowing review of the album and its accompanying live dates. Now, however, the best the *NME* (which, of course, had Elvis on the cover) could find to say was that the album was "quite good, actually".[36] The same week, in *Melody Maker*, Allan Jones found *Lust For Life* "perversely brash and brittle" compared to *The Idiot*, and was particularly disappointed with the lyrical content, which for him contained "no revelations, only titillating asides". *Rolling Stone*'s Billy Altman hit the nail on the head in his review a few months later, deciding that the album "leaves one with ambivalent feelings: glad that Iggy is alive, apparently well, and performing again, but upset because his new stance is so utterly unchallenging and cautious".[37]

"Here comes success, Iggy," Altman concluded, "and you deserve it more than just about any other performer I've ever seen or heard. I just wish there was some way that your music could be important and your life happy at the same time." Such a lament could, of course, be made about countless musicians, past and present, but in Iggy it seemed particularly true. And he knew it, too. The tour that accompanied the release of *Lust For Life* was bad-tempered and confrontational. Iggy stomped onstage in an old Nazi helmet, repeatedly spat at his audiences (but with real menace, as opposed to the anarchic glee of a Johnny Rotten), and did his best to search out and destroy the music his band was playing. All of a sudden, it seemed, he had become a singer who hated singing, a performer who hated performing, a star with nothing but abject hatred for stardom.

Perhaps this stemmed from a sense of disillusionment at the lack of fanfare afforded his new record by both his label and the popular-music press. If he wanted to drum up any interest in *Lust For Life*, going out on the road was his only option. This time around, however, he would have to do it without his trusty keyboard player. Bowie was getting ready to release *"Heroes"*, and intended to throw his full weight behind promoting it. There was no room in his schedule for a trek around Europe and America with Iggy.

Even if he had been able to make the time, it's unlikely that Bowie would have accepted. As much as he had enjoyed the Idiot tour, he hadn't found the lifestyle particularly conducive to his attempts to regain his health and stay off the drugs. "Touring with Iggy," he told *Q* magazine in 1993, "was very enjoyable for the most part. [But] the drug use was *unbelievable* and I knew it was killing me." Certainly, enough stories have emerged over the years to suggest that the behaviour of the musicians on the Idiot tour, particularly Hunt and Tony Sales, was pretty decadent. But, equally, some of those tales could well be as tall as the ones about Bowie bottling his urine and battling witches in Los Angeles. Both Ricky Gardiner (who would surely have had a reasonably accurate vantage point) and The Vibrators' Knox Carnochan claim neither to have experienced nor witnessed any drug use. ("It couldn't have been that much," notes Carnochan, "or they wouldn't have been able to play.")[38]

Wanting to maintain his chemical equilibrium is, in itself, justification enough for not wanting to go back out on the road with Iggy and the Saleses, but it's unlikely to have been the only reason Bowie passed on the Lust For Life tour. Bowie had clearly relished the opportunity to be just one of the guys in the band during March and April – he would attempt to manufacture a similar dynamic during 1989–92 with his much-maligned Tin Machine project. But having eased himself back into performing alongside Iggy, he would not logically have wanted to remain in that role forever. His rehabilitation programme complete, Bowie was ready to return his focus to his music.

Moreover, even if Bowie had been content to carry on playing in Iggy's band, it's entirely possible that Iggy would have turned him down anyway. In the handful of interviews he did to support *The Idiot*, and during the subsequent tour, it soon became clear to Iggy that a lot of people were beginning to see him as Bowie's lapdog. This is not a situation that anybody would have particularly enjoyed, but for someone in an industry as ego-driven as the record business, it was downright infuriating. The only way out of that, then, was for Iggy to prove himself, once again; and, this time, to do it on his own. "We have drifted away from each other," Bowie revealed two decades later. "I think there was a moment where Jim decided that he couldn't do a fucking article without my name being mentioned, and I don't think that's a very comfortable feeling. I think he had to physically take himself out of the picture to become autonomous again."[39]

In the short term, Bowie and Gardiner were replaced for the Lust For Life tour by another former Stooge, Scott Thurston, and Stacey Heydon, who had played on the Station To Station tour. Bowie would, however, end up working with all of the *Lust For Life* players again in the future, apart from Gardiner, for whom "children were on the way, so I priced myself out of the market".[40] Carlos Alomar, of course, remained as one of the key figures in Bowie's band until the mid 1980s (and, after a brief estrangement, has made regular guest appearances, onstage and on record, in the years since), while Hunt and Tony Sales, meanwhile, formed the nucleus of Tin Machine. Bowie and Iggy's paths have crossed on a number of occasions since 1977. Bowie made a one-off, unscheduled contribution to Iggy's 1980 LP *Soldier*, co-writing and singing backing vocals on 'Play It Safe'. Then, during the mid 1980s, he helped revive Iggy's fortunes again by recording disco-pop updates of 'China Girl', 'Neighborhood Threat', and 'Tonight', and then by producing and co-writing Iggy's *Blah Blah Blah*. None of these records were, in truth, representative of their creators' finest work, but were crucial in bringing Iggy back, once again, from the brink, and setting him on the way to his status as one of rock'n'roll's enduring animals.

IGGY POP: LUST FOR LIFE

Produced by The Bewlay Bros. Recorded by David Bowie.
Engineered by Eduard Meyer and Colin Thurston. Recorded and
mixed at Hansa Tonstudio 2, Berlin, Germany (May–June 1977).

LUST FOR LIFE 5:12
(Pop/Bowie)
Iggy Pop: vocals; **David Bowie**: piano, backing vocals;
Carlos Alomar: guitar; **Ricky Gardiner**: guitar;
Tony Sales: bass, backing vocals; **Hunt Sales**: drums, backing vocals.
■ Among the most famous rock'n'roll songs to have been written on a
ukulele, 'Lust For Life' is probably Iggy Pop's best known song, having
taken on a new lease of life, almost 20 years after its release, when it
was used in the cult classic movie *Trainspotting*. Bowie was reportedly
inspired to write the tune after hearing a Morse code-like theme to a
US Armed Forces Network news bulletin; he and the Sales brothers
then turned it into an irresistible rock'n'roll stomp that recalls, from a
rhythmic perspective, The Supremes' 1966 hit 'You Can't Hurry Love'.

Lyrically, however, 'Lust For Life' is pure Iggy, a five-minute
barrage of warped boasts and truisms, many of them made up, on the
spot, as he sang. The song is, in part, a rather hopeful dismissal of his
and Bowie's old ways – "No more beating my brains with liquor and
drugs" – supported (or perhaps refuted) by crazed ramblings about
stripteases, torture films, and government loans. Most memorably, Iggy
confirms himself to be a "modern guy" because, of course, "he's had it
in the ear". Bowie and the Saleses then chime in with breezy backing
vocals in the chorus.

SIXTEEN 3:27
(Pop)
Iggy Pop: vocals; **David Bowie**: piano, backing vocals;
Carlos Alomar: guitar; **Ricky Gardiner**: guitar;
Tony Sales: bass, backing vocals; **Hunt Sales**: drums, backing vocals.

■ Iggy's first-ever sole songwriting credit, 'Sixteen' is a raw, ragged, two-chord dirge on his favourite topic: warped, unrequited, obsessional love. Like *The Idiot*'s 'Tiny Girls', the focus appears to be on his preference for younger, less experienced ladies – perhaps not the wisest confession, in song or otherwise. "Tell me what I can do," he pleads, admitting that heartbreak has rendered him "an easy mark".

Although Iggy was nominally responsible for both words and music, Bowie clearly had a hand in the arrangement – notably the intro, which is driven by circular, barroom-style piano and Hunt Sales's fiercely hit cowbell. Then the drums kick in, providing a sturdy platform for Alomar and Gardiner to trade gritty guitar chords as Iggy yelps about being an "easy mark", "crying inside". As ever, there's no answer to his troubles, as the song merely fades out in the manner of so many of Bowie's songs of the era, leaving neither Iggy nor the listener sure of how things might play out.

SOME WEIRD SIN 3:40
(Pop/Bowie)
Iggy Pop: vocals; David Bowie: piano, backing vocals;
Carlos Alomar: guitar; **Ricky Gardiner**: guitar;
Tony Sales: bass, backing vocals; **Hunt Sales**: drums, backing vocals.
■ 'Some Weird Sin' is, in a sense, a retread of the themes already covered on 'Lust For Life'. This time, however, the music is slower and, it has to be said, rather less memorably insistent, and the lyric captures Iggy in rather less celebratory mood. Where once he found himself in a maelstrom of liquor, drugs, and stripteases, now he is "at the world's edge", being made to feel "sad and ill" at "the sight of it all". Like most of the songs on *Lust For Life*, 'Some Weird Sin' is straightforward enough that it doesn't require much in the way of analysis. From a musical perspective, the most interesting aspect of the song is the way that it shifts from gloomy discords, which briefly recall 'Mass Production', to more jaunty (if still rather uneasy) double-time rock. The rest is, essentially, the sound of Bowie, Iggy, and the rest letting

their hair down, from Ricky Gardiner's raucous, bluesy guitar-solo to the way Hunt Sales simply stops playing the beat at the end, allowing the song to collapse in a mess of distorted guitars and crashing cymbals.

THE PASSENGER 4:40
(Pop/Gardiner)
Iggy Pop: vocals; **David Bowie**: piano, backing vocals;
Carlos Alomar: guitar; **Ricky Gardiner**: guitar;
Tony Sales: bass, backing vocals; **Hunt Sales**: drums, backing vocals.

■ *Lust For Life*'s standout pop moment, 'The Passenger' is driven by one of the most infectious guitar-riffs of the late 1970s. It was written by Ricky Gardiner during a break between the end of the Idiot tour and the start of the *Lust For Life* sessions, and arrived, as the guitarist later recalled, in a moment of "Wordsworthian inspiration" in his walled garden. Hearing the riff for the first time a few months later in his Berlin flat, Iggy immediately came up with the beginnings of the lyric, borrowing liberally from Jim Morrison's poem 'Notes On Vision', which describes modern life in the context of "a journey by car" and makes reference to slicing through cities with "ripped backsides". The song has been interpreted by some as a straightforward depiction of the days Iggy spent shuttling around on Berlin's S-Bahn metro system and by others as a comment on the way Bowie seemed to pick up new musical ideas wherever he went; it's quite likely, given Iggy's spontaneous, free-thinking songwriting style, that it contains elements of both.

Alongside Gardiner's irresistible guitar-chords and Iggy's compelling monologue, the other main melodic hook of 'The Passenger' is the 'la la la' vocal of the chorus, which manages to sound nihilistic and impossibly catchy at the same time. Had it been released as a single, it might well have been the song that finally brought Iggy the mainstream success he seemed to both crave and fear in equal measure. Instead, it was issued only as the b-side to the lesser 'Success', which failed to chart at all. Like 'Lust For Life', it was given a new lease of life many years later after being used, somewhat inevitably, in a car commercial, whereupon it hit Number 22 on the UK singles chart. By that time it had also become Iggy's most covered song, having been recorded by everybody from Siouxsie And The Banshees to Michael Hutchence.

TONIGHT 3:38
(Pop/Bowie)
Iggy Pop: vocals; **David Bowie**: piano, synthesizer, backing vocals;
Carlos Alomar: guitar; **Ricky Gardiner**: guitar;
Tony Sales: bass, backing vocals; **Hunt Sales**: drums, backing vocals.
■ After four uptempo tracks, 'Tonight' brings side one to a rather more sombre close. It opens with Bowie and the Saleses wailing over a funereal dirge of guitar, drums, and treated piano, over which Iggy makes clear exactly to whom the song is addressed: a heroin-addicted young lover, whom he found in bed, "turning blue". At 0:52, the song abruptly changes pace, mutating all of a sudden into a more subdued take on 'Sound And Vision', complete with funky guitar-licks and slick, staccato drums. The rest of the lyric is similar to Bowie's subsequent "'Heroes'" in the way that Iggy seems to be kidding both himself and his lover with his declaration that "Everything will be all right tonight".

Seven years after *Lust For Life*, and having already turned 'China Girl' into an international hit, Bowie reimagined 'Tonight' as a cheery pop-reggae number on his 1984 album of the same name. In another of the rather odd series of duets he has performed over the years, he brought Tina Turner in to sing on it, but kindly spared her from having to sing the initial morbid monologue by dropping it altogether. One wonders exactly what Iggy might have made of this rather soulless working, but it did result in a few fat royalty cheques.

SUCCESS 4:23
(Pop/Bowie)
Iggy Pop: vocals; **David Bowie**: piano; **Carlos Alomar**: guitar;
Ricky Gardiner: guitar; **Tony Sales**: bass, backing vocals;
Hunt Sales: drums, backing vocals.

■ 'Success' picks up where the first half of *Lust For Life* ('Tonight' aside) left off: guitars duel playfully, drums bash and crash, and an exuberant Iggy, jumping the gun slightly, revels in his new life as a solo star. Bowie came up, once again, with the basic tune, but Iggy wasn't keen on the original melody. Bowie had wanted him to "sing like a crooner", but Iggy had other ideas. "I thought it was completely horrible," he revealed, to *Mojo* magazine, two decades later, "so I waited until he walked out of the studio and I changed everything." The reshaped vocal is fun, simple rock'n'roll, four minutes of call-and-response that have Hunt and Tony Sales echoing everything Iggy throws at them, from "Here comes my car" to "I'm gonna hop like a frog". As strange as some of the lines he comes up with might sound, most of them were rooted in some semblance of reality – he really had, for example, spent some of the *Lust For Life* advance on a Chinese rug.

As noted above, 'Success' was picked as the first single to be released from *Lust For Life*, but failed to chart and stunted the progress of the album as a whole. One of the most blindly optimistic songs Iggy has ever written, 'Success' casts an intriguing and bitterly ironic light on what came next. On the basis of this song, one might have expected Iggy to be priming himself for an assault on the musical mainstream when it came to releasing and promoting the album. Instead, the subsequent Lust For Life tour resulted in some of the most bad-tempered, spiteful, and badly played shows of his career – which in itself is no mean feat – not to mention a barrage of abuse for anyone who dared to mention Bowie's role in Iggy's resurrection.

TURN BLUE 6:53
(Pop/Lacey/Bowie/Peace)
Iggy Pop: vocals; **David Bowie**: keyboard; **Carlos Alomar**: guitar;
Ricky Gardiner: guitar; **Tony Sales**: bass, backing vocals;
Hunt Sales: drums, backing vocals.
■ 'Turn Blue' is the oldest song on *Lust For Life*, but sounds in the context of the album like an overlong, overwrought, and somewhat

unnecessary return to the ideas already covered, much more succinctly, on 'Tonight'. Bowie and Iggy made a vague attempt at recording the song during their brief and rather fruitless first attempt at recording together in Los Angeles in May 1975. Iggy later rewrote the lyric in collaboration with Warren Lacey, a poet and performing artist largely unheard-of outside his native L.A.

The music, which is pitched somewhere between *The Idiot*'s 'Dum Dum Boys' and 'Tiny Girls', stems from a song fragment written by Bowie and Warren Peace, one of the backing singers in his pre-*Station To Station* touring band. Bowie provides a pleasant enough backing-vocal towards the end, but by that stage the song has stop-started its way through almost six minutes of noodling that at times resembles The Velvet Underground at their least incisive. Ultimately, perhaps, 'Turn Blue' should have been left well alone after its authors failed to get it right the first time.

NEIGHBORHOOD THREAT 3:22
(Pop/Bowie/Gardiner)
Iggy Pop: vocals; **David Bowie**: piano, synthesizer;
Carlos Alomar: guitar; **Ricky Gardiner**: guitar;
Tony Sales: bass; **Hunt Sales**: drums.
■ After the rather drawn-out diversion of 'Turn Blue', 'Neighborhood Threat' brings *Lust For Life* back into focus with another excellent, circular guitar riff from Ricky Gardiner, the song's co-author. Whereas the majority of the tracks on the album are loose and relatively straightforward, 'Neighborhood Threat' is taut and atmospheric, and full of intricate details – spidery, criss-crossing guitars, eerie synths, dark piano-chords – that recall the more insular sound of *The Idiot*. So, too, do the lyrics, a series of bleak, fragmentary observations about people who want to "kiss your trash".

'Neighborhood Threat' was another of the songs from this period that Bowie reprised in a more pop-orientated setting in the 1980s, but he was unable to repeat the 'China Girl' magic here. The version included on Bowie's *Tonight* LP is hopelessly ill-judged, and sounds, bafflingly, like the work of somebody with no idea whatsoever of what made the original work.

FALL IN LOVE WITH ME 6:30
(Pop/Bowie/Sales/Sales)
Iggy Pop: vocals; **David Bowie**: organ; **Carlos Alomar**: guitar; **Ricky Gardiner**: drums; **Tony Sales**: guitar; **Hunt Sales**: bass.

■ *Lust For Life* ends with one of its most spontaneous, inspired songs, an epic of lust and yearning in the classic Iggy Pop style. Like so many other great musical moments, it came about almost by accident. During a lull in the recording sessions, Tony Sales picked up a guitar; his brother, Hunt, a bass; and Ricky Gardiner found himself behind the drum kit. Out of nowhere, 'Fall In Love With Me' was born.

Fortunately for all concerned, the tape was still rolling, capturing the original performance of the song in all its ramshackle glory. Bowie added a simple organ part and Alomar a sequence of lithe guitar-lines, to which Iggy responded with one of his finest sets of lyrics. Beginning his tale in "an old saloon" in West Berlin, he manages to make his favourite theme – unrequited love – sound as fresh and vital as ever. He then brings both song and album neatly to a close with the line: "When you're tumbling down / You just look better." He could be singing to himself, about Bowie, about Esther Friedmann, or any of the other characters in his life – or, indeed, to the lot of them, all at once.

FÜR EINEN TAG

By the summer of 1977, David Bowie might not quite have been fighting fit, but he was in much ruder health, mentally and physically, than he had been a year earlier. The past year had been one of gradual recovery tempered by not inconsiderable setbacks – collapsing relationships, both personal and professional, and significant lapses in sobriety – which Bowie, nonetheless, seemed just about able to overcome. He had also, of course, undergone a complete artistic rebirth which, in twelve short months, had resulted in three albums – one of his own, and two for Iggy Pop – that would help shape the musical landscape of the coming years. His *Low*, however, for all its unquestionable artistic merit and pronounced effect on what followed, was a very insular record, reflected not just in its musical and lyrical content but also by the fact that its creator refused to promote it in any way.

Now, bolstered by his work with Iggy, onstage and on record, Bowie was ready to re-engage with the world. Just before serious work began on his new album, he undertook his first solo media engagements in over a year, for which he travelled to Paris. The last time Bowie was in the French capital, it was very much under duress. He had been called away from the *Low* sessions to attend meetings with his lawyers, from which he returned drained, dejected, and barely able to function, let alone work. This time he made two trips to the city out of choice rather than necessity. On June 21st he shot a promo video for his current single, 'Be My Wife', a simple performance piece directed by Stanley Dorfman, in which an anguished Bowie sings and plays a red Stratocaster in an empty room bathed in white light.

Bowie returned to Paris on June 27th to tape interviews for a pair of relatively high-profile shows on the French TF1 network. He appeared first on *Actualités*, a current-affairs discussion show, and then, later the same day, turned up on *Midi Première*. He also spoke to a pair of journalists from *Rock Et Folk* magazine, Phillip Manoeuvre and Jonathan Farren, to whom he enthused about the positive effect Berlin was having on his writing and music-making. A couple of days later, he attended the French premiere of *The Man Who Fell To Earth* at the tiny Gaumont Theatre on the Champs-Elysées. That evening he was spotted out on the town with Sydne Rome, an American actress based in Italy, with whom he hoped to star in *Wally*, a film about the Austrian expressionist painter Egon Schiele. (*Wally* never made it past the planning stage, but Bowie and Rome would be united on the silver screen a year later for *Schöner Gigolo, Armer Gigolo*, known in English as *Just A Gigolo*.)

Bowie's immediate focus, however, was on making a new album. Almost immediately after completing work on Iggy's *Lust For Life*, Bowie had called Eno to Berlin to begin preparations for their second full-length collaboration. Eno had kept himself as busy as ever in the time since he had worked on *Low*, recording albums with Cluster and Phil Manzanera's 801 project, co-producing *Ultravox*, and overseeing several noteworthy recordings of works by contemporary composers on his Obscure label. He had also devoted a fair amount of time and effort to his own as-yet incomplete *Before And After Science*, which, like "*Heroes*", contains ten songs split between up-tempo art-rock on side one and more pastoral material on side two. Eno spent two years recording dozens of songs for the album with collaborators ranging from Phil Collins to Can's Jaki Liebezeit. Taking a break to work with

Bowie, it seems, helped reinvigorate the project, which Eno finally completed shortly thereafter.

Bowie and Eno spent a couple of weeks together working informally on a series of rough concepts and ideas that would form the basis of the record. This period of 'pre-production' was extended by a week because of the late arrival of Tony Visconti, who had been held up, much to Bowie's irritation, by "last minute hitches" with a Thin Lizzy album he had been producing in Toronto.[1] The album was called *Bad Reputation*, which seems rather fitting, since that's exactly what Bowie thought his producer would end up with if he continued to work with such awful bands.

For *"Heroes"*, Bowie booked out Hansa's largest room, the Meistersaal or Studio 2, famed for its close proximity, at the time, to the Berlin Wall. The wall – or Anti-Fascist Protective Rampart, as it was known in East Germany – was several hundred yards from Hansa, but it was possible to see the armed border-guards patrolling it from the studio window. (Some romanticised retellings even have the guards peering in through binoculars, rifles at the ready – unlikely, perhaps, but such a thing, real or imagined, would certainly have had an impact on the mood and intensity of the musicians as they worked.) The studio's other important feature was its vastness. A Weimar-era former ballroom that had, by all accounts, also been used to host Nazi Party soirees, Studio 2 – the 'hall by the wall', as it became known – was big enough for a 100-piece orchestra. This made it something of a producer's dream: the room itself provided cavernous natural reverb, which the producer captured with a lone ambient mic at one end. And with only Bowie, Eno, and the regular trio of Carlos Alomar, Dennis Davis, and George Murray to fill the space, there was little chance of problems with the separation between the instruments.

With a modus operandi already established during the previous year's *Low* sessions, the band worked incredibly quickly, completing basic backing tracks for the songs on side one of *"Heroes"* within the first two days. Visconti wisely stuck to the same principles he'd followed on *Low*. Once again, Dennis Davis's drums were given a distinctive, high-tech sheen by the Eventide Harmonizer. This time around, taking advantage of the spacious environs, the drummer augmented his regular kit with congas and timpani. "Although those fills may sound like overdubs," Visconti later recalled, "that's actually Dennis playing live. [He's] one of the best drummers I've ever worked with." Alomar and Murray, too, were "amazing musicians … you'd just throw a few chord changes at them and they'd run with it".[2] Bowie himself played piano throughout, his proficiency and confidence on the instrument having grown significantly following his recent stint as Iggy's sideman.

This initial phase of recording was "all done in a very casual kind of way", Eno told the *NME* later in the year. Bowie would give a "very brief instruction", perhaps to request that one part of a song be extended, or shortened, and then the band would start playing. Eno, who hadn't been around for the first phase of recording *Low*, and who tended to labour for months on the foundations of his own records, found the whole thing rather disconcerting: "I thought, 'Shit, it can't be this easy.'" But it was. Most of the rhythm tracks heard on *"Heroes"* are first takes. "We did second takes," Eno recalled, "but they weren't nearly as good."[3] Eno's presence right from the outset made *"Heroes"* a much truer collaboration between him and Bowie than *Low*, on which he was only sporadically involved. The fact that he is listed as co-author of four of the album's ten songs reflects Eno's increased role in the general direction of the sessions as a kind of assistant director to Bowie. He would regularly suggest new – and often unusual – ways of approaching each song, which for some of the musicians wasn't always particularly easy to take. Dennis Davis, a little more diplomatically, described Eno as "difficult at first. But we learned to work together".[4]

Of all of Eno's interventions on *"Heroes"*, the one that drew the most resistance was the deployment of his Oblique Strategies. These are contained on a set of around 100 cards he first produced in 1975 in collaboration with the artist Peter Schmidt; each features a non-linear instruction designed to help the musician or artist in question overcome a creative block. "The kind of panic situation you get into in the studio is unreal," Eno said in 1978. "The function of the cards was to constantly question whether [the direction the music took] was correct. To say 'How about going that way?'"[5] Eno has continued to use Oblique Strategies during the three decades since, adding to and subtracting from the list depending on their relevance. "Some cards," he told Alan Moore in 2005, "their ideas have entered the culture so much that you don't need to say them any longer. Other ideas still seem fresh."[6] He and Schmidt have published five subtly different sets of the cards over the years; prior to the release of the fifth edition, in 2001, older decks were changing hands for up to $1,500 on eBay. For some at Hansa, however, notably Carlos Alomar, the Oblique Strategies were simply too much. Fortunately, Eno resisted calling on the cards too often during the initial phase of recording, waiting instead until it was just him and Bowie working together like a couple of eccentric professors.

This next phase of the *"Heroes"* sessions progressed at a considerably slower pace than had the initial rush of recording backing tracks. Eno, for example, spent the best part of a week perfecting the multi-layered wave of oscillating EMS Synthi A that gradually overwhelms the title track. Bowie, meanwhile, is as prominent as an instrumental player here as he was on *Low*. Much of the first side of *"Heroes"* – once again the more accessible, 'song-based' side – is underpinned by his piano playing, all recorded live with the band. His Chamberlin also puts in regular appearances, while his punchy sax helps bring the dreamy 'Sons Of The Silent Age', 'V–2 Schneider', and 'Neuköln' into focus.

Tony Visconti's main role during the first couple of weeks of recording was to manually edit the songs into shape. As most of them had emerged from spontaneous jamming around loose and largely unstructured ideas, they tended to run on longer than was strictly necessary. '"Heroes"', for example, initially ran to eight minutes before Visconti trimmed it to a more manageable six. In the days before digital editing, this was quite a delicate procedure. It required not just a keen eye – and a steady hand – to make the edits in exactly the right place, but also good judgement and a confident, decisive nature, as too many cuts and splices would render the tape unusable. The pressure on Visconti didn't end there. He would often find himself short of tracks following the latest spate of Bowie/Eno overdubs, and so would have to create sub-mixes of, for example, some of the drum tracks in order to free up space for new additions. This meant that the tracks in question would have to stay as they were at this mid-recording point, levels and all, but that suited Bowie. "Once I've made up my mind," he told Visconti, "I don't want to change it."

The producer's job was made easier by the presence of Hansa's in-house engineer, Eduard Meyer (whom eagle-eyed Bowie fans would already have recognised as the cellist on the previous album's 'Art Decade'). While making *Low*, Visconti was left flabbergasted by what at times seems to have been a complete lack of studio staff. Hansa, by comparison, was a much tighter ship; Meyer was instrumental in helping to maintain, as Visconti later recalled, a stable working environment. The producer kept a two-track tape recorder running at all times, having learnt from previous Bowie sessions not just that inspiration could strike at any minute, but also that, given the frequency at which ideas tended to pop up, it could be forgotten at any minute, too. Time and again, he found himself playing back the tapes to remind the musicians of what they ought to be aiming for.

"All of the rhythm tracks used on the album are in fact rehearsal tracks," recalled George Murray. "Tony had the insight to see what was happening at rehearsals so he just switched on the tape machines and let them run."[7] "It came in handy many times," the producer himself recalled in 2004, "because we'd get lost. We'd start with an idea and then we might go in the wrong direction, and after an hour we'd say 'How did this start again?'"[8]

The general mood at Hansa Tonstudio 2 was much brighter than it had been when much the same group of musicians had assembled at the end of the previous summer to make *Low*. Despite the fact that they found themselves in what was, essentially, a tiny enclave of Westernism deep in Soviet-controlled East Germany, overlooked by border guards, the musicians involved felt less isolated than they had while holed up in the French countryside. Bowie, for his part, was in a brighter and more optimistic frame of mind than he had been a year before. While making *Low*, he had been withdrawn and depressed for long periods; now he seemed to enjoy a sense of comradeship, particularly with Tony Visconti, with whom he would go out to galleries and clubs during breaks from work in the studio. The producer has fond memories of the two months he spent in Berlin while making *"Heroes"*. His autobiography is peppered with recollections of dining with local musicians and artists, among them Tangerine Dream keyboardist Edgar Froese; giving Bowie and Iggy severe, impromptu haircuts; taking tentative trips into East Berlin; and enjoying cabaret nights at clubs whose "interior hadn't changed since the 1920s". In one such club Bowie and Visconti met a jazz singer, Antonia Maass, who ended up providing backing vocals on *"Heroes"*, not to mention inadvertently inspiring part of the lyric for the album's most famous song.

The improved mood of the *"Heroes"* sessions wasn't, however, reflected in the music that Bowie, Eno, and Visconti fashioned, which tends towards much harsher, bleaker extremes than their previous collaborations. On *Low*, Bowie seems almost catatonic on some songs, while the instruments around him sound at times as though they have been wrapped in cotton wool. On *"Heroes"*, by comparison, Bowie is unmistakably alert, manic even, and the music, too, adopts a similar sensibility. The songs on the album were designed, as Bowie later explained, to reflect "the street life in Berlin", and as such are "a lot more radical in [their] expression … the kind of lush, decadent thing that's thrown around about Berlin [is] entirely wrong".[9]

The arrangements on *"Heroes"* are, by and large, much more atonal and confrontational than anything on its predecessor, with noisy, distorted, multi-tracked electric guitar very much at the forefront on side one, particularly on the first two songs, 'Beauty And The Beast' and 'Joe The Lion'. The return to prominence of the six-string had a lot to do with the choice of guest player: Robert Fripp, an old friend and collaborator of Eno's, whom Bowie later described as "one of the only virtuosos that I liked".[10] Born in Dorset, England, in 1946, Fripp began his musical career in his late teens as the organist in a little-heard trio by the name of Giles, Giles, And Fripp. His next move was to form King Crimson, quickly established as one of Britain's premier psychedelic-rock bands of the late 1960s and early 1970s, with whom Fripp recorded seven albums in five years, including the landmark debut *In The Court Of The Crimson King*. By the mid 1970s, however, Fripp had decided to put the band, which had already been through a number of line-up changes, on indefinite hiatus. He had already started to work with other musicians, most notably Eno, on albums such as the proto-ambient *No Pussyfooting*. Bowie and Iggy reportedly demonstrated their appreciation for the album midway through the *Low* sessions by humming parts of it, note for note, to a pleasantly stunned Eno. Fripp had also spent a fair amount of time away from music, some of which he spent studying the works of the Armenian mystic G. I. Gurdjieff. During 1976–7, he had begun to ease himself back into his day job (in much the same way as Bowie did with Iggy) by touring, under the pseudonym 'Dusty Rhodes', with Peter Gabriel.

Fripp famously recorded his guitar parts for *"Heroes"* at a pace that rivalled even Bowie's rhythm section. He arrived at Hansa late one evening, straight off a plane from New York, and suggested, according to Eno, that he "might as well try a few things".[11] Almost as soon as he had unpacked his guitar, he was plugging into Eno's EMS briefcase synthesizer, which Eno manipulated live, in true Frippertronics style, producing a battery of wild and wonderful sounds that often barely sound like they could have come out of a guitar. From there he simply started playing, apparently without having heard the songs first. Bowie, as ever, resisted the opportunity to give the new arrival anything approaching a tangible instruction, suggesting only that he "play with total abandonment, and in a way that he would never consider playing on his own albums".[12] That seemed to do the trick, as Fripp proceeded to record all of his contributions to the album in six intensive hours. The best bits, he later noted, went onto tape "before I learned the chords. It's an immediate reaction to what I'm hearing for the first time".[13] In quite a few cases, however, what's heard on the record is actually a composite mix, pieced together by Tony Visconti, of several attempts at a particular guitar part. The most striking example of this is the title track, for which Visconti pulled together four passes of Fripp's sinuous, feedback-laden, Enosified drones.

The following morning Fripp packed up and left, his work completed in record time. And, with that, the first side of *"Heroes"* was, for all intents and purposes, complete – except, of course, for the vocals, to which Bowie had not yet given any thought whatsoever. But there was still plenty of work to be done on the more experimental material that dominates the second half of the album. This time around, however, the split between the two sides of the album is a little less pronounced – perhaps because this time Bowie and Eno worked on both concurrently, rather than recording the more conventional songs first and the instrumentals second, as had been the case with *Low*. Thus side two of *"Heroes"* opens with 'V–2 Schneider', which, while certainly unconventional, still has most of the hallmarks of a 'song', and features several of the musicians from side one. The closing track, meanwhile, 'The Secret Life Of Arabia', is perhaps the most pop-orientated moment on the album.

Sandwiched between those two songs are three instrumental pieces, two of them co-written by Eno, that build on the ideas he and Bowie had begun to explore the previous year. The basic methodology was similar, broadly speaking, to the way that Bowie and Eno had created the music on side two of *Low*: that is, by building up instrumental textures over an instrumental pulse of a pre-defined length, and generally avoiding regular song-structures. Of the four 'ambient' tracks on *Low*, Bowie and Eno were essentially responsible for two each – Eno did most of the work on 'Warszawa' and 'Art Decade' while Bowie met with his lawyers in Paris; likewise, Bowie recorded 'Weeping Wall' on his own. The *"Heroes"* material, however, was compiled in a much more collaborative fashion. "We both worked on all the pieces all the time," Eno told Ian MacDonald of the *New Musical Express*, shortly after the album's release.

Bowie and Eno also imposed various rules and constraints on the recording process that helped lend the material a tension to match the songs on side one. Their musical path would often be led by Eno's Oblique Strategy cards, which frequently took both off in unexpected directions. Sometimes this meant leaving the outcome entirely to chance. The most tangible example of this is when each would record a track (or several) on his own and then, before the other added his, push down the sliders, leaving them both unsure as to exactly what they were working with. Then, at a predetermined end-point, they would bring up the faders and listen, for the first time, to what they had produced. The chance element meant, of course, that there were no guarantees as to whether the end result would be usable. Often, it would simply be too disjointed. But it was equally possible for this methodology to throw up juxtapositions that, because of the way the brain assimilates and responds to what it hears, would have been unlikely to have come out of working in a more linear fashion.

In an interview to mark his 50th birthday, Bowie told Alan Yentob (who, in the years since making *Cracked Actor*, had risen to the post of BBC Director Of Programmes) that, in Eno, he had found "someone who really understood the illogic of putting together different systems". The pair had formed a New School Of Pretension, Bowie said (tongue perhaps slightly in cheek), and had set their sights on capturing "playfulness" and the "evocative feeling" it brings to art. Provided one can get past the top-level bleakness and any simplistic, predescribed notions of what makes music 'up' or 'down', such playfulness can be found in abundance in the music Bowie and Eno made together between 1976 and 1978, notably on the third of their three 1970s collaborations, *Lodger*, but also here, on the second side of *"Heroes"*.

As austere as tracks such as 'Neuköln' and 'Sense Of Doubt' might be, there is also a sense beneath the surface of them being created by a pair of musicians delighting in playing musical tricks on one another and engaging in a drawn-out game of one-upmanship. Bowie and (in particular) Eno are often presumed to be pompous and humourless, but that simply isn't the case. The most overt and surprising rejoinder to such a claim is the fact that, while working on *"Heroes"*, Bowie and Eno weren't so much David and Brian as Derek and Clive. "We've developed these two characters that we play, who I guess are loosely based on Peter Cook and Dudley Moore,"[14] Eno explained in 1978. "We certainly had our share of schoolboy giggling fits,"[15] Bowie confirmed more recently, while in 2005 Eno noted, "We hardly ever have a conversation in any other voice."[16] A new school of pretension it might have been, then, but not perhaps in the most widely expected use of the word.

Bowie and Eno spent about two weeks on the four-song suite of *"Heroes"* instrumentals, after which Eno returned to Britain to finish *Before And After Science* and Bowie turned his attention, finally, to lyrics and vocals. The pace of the *"Heroes"* sessions had slowed considerably since the first few frenzied days, with this final stage being characterised by sporadic bursts of inspiration surrounded by longer stretches of contemplation. As with *Low*, very few vocal or lyrical ideas were present as the instrumental parts went onto tape, and most of the songs only had working titles. Bowie would spend long periods sitting at the studio piano, waiting for an idea to form. Sometimes he would come up with a line or two, record them, and have Visconti stop the tape while he thought out the next couplet. Most of the time, once he got going, Bowie tended to finish the songs fairly quickly, taking a leaf out of Iggy Pop's book and writing 'on the mic'. Often only an hour or two would pass between Bowie coming up with a basic idea and recording the lead vocal, usually within one or two takes. He and Visconti would then tape the backing vocals in similarly spontaneous fashion. Bowie's vocal performances are magnificent throughout, switching effortlessly from histrionic falsetto to low, warm, conversational tones. From a pure singing perspective, he had never sounded as good, and perhaps never would again.

Sometimes the mood of the music already on tape seemed to dictate the theme of Bowie's lyrics, consciously or otherwise. Brian Eno later recalled leaving the studio feeling that the song that became the album's title track sounded "grand and heroic". "I had that very word [Heroes] in mind," he told Ian MacDonald. "And then David brought the finished album round to my place and that track came up … I just shivered."[17] Much of the rest of the album, however, takes the form of a scattershot collection of displaced phrases pieced together using the cut-up technique Bowie had copped earlier in the 1970s from William Burroughs, and covering topics as diverse as the performance artist Chris Burden and Hitlerian Supermen plotting dark deeds in rooms with "a cell's dimensions".

It was mid-August by the time Bowie and Visconti had finished recording and begun to mix *"Heroes"*. The final stage of the mixing process was completed not at Hansa but at the state-of-the-art Mountain Studios in Montreux, Switzerland, the country that was still, officially, Bowie's home. The changeover was facilitated by the fact that both studios had installed similar Neve desks, allowing Visconti to pick up pretty much exactly where he had left off in Berlin.

Taken as a whole, the songs on *"Heroes"* are less obviously personal than those on *Low*, which repeatedly returned to the theme of Bowie shutting himself away from the world in Los Angeles. There are, however, plenty of self-referential moments to be found. 'Beauty And The Beast' opens the album with what reads like an attempt to draw a line under the Thin White Duke era, while 'Blackout' seems to refer at least in part to Bowie's collapse after a night out with his wife in late 1976. These are also a number of allusions to drinking and drunkenness: bars serve as central locations in 'Joe The Lion' and 'Sons Of The Silent Age', while the narrator of 'Blackout' cries out to see a doctor after drinking "rotten wine". Perhaps most striking of all is the singer's stark confession, midway through '"Heroes"', that "I drink all the time".

The natural conclusion to draw in the face of these repeated references is that Bowie was writing about himself. Although he was unquestionably healthier and brighter of spirit than he had been a year earlier, hauling himself back from the brink of self-destruction was "a good two-to-three year process".[18] It is well documented, too, that for the first couple of years after he left Los Angeles, alcohol took the place of cocaine in the singer's chemical constitution. But it would be wrong to suggest that the songs that came out of this period are purely autobiographical in nature, for *"Heroes"* is very much an album not just about David Bowie but about the city he would subsequently characterise as being "made up of bars for sad people to get drunk in".[19] Indeed, *"Heroes"* is the only one of Bowie's late-1970s records that can truly claim to be a 'Berlin album' – a powerful testament to both the city itself and to the Wall and the wedge it drove, literally and symbolically, right through it. The other parts of Bowie's so-called 'Berlin trilogy' had a much more international upbringing: *Low* was made mostly in France and inspired not so much by Bowie's arrival in Berlin as by his rather insular journey to it, while *Lodger* found its way onto tape in Montreux and New York. Only *"Heroes"* was conceived and recorded entirely in Berlin, and as such it is the album on which the culture, the history, and the very essence of Berlin come to bear most fully on Bowie's work. The fact that he and his fellow musicians were working directly in the shadows of the Wall, and surrounded not just by echoes of wars past but by reminders of the contemporary conflicts between East and West, instilled a drive and seriousness into their work. Living in Berlin, Bowie had told *Rock Et Folk* immediately before the *"Heroes"* sessions began, had taught him to write "only the important things". Now it was having the same effect on his band, encouraging them to play with a renewed energy and economy.

Berlin's multiculturalism also shines through on the album, most obviously on the last two songs: 'Neuköln', which Bowie later revealed to have been named after "the area of Berlin where the Turks are shackled in bad conditions"[20], and 'The Secret Life Of Arabia', which from its title down is a typically cinematic rendering of the Middle Eastern influence on the city, its people, and its music. 'Moss Garden', meanwhile, makes good on the "Japanese influence" Bowie mentions on 'Blackout'. This kind of cross-fertilisation of different musical and cultural concepts is something he would develop further on his next two full-length albums, *Lodger* and *Scary Monsters*. Elsewhere on *"Heroes"*, however, Bowie's touchstones are more obviously Germanic. The title track, in fact, bears the clearest example yet of the impact of the insistent, gradually shifting textures of 'Conny' Plank and Neu! on Bowie's work, while other parts of the album offer faint echoes of Faust in their resolute determination to stick with and resolve unusual ideas.

The line generally taken about *"Heroes"* is that it is both a more extreme take on *Low* and a refinement of the musical ideas of its predecessor, which indeed it is. The songs are sharper and more clearly defined than *Low*'s stillborn soundscapes; the playing is harder and more expansive; the lyrics and vocals are markedly more anguished; and the instrumental tracks go several steps further beyond the normal boundaries of conventional popular music. To some, not least the album's producer, Tony Visconti, *"Heroes"* is simply a better album all round – certainly, the way it was subsequently received by the press would suggest as much. And on an individual, song-by-song basis, such exemplary material as '"Heroes"', 'Sons Of The Silent Age', and 'Joe The Lion' have the edge over *Low* – with '"Heroes"' itself widely accepted to be one of the greatest songs of the 1970s. The five-song suite that makes up side one, in fact, is perhaps the strongest sequence of songs on any Bowie record. But in terms of overall canonical importance and sheer artistic bravery, *Low* has the overwhelming advantage of having been released first, and as such being the marker for the greatest and canniest musical move of Bowie's career. It seems perverse to criticise *"Heroes"* for lack of invention when, judged against most other records from 1977, it sounds like a blast from the future.

But it is, essentially, a revision and re-evaluation of the groundwork laid out on its predecessor – something that Bowie himself would acknowledge as early as 1978, when he noted that he had "gone against myself" by bringing out "two [albums] now of the same nature".

That said, *"Heroes"* remains one of Bowie's finest recorded works, and indeed one of the key albums of the 1970s. Its visceral, electrifying songs served a dual purpose in 1977: both an antidote to the messy irreverence of punk and a confirmation that, in a volatile, revolutionary musical climate, Bowie would not go the same way as so many of his once-cool peers, now condemned as irrelevant old fogies. Bowie's standing in music at the time, in fact, was pretty much unique among popular music stars of the time, and best summed up by the line RCA used to advertise the record in the midst of the media blitz that would accompany its release: *There's old wave. There's new wave. And there's David Bowie.*

DAVID BOWIE: "HEROES"

Produced by David Bowie and Tony Visconti. Engineered by Tony Visconti, Colin Thurston, and Eduard Meyer. Assistant mix engineering by Eugene Chaplin and David Richards. Unless otherwise noted, recorded at Hansa Tonstudio 3, Berlin, Germany (July 1977) and mixed at Hansa Tonstudio 3 and Mountain Studios, Montreux, Switzerland (August 1977).

BEAUTY AND THE BEAST 3:32

(Bowie)

David Bowie: vocals, piano, Chamberlin; **Brian Eno**: guitar treatments; **Robert Fripp**: lead guitar; **Carlos Alomar**: guitar; **George Murray**: bass; **Dennis Davis**: drums; **Antonia Maass**: backing vocals.

■ Whereas *Low* began with the bright, up-tempo 'Speed Of Life', *"Heroes"* opens with a jerky, one-chord vamp that sets the tone perfectly for the 40 minutes of paranoid, unhinged music to follow. The opening half-minute sounds, in fact, like a less restrained take on the front end of 'Station To Station': both songs feature a tick-tocking piano line underpinned by tight bass and drums, gradually overwhelmed by guitar feedback that brings to mind a train whistle. This time around, however, the train sounds as though it might derail at any moment, until Alomar, Davis, and Murray haul a brutal, unyielding funk riff from the wreckage, over which Eno weaves Fripp's lead guitar into a mangled, dissonant web. All of the guitar parts on the song, of which there are at least four, are subjected to effects and filters to the extent that, at times, they barely sound like guitars at all. Fripp's lead part during the post-chorus bridge, for example, sounds almost like a flute.

Above the cacophony, Bowie calls time on his Thin White Duke character – fittingly, given the initial musical reference to *Station To Station*. Recalling a time of "slaughter in the air" and "protest in the wind", he laments the extent to which he had 'become' the Duke, claims to have really only "wanted to be good", and thanks his lucky stars that

174

he's managed to make it through the past couple of years. Bowie is joined on vocals for the central warning of the song – "You can't say no to the beauty and the beast" – by Antonia Maass, whom he and Visconti had met midway through the *"Heroes"* sessions at a Berlin nightclub.

'Beauty And The Beast' was chosen, somewhat surprisingly, as the second single to be taken from *"Heroes"*, following the title track. Perhaps less surprisingly, it barely scraped into the UK singles chart, peaking at Number 39 in January 1978, and couldn't find its way onto the *Billboard* Hot 100 at all – most likely because, as Roy Carr and Charles Shaar Murray note in their *Bowie: An Illustrated Record*, it was "one of the most menacing singles of a menacing year".

JOE THE LION 3:05
(Bowie)
David Bowie: vocals, guitar, piano; **Brian Eno**: guitar treatments; **Robert Fripp**: lead guitar; **Carlos Alomar**: guitar; **George Murray**: bass; **Dennis Davis**: drums; **Tony Visconti**: backing vocals.

■ 'Joe The Lion' takes off almost exactly where 'Beauty And The Beast' left off, hurtling into action with an avalanche of processed, multi-tracked guitars, each tumbling in and out of time with the others. As extreme and chaotic as *"Heroes"* gets, 'Joe The Lion' is the Bowie song that most closely recalls the sound and approach of kosmische pioneers Faust, although the raucous, interwoven guitar parts were reportedly inspired by Bowie's instruction to Fripp to play in the style of blues legend Albert King. As ear-catching as Fripp's playing is, however, the most striking section of the song occurs at 1:20, when the band is at its quietest. Over a more restrained arrangement of piano, bass, drums, and a single, lightly distorted guitar, Bowie announces that "it's Monday" in the serene tones of a newsreader, before launching, seemingly out of nowhere, into an extraordinary rising-and-falling vocal passage.

Bowie reportedly wrote and sang the elliptical, free-associative lyric in less than an hour, singing each line straight onto tape as he wrote it.

"It was something I learnt from working with Iggy," he confirmed in 2001. "I thought it a very effective way of breaking normality in the lyric."[21] And indeed it was. The song is in part about the American performance artist Chris Burden, and in particular his 1974 piece *Trans-fixed*, for which he nailed himself to the hood of a Volkswagen. The lines about buying a gun, meanwhile, are most likely in reference to an earlier Burden performance, *Shoot*, in which his assistant was instructed to shoot him in the arm from a range of five metres. Elsewhere in the song, Bowie probes the gap between dreams and reality, issuing a repeated command to "get up and sleep". Although Bowie made clear in interviews to promote *"Heroes"* that he had discarded the idea of character-based songs on this album and its predecessor, 'Joe The Lion', about a visionary artist "made of iron", is a notable exception to the rule.

(The 1991 reissue of *"Heroes"* includes a thoroughly pointless remix of 'Joe The Lion', mixed by David Richards, that leaves the song's structure pretty much intact but brings in stadium drums and thicker reverb – perhaps with the questionable intention of making it sound more like Tin Machine.)

"HEROES" 6:09
(Bowie/Eno)
David Bowie: vocals, piano, Chamberlin, percussion;
Brian Eno: guitar treatments, synthesizer; **Carlos Alomar**: guitar;
Robert Fripp: lead guitar; **George Murray**: bass;
Dennis Davis: drums; **Tony Visconti**: backing vocals, percussion.
■ The most famous and, by most reckonings, finest individual song in Bowie's late-1970s catalogue, '"Heroes"' brings in an immediate sense of grace and majesty to its parent album after the frenetic expulsions that precede it. In its earliest form, '"Heroes"' was a simple, stately rock track, built on a solid foundation of major piano chords, a gently walking bassline (echoed on guitar, in a higher register, by Carlos Alomar, who also came up with the sweet melodic hooks in the bridge

and chorus), and unfussy drums. In its final form, however, the song is, of course, a much more complex and conflicted animal.

Twenty years after "'Heroes'" was recorded, Brian Eno recalled how he had felt, during the first wave of kosmische music in the early 1970s, that bands such as Can had "picked up the gauntlet that The Velvet Underground had thrown down". "'Heroes'", for which Eno co-wrote the music and spent the best part of a week shaping the sound, is pitched somewhere between the disciplines of those two bands. At its root, the song sounds like a more stately take on the Velvets' 'I'm Waiting For The Man' – a song that Bowie has performed, on and off, for four decades – run through the motorik wringer.

Once Bowie, Alomar, Murray, and Davis had put down the basic structural elements, Eno set to work on shifting the song's focus in less traditional directions. What this meant, first of all, was building up multiple layers of trembling low frequency oscillations that, in true kosmische style, are barely audible to begin with, but by the end of the song take on the form of a volcanic eruption. The next step was for Robert Fripp to add his searing, semi-improvised lead-guitar to the mix, which he played through Eno's EMS Synthi. He had, as was the case with all of the *Heroes* tracks he contributed to, not even heard the song before he started play. What is heard on the record is a composite mix, by Tony Visconti, of Fripp's four runs through the song, each manipulated in real time by Eno using the joystick and oscillator banks of his briefcase synthesizer. Fripp's exemplary playing shows off his precise method of generating pitched feedback, which he produced by standing at certain distances away from his amp, depending on which note he wanted. Fripp had this worked out to a "fine science", according to Visconti. "He had a strip that he would place on the floor," the producer recalled, which showed him where he needed to stand to produce each note.[22]

Even after Eno, and then Fripp, had made their contributions, there was still work to be done. Bowie added a synthesized brass part with his Chamberlin, and then he and Visconti, after a fruitless search for a cowbell, added another layer of percussion by banging on a large, empty tape canister. For several weeks, the song was left as an instrumental – some commentators have suggested that Bowie, right until the end, was planning to leave it that way. Then, one day, he asked Visconti to leave him alone for a while so that he could concentrate on coming up with some lyrics. Bowie reportedly had several themes in mind for the lyric, an epic tale of lovers torn apart by the Berlin Wall. One was Otto Mueller's painting *Lovers Between Garden Walls*, which Bowie had found himself drawn to in Berlin's Die Brücke museum, and which, in its depiction of a strained and perhaps final pre-war embrace, bears an obvious stylistic similarity to '"Heroes"'.

Another, as Bowie revealed in his foreword to *I Am Iman*, which his second wife published in 2001, was the post-war Italian love story *A Grave For A Dolphin* by Alberto Denti di Pirajno. There are also suggestions of Bowie's own situation at the time: his first marriage, like the relationship between the song's protagonists, was on the verge of collapse; he most likely did, at that point, "drink all the time"; and he really wasn't (and by all accounts still isn't) able to swim, like a dolphin or otherwise. But the most important germ of inspiration came to him by accident. Sitting in the control room of Hansa Tonstudio 2, Bowie observed a couple come together beneath the shadows of the Wall and share a brief, illicit embrace: Tony Visconti and Antonia Maass. Bowie kept this information under wraps for the next two decades – Visconti was still married to Mary Hopkin at the time – but finally confirmed, around the time of the song's 25th anniversary, that he had indeed rumbled his producer.

When Visconti returned to the studio – not yet aware of his role in the formation of the lyric – he immediately set about recording Bowie's vocal. For this, Visconti devised a system every bit as inventive as the method of mangling Dennis Davis's drum kit he had unveiled on *Low*. Bowie's vocal – the finest he has ever recorded – begins in a low, conversational tone but gradually rises to a terrific, anguished cry by the song's end. In part because he was running out of tracks, and also because he wanted to try to capture a full, live vocal, Visconti set up three separate microphones around Tonstudio 2. The first was placed where one would expect it to be: six inches or so in front of where Bowie stood to sing. The other two were positioned around 15 and 20 feet further back, in order that they might take advantage of the excellent acoustic properties of the studio itself. Visconti placed noise gates on both of these, setting them so that they would only open – and thus become active – when Bowie's voice reached a certain volume. The result of this marvellous innovation was that, in a single take, his voice could shift from a warm intimacy to a distant wail. And it is this, alongside the unparalleled power of Bowie's vocal delivery, which lifted "'Heroes'" up from its status as merely a great song to the realm of the all-time classic.

Despite its unquestionable musical merit, however, "'Heroes'" was only the most minor of hits when issued – as an edit almost half the length of the six-minute original – as the first single from its parent album. Bowie clearly had high hopes for the song: he shot a promo video for it, performed it on numerous musical television shows around Europe, and even re-recorded it, in French and German, as "Héros" and "Helden", the latter having been translated by Antonia Maass. In the UK, however, it scraped in at Number 24; in the US, it didn't even chart at all. In the three decades since, however, it has risen in stature and reputation, having been covered by countless other acts, used to soundtrack sporting events and advertising campaigns, and chosen by the Brit Awards as one of the greatest British songs of the past three decades (losing out by some distance in the subsequent public vote to a rather dubious victor, Robbie Williams's 'Angels').

For all of its latter-day recognition, however, "'Heroes'" is still widely mistaken to be an anthem to fist-pumping optimism, when in fact Bowie is singing about the self-delusion of clinging to a relationship that might last, at best, "just for one [more] day". The title, moreover, is framed in what Bowie would later refer to as ironic quotation marks – suggesting that the "only truly heroic act" available, as he told *Melody Maker*'s Allan Jones shortly after the song's release, was to enjoy "the very simple pleasure of being alive".

SONS OF THE SILENT AGE 3:15
(Bowie)
David Bowie: vocals, saxophone, Chamberlin, percussion;
Brian Eno: guitar treatments, synthesizer; **Carlos Alomar**: guitar;
George Murray: bass; **Dennis Davis**: drums;
Tony Visconti: backing vocals.

■ Following a song as potent as "'Heroes'" could scarcely have been more difficult; anything in remotely the same vein would surely have paled by comparison. So Bowie wisely chose to place after it a song that represents a distinct change of tack, and one that stands apart among the other tracks on side one of *"Heroes"* – a dreamy mood-piece closer in sound and feel to *Low* than to the songs that surround it, which are very much wide-awake.

'Sons Of The Silent Age' was, according to Eno, the only song on the album that Bowie had written in advance of the *"Heroes"* sessions. It is, certainly, a carefully constructed piece made up of two distinct sections. The intro places Bowie's marauding saxophone over an inviting bed of slow-moving drums, subtly shifting synths, and several tracks of guitar, each of them subjected to extreme phasing. Bowie's double-tracked vocal is similarly lackadaisical, and delivered in a whimsical tone reminiscent of his great British idol, Syd Barrett. (The vocal melody is also similar to the one Bowie would give, a few years later, to the excellent 'Ashes To Ashes'.) The lyrics, meanwhile, mark a return to the dark territory of earlier songs such as 'The Supermen' and 'Cygnet Committee' as the "sons" of the title plot and scheme in little rooms, preparing to rise up and "make war". (There's a further hint of supernature later on in the way that they "glide in and out of life" and "never die, they just go to sleep one day".)

Just under a minute in, the song is woken from its slumbers by a clatter of drums, as Bowie shifts gears and unveils a much brassier, Anthony Newley-style pastiche of big-band pop. The lyrics change direction too, as Bowie declares, abruptly, that he'll "never let you go", a rather vague announcement that serves only to add to the general sense of unease. Tony Visconti joins in on harmonic backing vocals before Bowie's sax hauls the song back round into the verse. After a second run through, a neat key change introduces a final, fading coda of celestial, multi-tracked vocals and synthetic strings. All in all, 'Sons Of The Silent Age' sits among the most underrated tracks of Bowie's late-1970s oeuvre as an effortless tying together of various strands of his earlier work.

BLACKOUT 3:50
(Bowie)
David Bowie: vocals, piano, percussion; **Robert Fripp**: lead guitar;
Brian Eno: guitar treatments, synthesizers;
Carlos Alomar: guitar; **George Murray**: bass;
Dennis Davis: drums; **Tony Visconti**: backing vocals.

■ Side one of *"Heroes"* ends with a song that, like *Low* tracks such as 'Breaking Glass', could well have started life as a straightforward rock'n'roller, but in its final form is full of musical depth and detail. At its root are Bowie's boogie-woogie piano and a bruising, disco-inflected rhythm, but more striking are Robert Fripp's dissonant lead-guitar and Eno's insistent, chirruping synthesizers (which recall his contribution to another *Low* track, 'What In The World'). Dennis Davis then comes to the fore during the pre-chorus breaks, unleashing a series of dizzying live fills that involve not just his own kit but also a set of congas he'd found in a corner of the studio.

While the music verges on hyperactivity, the lyrics are bleak and unforgiving. In interviews to promote *"Heroes"*, Bowie claimed to have written the song in response to events earlier in the year in New York, where lightning strikes left the city without power for 25 hours. Most contemporary reviewers, however, found it hard to ignore the parallels with Bowie's own life. In the song, the narrator is anxious that "someone's back in town", and ends up blacking out after drinking too much; a little under a year earlier, Bowie had collapsed and been taken to hospital in similar circumstances after a visit from his estranged wife. Elsewhere in the song, Bowie claims to be "under Japanese influence"

– a motif he would return to on side two of the album by gently plucking a koto on 'Moss Garden'.

V–2 SCHNEIDER 3:10

(Bowie)

David Bowie: vocals, piano, saxophone; **Robert Fripp**: guitar; **Brian Eno**: guitar treatments, synthesizer; **Carlos Alomar**: guitar; **George Murray**: bass; **Dennis Davis**: drums; **Tony Visconti**: Vocoder.

■ Side two of *"Heroes"* opens with a track that, like *Low*'s 'A New Career In A New Town', bridges the gap between the 'rock' songs of the first half and the more atmospheric material that follows. After the psychotic angst of side one, 'V–2 Schneider' fades in to the sound of synthesized airplanes passing in the distance before Davis and Murray work up a lithe, circular groove that manages to be both insistent and unthreatening. Bowie himself then brings a little more urgency to proceedings, hammering away at the same piano chord and blasting out several delightfully offbeat sax parts. Eno, Fripp, and Alomar meanwhile content themselves with throwing disparate sounds around in the background to see what sticks.

The only words to speak of come from a robo-Bowie gently intoning the title over the song's quieter moments. The effect on his voice was achieved, as suspected by a handful of bat-eared reviewers and later confirmed by Tony Visconti, by taking the vowel sounds from a primitive Vocoder, and then having Bowie overdub the consonants himself through a heavily processed microphone.

'V–2 Schneider' was named in homage to Florian Schneider of Kraftwerk, who had themselves referenced Bowie on their recent *Trans-Europe Express*, which came out in German, French, and English-language versions (the same languages in which the ever-resourceful Bowie recorded '"Heroes"' a couple of months later). The title track includes a line about travelling "from station to station back to Düsseldorf city" to "meet Iggy Pop and David Bowie".

SENSE OF DOUBT 3:57
(Bowie)
David Bowie: piano, Chamberlin, synthesizer;
Brian Eno: synthesizers.

■ 'Sense Of Doubt' begins a suite of moody instrumentals that Bowie might, had he been feeling particularly precious, have labelled as three movements of the same 13-minute piece. On *Low*, as bleak as things got, there was still a certain warmth of emotion, even to tracks such as 'Warszawa'. 'Sense Of Doubt', however, is unremittingly cold. The closest it gets to a melody is when a piano tumbles down the four semitones (half-steps) from C to A like a drunk on a staircase. Underneath, from the basement, Bowie and Eno conjure up waves of synthesized sound and effects that evoke the trembling terror of ducking from searchlights on a dark, windy night.

If it sounds as if Bowie and Eno were working against each other on 'Sense Of Doubt', rather than in collaboration, that's because that is, essentially, what they were doing. The piece was recorded entirely at the mercy of Eno's Oblique Strategies, to unintentionally comical effect. Each picked a card at the start, kept its instruction a secret from the other, and tried to work as closely as possible to it. "As it turned out," Eno recalled, "they were entirely opposed to one another. Effectively mine said 'Try to make everything as similar as possible' ... and [Bowie's] said 'Emphasise differences'."[23] Hence the constant sense not just of doubt but also of conflict, which Bowie and Eno struggle to resolve throughout, eventually allowing the song to drift, amid crashes of synthesized wind, into the more reassuring 'Moss Garden'.

MOSS GARDEN 5:03
(Bowie/Eno)
David Bowie: koto, synthesizer; **Brian Eno**: synthesizer.

■ The least Germanic-sounding piece of music on *"Heroes"*, 'Moss Garden' offers a peaceful refuge between the dark, tense instrumentals either side of it. According to Eno, it came about as a result of Bowie wanting to record a "very descriptive" piece about the Moss Garden in Kyoto, Japan.[24] The pair of them duly laid down several layers of slow-moving synthesizer chords, which rock gently from one speaker to the other beneath Bowie's lead part, which he played on a koto, a 13-stringed traditional instrument developed in 7th century Japan in response to the Chinese guzheng (a kind of zither).

Bowie's interest in Far Eastern culture was longstanding and well known, but 'Moss Garden' was the most explicit musical reference to date to the "Japanese influence" he had called to attention earlier on the album (on 'Blackout'). As well as seeking inspiration from Japan's music, he even appeared to be considering the country as a potential new home, once he tired of Berlin. "I think I'll plump for Kyoto," he announced a month after *"Heroes"* was released, "because I want something very serene around me for a few months to see if that produces anything."[25]

Although in the end he wouldn't go so far as to settle permanently in Japan, Bowie did spend an extended period in Tokyo after completing his 1978 world tour, and has returned to Japanese themes on a number of subsequent recordings, notably *Scary Monsters'* 'It's No Game'. For all its cultural curiosity, however, 'Moss Garden' is one of the least involving Bowie recordings of the period. Each of the other instrumental tracks on *Low* and *"Heroes"* contains some form of melodic or harmonic development; 'Moss Garden' merely drifts in and out, working well enough in the context of the album, but not quite doing enough on its own to leave a lasting impression.

NEUKÖLN 4:34
(Bowie/Eno)
David Bowie: saxophone, Chamberlin;
Brian Eno: synthesizers, treatments; **Robert Fripp**: guitar.
■ The penultimate track on *"Heroes"* provides the most unsettling moment on the album. Bowie devised it with Berlin's impoverished, itinerant Turkish community in mind, even going so far as to adopt a Middle Eastern modal scale for his saxophone part. As on the previous

track, Bowie plays the 'lead' instrumental part over an expansive, multi-tracked backing that this time rises and falls on sustained organ chords, mangled, distorted guitar, and birdlike, staccato synthesizers.

From the opening assemblage of twittering musique concrète to the final blasts of mournful, squawking sax, the overall effect is reminiscent of the murky, nightmarish undertones of David Lynch's *Eraserhead*, which became a cult favourite almost immediately upon its release, six months before *"Heroes"*.

THE SECRET LIFE OF ARABIA 3:46

(Bowie/Eno/Alomar)
David Bowie: vocals, piano, handclaps;
Brian Eno: synthesizers, handclaps; **Carlos Alomar**: guitar;
George Murray: bass; **Dennis Davis**: drums;
Tony Visconti: handclaps, backing vocals.

■ After almost a quarter of an hour of slow-moving, heavily synthesized instrumentals, 'The Secret Life Of Arabia' provides a final jolt of life to what is, taken as a whole, a frantic, impassioned album. Carlos Alomar, who co-wrote the song, opens proceedings with an emphatic, Latin-inflected guitar part, over which is draped a vaguely Eastern motif that ushers in the rest of the band. Murray and Davis are at their funkiest since *Station To Station*'s 'Stay', Eno provides a bed of squealing synths, and Bowie plays disco-style piano. His yearning falsetto, meanwhile, recalls 'plastic soul' moments such as 'Word On A Wing'. (Demonstrating the full extent of his vocal ability, he also drops effortlessly to a deep bass-baritone midway through the title phrase.)

The lyrics also hark back to days gone by as Bowie returns to one of his favourite themes, the blurring of the line between art and reality, even finding time to reference his previous album by "running at the speed of life". Then he sees a pair of eyes "at the cross fades", and falls back into a dreamy, cinematic world perhaps intended to evoke David Lean's *Lawrence Of Arabia*. Musically, 'The Secret Life Of Arabia' is as uptempo and immediate as anything that Bowie had released since

'Golden Years'. After a couple of loosely defined verses and choruses, the song gives way to the kosmische model of subtle shifts and endless revolutions of the central idea, which are augmented, from the midway point on, by that old rock'n'roll staple: handclaps.

Some commentators, notably Bowie biographer David Buckley, have suggested that 'Neuköln' should have been the last song on *"Heroes"*; that Bowie's desperate, unencumbered saxophone would have provided a fitting conclusion to the record, and that 'The Secret Life Of Arabia', by extension, jumps out like a particularly sore thumb. But while there is a certain sense of closure (of death, even) at the end of 'Neuköln', it would have made for a distinctly dark finale. *"Heroes"* may not be the record of joy and triumph that its title – without the ironic quotation marks – would imply, but it is a collection of impassioned, living, breathing songs. It's enough, then, that 'Neuköln' resolves the album's trio of stark instrumental pieces, while still leaving room for this more cheery, escapist final act. Like *Low*'s 'Subterraneans', 'The Secret Life Or Arabia' doesn't offer any real sense of resolution, but does, in its seemingly interminable looped coda, imply that Bowie is content in his musical world and coming to terms (again) with the one beyond it.

ABDULMAJID 3:30
(Bowie/Eno)
Mixed at Mountain Studios, Montreux, Switzerland (summer 1991).
David Bowie: piano, synthesizers;
Brian Eno: synthesizers, drum machine, bass.
■ Not much is known about 'Abdulmajid', which was mixed in 1991 as part of Rykodisc and EMI's programme of Bowie remasters and included on that year's reissue of *"Heroes"*. It would, originally, have been called something else, if indeed Bowie bothered to name it at all; he gave it its current title in 1991 in tribute to Iman Abdulmajid, whom he married the following year. The sleeve notes say only that it was recorded at some point during 1976–9, but the Middle Eastern

undertones suggest it to be an off-cut from the sessions that produced 'Neuköln' and 'The Secret Life Of Arabia' – as indeed does the fact that it was tacked onto the end of *"Heroes"*, rather than *Low* or *Lodger*.

That aside, there's little to tie 'Abdulmajid' to the rest of the *"Heroes"* material. While the three instrumentals included on the album are slow, moody, and beatless, this one is driven by an insistent, reverb-drenched drum machine and subtly funky bass, over which Bowie and Eno applied multiple, interwoven tracks of horror-soundtrack synthesizers. The overall result, while admirably forward-thinking for its time, is a fairly one-dimensional piece pitched somewhere between Kraftwerk at their darkest and the rhythmic 'world music' Eno would subsequently make with Talking Heads frontman David Byrne. It's also strangely similar to the work of early industrial groups such as Cabaret Voltaire and Throbbing Gristle, whose first recordings emerged right around the time 'Abdulmajid' was (probably) recorded. Whether or not it was actually inspired by those acts, however, is nigh on impossible to determine.

PART 3
PEACE ON EARTH

STAGE & SCREEN

"Hello," says David Bowie, pretending, for a moment, not to recognise one of the titans of American popular music. "Are you the new butler?"

"It's a long time since I've been the new anything," says Bing Crosby, welcoming Bowie, who apparently "live[s] down the road", into the hallway of an old English mansion all decked out for Christmas. They are on the set of *Bing Crosby's Merrie Olde Christmas*, a one-off TV special based around the conceit that the ageing vocalist and entertainer, in his 51st year in show business, has taken over the home of a rich English relative, 'Sir Percival'. Bowie and Bing make their way into an adjoining room for a minute's uneasy small-talk about the coming holiday season and the current popular-music scene; Bowie namechecks John Lennon and Harry Nilsson, having perhaps concluded that this isn't quite the right forum for a eulogy on the unique sonic properties of Tangerine Dream.

He and Crosby then find their way into a sugary, grandiose reading of 'Peace On Earth / Little Drummer Boy', with the former Thin White Duke singing the counterpoint.

David Bowie's career has been marked, since the late 1960s, by all sorts of strange and sometimes faintly comical moves, from 'The

Laughing Gnome' to *Labyrinth* to Tin Machine. But the one that stands out above all others came here, at the start of the promotional tour in support of his recently completed *"Heroes"*, the latest and in many ways most uncompromising of his run of classic albums of the 1970s. One might have expected the deadly serious appearances on outré European television shows, performing works of dissonant ambience and strained, epic post-rock, or the guarded interviews with established members of the British rock press. But a spot on a festive TV special hosted by a 74-year-old crooner, whose other guests included the 1960s model and pop icon Twiggy? If proof was needed that Bowie was ready to reassert his status as a maverick pop star after two years of paranoid seclusion and experimentation, this was it.

The release of *Low*, nine months earlier, had been marked by Bowie's complete refusal to promote it. Whether or not this contributed to the lacklustre critical response to the record is difficult to quantify; what is clear is that by the time *"Heroes"* went on sale, in the week of October 14th, 1977, Bowie had already spent the best part of a month giving interviews and appearing on television shows in support of it, and that, perhaps as a consequence of this, the album fared much better with reviewers than its predecessor did. The response was still mixed – perhaps unsurprisingly, given the uncompromising musical stance Bowie continued to take – but there were certainly more yays than nays.

Earlier in the year the *New Musical Express* had been so unsure of *Low* that it published two contrasting responses to it, one of them full of admiration, the other by a critic tearing his hair out with disgust. Now, however, there were no such concessions to democratic opinion, just the lone voice of Angus MacKinnon, who declared *"Heroes"* to be "Bowie's most moving performance in years". In *Melody Maker*, meanwhile, Allan Jones hailed the album as "further, and occasionally considerable, evidence of [Bowie's] artistic maturity" and "truly modern music for a modern world ... its courage cannot be denied". Both publications subsequently chose Bowie's tenth studio LP of the decade as their album of the year, ahead of a strong field that included *Never Mind The Bollocks Here's The Sex Pistols*, *My Aim Is True*, *The Clash*, *Marquee Moon*, and *New Boots & Panties*. Bowie also fared particularly well, given the supposed omnipresence of punk, in the *NME* Readers' Poll. He beat Johnny Rotten to the title of 'best male singer', and was named third best 'miscellaneous instrumentalist' behind Mike Oldfield and Brian Eno.

Elsewhere, Patti Smith was significantly impressed with the album that she felt compelled to write a "communiqué" on *"Heroes"* for *Hit Parader*, describing it as "a cryptic product of a high order of intelligence". In *Rolling Stone*, Bart Testa was similarly impressed. While *Low* was, he felt, "just another auteurish exploitation", *"Heroes"* "prompts a much more enthusiastic reading of the collaboration [with Eno], which here takes the form of a union of Bowie's dramatic instincts and Eno's unshakeable sonic serenity". Testa heaped further praise on the often-unsung heroes of the rhythm section, who had managed, unlike their predecessors, to hang on to their places in Bowie's band for three consecutive albums, and for good reason. A number of other quarters of the American press were, however, less effusive in their praise. *Billboard* surmised that Bowie was on a journey that only "[he] himself can define", while Robert Hillburn in *The Los Angeles Times* lamented the way his "fluctuating pop interests caused him to shift from style to style faster than his ability to master them".

Bowie made a conscious decision, it seems, to stand up for his art this time around. "The only reason I've decided to do these interviews," he told *Melody Maker*, bluntly, in October, "is to prove my belief in the album." Some people had, he noted, taken his decision not to promote *Low* to mean that his "heart wasn't in it", when in fact "I believe in the last two albums … more than anything I have done before".[1] Which he unquestionably did, at the time (and probably still does), although it's worth setting this statement against his admission, to Cameron Crowe a couple of years earlier, that "nothing matters except whatever it is I'm doing at the moment".[2] But one gets the impression, too, that Bowie couldn't have stood up for *Low* even if he'd wanted to – he wasn't in the right physical or mental shape then to throw himself into the lion's den. Now, with *"Heroes"* on the horizon, he was.

After taking a holiday in Spain at the end of August to celebrate completing work on the album, Bowie began his most vigorous media blitz in some years with a pair of oddball television appearances. The first of these was a hastily arranged spot on the final episode of Marc Bolan's Granada TV show, *Marc*, taped on September 9th in Manchester. The main purpose of Bowie's appearance was of course to perform his new single, '"Heroes"', due for release on September 23rd, but he also ended up taping a rough-and-ready duet of a song he and Bolan had written together earlier in the day, entitled 'Standing Next To You'. The performance came to an abrupt end when Bolan slipped from the stage midway through, having reportedly indulged, with Bowie, in some illicit substance or other during the afternoon. But that ended up being the broadcast take, owing to delays earlier in the day while two other bands, X-Ray Spex and Eddie & The Hot Rods, filmed their spots, and the refusal of the crew to do the overtime required to shoot a second run through Bowie and Bolan's song.

The whole show was, according to *Melody Maker's* eyewitness spy, Chris Welch, a "shambles", beset throughout by technical interruptions and conflicts between the two younger bands and the crew. Furthermore, Bowie was none too pleased to find that Bolan's resident bassist was a certain Herbie Flowers, with whom he had come into conflict during the Diamond Dogs tour and not seen since. (Flowers led a vociferous musicians' revolt at the Tower Theater in Philadelphia, demanding, quite rightly, that he and the rest of the band be paid more since the gig was to be recorded for posterity as *David Live*; he and several of his colleagues were subsequently replaced for the second leg of the tour.) Shambolic as it might have been, Bowie's stint on *Marc* did at least give '"Heroes"' an airing on nationwide, primetime television during the week of its release.

Bowie was back in Manchester two days later to film his appearance on *Bing Crosby's Merrie Olde Christmas*, which rivals even his guest spot on *The Cher Show* a couple of years earlier for sheer incongruity. He sang "'Heroes'" again, but the real draw was his festive duet with Crosby on 'Peace On Earth / Little Drummer Boy', which became an international hit single when it was released by RCA five years later. Bowie was reportedly invited to appear on the show, alongside Twiggy and a selection box of ageing actors and comedians, because Crosby's children were fans of his. Neither he nor Crosby knew much about each other. "I just knew my mother liked him," Bowie recalled in 1999.[3]

Bowie's appearances on *Marc* and *Bing Crosby's Merrie Olde Christmas* form the crux of an eerily morbid coincidence. By the time the two shows hit the airwaves, both hosts were dead. On September 16th, a week after filming his duet with Bowie, Marc Bolan was killed in a car accident in southwest London, just short of his 30th birthday. Bowie subsequently attended Bolan's funeral, in Golders Green, and helped set up a trust fund for Bolan's two-year-old son, Rolan. By the time *Merrie Olde Christmas* aired on Christmas Eve, meanwhile, Bing Crosby had been dead for two months, having suffered a heart attack shortly after completing a round of golf in Madrid, Spain, on October 14th. In the wake of these two deaths, Bowie was understandably reluctant to guest on anyone else's TV show – it was some years, in fact, before he performed another televised duet.

The rest of Bowie's promotional engagements for *"Heroes"* passed largely without incident. He shot several promo videos with director Nick Ferguson, including the one for "'Heroes'", and appeared on television and radio shows in Italy, Germany, France, the Netherlands, and Britain. Most notably, he decided, in typically contrary fashion, to treat viewers of the Italian show *Odeon* to a performance of the doomy instrumental 'Sense Of Doubt'. For *Top Of The Pops*, meanwhile, he assembled an odd hybrid of old and new band members that included Tony Visconti on bass for the first time since the early 1970s and Sean Mayes, who would subsequently join the *"Heroes"* tour, making his debut on keyboards.

Bowie's television appearances and press photographs during the autumn of 1977 introduced yet another new look ... or rather a non-look. Bowie's new mode of dress seemed to take its cue from "'Heroes'" and its suggestion that "we can be us / Forever and ever", the lavish costumes of old replaced by jeans and plain shirts, the shock of coloured hair brushed simply back and left in its natural shade of brown. For this new, everyman Bowie, even the pleated trousers of the Station To Station tour were too much. Despite the abrasive, epic sound of the record he was busily promoting, Bowie the man looked at pains to blend quietly into the space behind the music. The sleeve of the *"Heroes"* album – Bowie's take on *Roquairol* by Erich Heckel, on which *The Idiot* had also been modelled – is similarly restrained. Softly lit in black-and-white, it depicts an older, wiser Bowie, no longer interested in casting himself as Nietzschean superman or rock'n'roll prophet from Mars, but keen instead to paint a stark, serious picture of the world around him.

Similarly, the interviews Bowie gave during the autumn of 1977 reveal a quietly determined character, sure enough of himself now that he no longer felt it necessary to play the 'star' card at every turn. "I'm becoming incredibly straight, level, assertive, moderate," he told Charles Shaar Murray. He was, however, still conscious of the need to steer well clear of anything approaching a 'normal' life. "I have never got round to getting myself a piece of land, putting a house on it, and saying this is mine, this is home," he continued. "If I did that, that would just ruin everything. I don't think I'd ever write again."

This sense of needing to travel, to find new environments into which to throw himself to inspire new songs, was another common theme. Despite the fact of its having provided so much inspiration for his two most recent albums, Bowie seemed to be preparing to draw a line under his Berlin period already. "I've written in all the Western capitals," he had told *Rock Et Folk* magazine in June, shortly before starting work on *"Heroes"*, "and I've always got to the stage where there isn't any friction between a city and me." Now, it seems, mere weeks after completing work on the album, there was a growing danger of the same thing happening in Berlin. Certainly, he was already musing, publicly, about where to take himself next: Japan, perhaps, or maybe Israel.

His next immediate move was, however, not a full-scale relocation but a lengthy holiday in Kenya. Having fulfilled his commitments with the European media, Bowie flew out from Heathrow at the end of October and spent six weeks there with his son, Joey, during which time he stayed at the famous Treetops resort, went out on safari, and spent time with Masai tribesmen. Once again, new places and new experiences would bring new songs, notably 'African Night Flight' on *Lodger*, his final studio album of the decade.

While he might well have been gathering new ideas and concepts for it almost as soon as he had completed *"Heroes"*, Bowie didn't start work on *Lodger* until the latter part of 1978, and would not have the album ready for release until the following March. This next phase of his career would, in fact, be marked by his longest break from the recording studio – and the biggest gap between album releases – since the start of the 1970s. Instead, he would focus for the next year on two more exhibitionist aspects of his career: acting and touring. The only exception came at the beginning of December, 1977, when Bowie flew into New York, from Kenya, to make his contribution to a project that, were it not for his appearance on *Bing Crosby's Merrie Olde Christmas*, would certainly have been heralded as his most surprising career-move of the era.

Almost immediately upon touching down in New York, Bowie was in RCA Studio B, providing the narration for a new version of Sergei Prokofiev's *Peter And The Wolf*, one of several works the composer completed during the 1930s with the aim of introducing young people to orchestral music. It tells the story, through words and music, of a small boy who goes out beyond the confines of his grandfather's garden in search of a big bad wolf, with a different instrument representing each animal (Peter's pet cat is represented by a clarinet, the wolf by a trio of French horns, and so on). The recording of *Peter And The Wolf* that Bowie became involved in was by no means the first of its type, nor indeed the first time it had been used to bridge separate artistic domains. Prokofiev's work had, in fact, formed part of the 1946 Walt Disney feature *Make Mine Music*, while various record labels had cottoned on to the idea of attaching the voices of big-name stars to the project. Decca, for example, had issued a version narrated and conducted by Leonard Bernstein in 1960, while Sean Connery – at the height of his fame, having just starred in *Diamonds Are Forever* – recorded his take on the story in 1971, backed by London's Royal Philharmonic Orchestra. In between times, Hammond Organ whiz 'The Incredible' Jimmy Smith had cut an improvisatory, wordless version in 1966.

Bowie, in fact, was not even RCA's first choice for narrating their version of *Peter And The Wolf*: a pair of high-profile actors, Alec Guinness and Peter Ustinov, both reportedly turned the job down before the label turned to its biggest contemporary star. (Guinness would, however, narrate a later version for BMG.) Bowie has since claimed that he decided to do it as a Christmas gift for his son, which seems fair enough. While projects such as this are easy to mock, only the most hard-hearted of listeners could deny that both Bowie, with his wide-eyed, enthusiastic delivery, and the Philadelphia Orchestra (conducted by Eugene Ormandy) made a fine job of it. Released during the spring of 1978, with a recording of Benjamin Britten's *Young Person's Guide To The Orchestra* on the flipside, the album sold fairly well, even making a small indentation on the lower reaches of the *Billboard* Top 200 – no mean feat for a record such as this, so completely out of phase with contemporary trends.

But for a few radio interviews, recording *Peter And The Wolf* was Bowie's final significant professional act of the year. He stayed on for a little while longer in New York, principally so that he could fulfil his duties as best man at the wedding of Tony Mascia, his bodyguard and indeed co-star in *The Man Who Fell To Earth*. The wedding was also attended by Iggy Pop, fresh from his own tour in support of *Lust For Life*. Interviewed about Bowie a decade later, Mascia noted, "I'm like his father."[4] Coco Schwab aside, he was the most trusted and longest serving member of Bowie's slimmed down, post-Lippman entourage; he worked for the singer right up until his death in 1991.

Bowie also took advantage, while in the cosmopolitan environs of New York City, of the opportunity to convene with the hotly tipped new-wave five-piece, Devo. Bowie had become aware of the group earlier in the year, on his last trip to New York, with Iggy Pop, when the pair of them had seen the group's self-made short film *The Truth About De-Evolution*. Bowie's patronage then reportedly helped the group secure a lucrative deal with Warner Bros. Here he solidified his relationship with the band by introducing them onstage at Max's Kansas City in New York on December 17th. He also made a loose agreement to produce their debut album, but in the end had to drop out because of his touring commitments, which took up most of his 1978. (Brian Eno ended up producing the album instead.)

For Christmas, Bowie returned to his official residence in Switzerland to spend the festive season with his son. In a series of incidents that have since received more coverage than they deserved, Angela Bowie spent the holidays elsewhere, and then returned, on January 2nd, to find David and Joey gone – to Berlin, as it turned out. She subsequently attempted suicide, although probably not with the intention, really and truly, of ending her life. (She made a second, more concerted attempt three months later, and ended up with a rather painful and unintended reminder of the fact when, as she later wrote, the paramedics who came to her rescue "dropped me down two flights of stairs on the way to the ambulance, breaking my nose".[5])

A week after his wife's first suicide attempt, Bowie issued a statement intended both to play down the incident and to deny any wrongdoing on his part, noting that, during the entire time he was in Switzerland, "she didn't phone me or the boy to say where she was". The situation was then officially resolved when Bowie allowed his son to be returned to Switzerland in the care of his Scottish nanny a few days later. In reality, however, his wife's actions over the Christmas period only served to confirm his feelings towards her. But for the legal formalities, their marriage had long since been over. Mr. & Mrs. Bowie would not reconvene in the flesh until 1980, and then only to exchange divorce papers.

With his son safely back at Clos des Mésanges, Bowie turned his attentions to the first of his two big projects for 1978: his second major acting role, in David Hemmings's *Schöner Gigolo, Armer Gigolo* (or *Just A Gigolo*, as it is more widely known outside Germany). Initially, the project must have sounded like the perfect fit for Bowie The Actor: a film about depressed, decadent Berlin during the 1920s, to be filmed on location.

Since starring in *The Man Who Fell To Earth* a couple of years earlier, Bowie had been offered a series of similar roles, but none demonstrated much in the way of imagination from their respective casting directors. Each of these offers was for a different spin on roughly the same sci-fi yarn – the lead in a proposed adaptation of Robert A. Heinlein's *Stranger In A Strange Land*, for example. Bowie, conscious of being typecast so early in his acting career, was dead against anything even remotely in that vein. "I'd be alien for life," he remarked at the time. "All I'd be offered would be people with green skins and varying colour hair."[6]

Just A Gigolo, on the other hand, sounded like just the kind of role he had been waiting for. Bowie's fascination with the time and place in which the film was to be set was such that it had been one of the overriding factors in his decision to relocate to Berlin two years previously. Indeed, Berlin during the 1920s was, by anybody's reckoning, a thoroughly intriguing period. It was a city trying desperately to uphold its pride in the wake of Germany's defeat in the First World War, and one marked by its growing liberal subcultures – exemplified by the cabaret clubs later brought to wider recognition by one of Bowie's great literary idols, Christopher Isherwood – and fierce street-battles between opposing political factions.

The script, by Ennio de Concini and Joshua Sinclair, touched on each of these areas, which would doubtless have appealed to Bowie, but even beyond that there were several other key factors behind his decision to star in the film. Firstly, from the outset, he got on very well with the director, just as he had with Nicholas Roeg. This was doubly important as David Hemmings was set to star in the film, too – he had made his name as an actor in Michelangelo Antonioni's *Blow-Up*, the definitive big-screen depiction of London during the 1960s. Bowie hoped, meanwhile, that taking the role of Paul von Przygodski, a shell-shocked Prussian soldier returning from the war and struggling to fit in with the 'new' Berlin, would provide him with a suitable opportunity to prove himself as a serious actor – something he certainly craved, particularly since a significant number of reviewers had surmised that becoming Thomas Newton in *The Man Who Fell To Earth* hadn't required any acting whatsoever.

On top of that, there was the lure of Bowie's female co-stars. Somehow, for reasons that have never been adequately explained, David Hemmings and his German producer, Rolf Thiele, managed to put together an almost unparalleled assemblage of cinematic sex symbols, past and present. Representing the current wave of European cinema was the expatriate American actress Sydne Rome, who plays Cilly, Bowie's main love interest in the film. Alongside her were three screen legends from days gone by, each making something of a comeback. The Austrian actress Maria Schell had technically retired in 1963, but continued to take on film roles sporadically right up until 1990. Here she plays Paul's mother (having also recently filmed a brief cameo in *Superman: The Movie*). Similarly, Kim Novak, best known for her starring role in Alfred Hitchcock's *Vertigo*, had all but retired by the 1970s, but was coaxed by Hemmings into playing Helga von Kaiserling, a socialite with whom Paul, in his gigolo guise, has a fling.

Just A Gigolo's biggest draw was, however, the first speaking role in almost two decades for Marlene Dietrich, one of the greatest screen icons of the 20th century, who here makes a cameo as elusive as Marlon Brando's in *Apocalypse Now*. Having begun her career as a cabaret singer and actress during the very Weimar-era Berlin in which the film is set (she was born in Schöneberg, where Bowie now lived), Dietrich set sail for Hollywood in the 1930s and became one of American cinema's biggest stars of the next two decades. From the 1950s onwards, she concentrated almost exclusively on stage work, but had effectively retired in 1975 after breaking her leg during a performance in Australia. But now, at the age of 76, she had agreed to two days of filming – "with pride", according to the opening credits – for a reported fee of $250,000.

When asked what had, ultimately, led him to agree to star in the film, Bowie answered, simply, that "Marlene Dietrich was dangled in front of me".[7] Sadly for Bowie – and perhaps for Dietrich, too – they were never actually on the same set, or even in the same country, during the making of the film. Dietrich had, since her accident, become something of a recluse. She rarely left her apartment in Paris, and was particularly adamant that she wouldn't travel to Berlin to shoot her scenes. Her relationship with her homeland was a difficult, complex matter. Having become a naturalised American citizen in 1939 and sided in no uncertain terms with the Allies during World War Two, she had only returned to Germany once in the years since, and on that occasion received something of a mixed reception. As a result, after much deliberation, Dietrich's scenes were shot in Paris and inserted – rather awkwardly, in some instances – into what had already been filmed in Berlin.

This would, in the end, be her final public act. She spent the remaining 14 years of her life hidden away in her Parisian home, writing books and letters and making lengthy, expensive telephone calls to a wide cast of characters that ranged from her biographer, David Bret, to the former Russian premier Mikhail Gorbachev.

Back in Berlin, principal shooting of *Just A Gigolo*, much of which took place at the Café Wien on the Kurfürstendamm, passed without incident. Just as had been the case during the filming of *The Man Who Fell To Earth*, Bowie was visited by a couple of members of the British and American music press while on set, each of whom was impressed by what seemed to be a fit, happy, and determined figure. Physically, Bowie was barely the same person as the one who had rolled into Berlin at the end of the Station To Station tour. Back then he was pale and thin, his pasty white complexion given further emphasis by his shock of dyed hair. Now, however, he looked much more like what one would expect from a 32-year-old actor and musician. He had let his hair grow back to its natural, mousy brown, and his skin was a much healthier colour – a by-product, perhaps, of his recent time in Africa. He had also begun to put back on some of the weight he had lost in recent years, a consequence no doubt of an improved lifestyle and stronger appetite. *Melody Maker*'s Michael Watts noted, in his on-set report, that Bowie ate steak, eggs, and chips for lunch.

In most instances, details such as these about a celebrity's dietary habits might rightly be dismissed as idle, tabloid-style gossip. Here, however, they are indicative of a pronounced and crucial turnaround. Put simply, had Bowie continued in the lifestyle he had followed in America during 1974–5, and during the early part of his return to Europe in 1976, he would most likely not have made it through to the end of the end of the decade. In an interview with *Crawdaddy* published while he was filming *Just A Gigolo*, Bowie described how it took the intervention of an unnamed close friend just before Christmas, 1975, to make him realise how low he had sunk. "If you continue to be the way you're being at the moment," this friend had told him, "you're never going to see me again."[8] Fortunately, he had, in the two years since, made significant changes; he would even, soon, be extolling the virtues of going to bed early and getting up "in the morning instead of halfway through the day".[9] By the beginning of 1978, even the decadent nightspots of Berlin – which had, of course, risen from the ashes of the places in which *Just A Gigolo* was set – had, for Bowie, lost their lustre.

Instead, if he wasn't filming or working on music, he would stay in and work on his post-expressionist paintings and woodcuts.

On the set, Bowie played a character in some ways as cold and lacking in emotion as Thomas Newton in *The Man Who Fell To Earth*. *Just A Gigolo* is, according to its director, "about a boy trying to find his own way in a time and situation which was changing so rapidly that no one knew what they wanted".[10] That boy, Bowie's Paul von Przygodski, is first seen as a German soldier in the Great War, announcing to his superiors that "heroism is my destiny". We then flash forward to 1921, and learn that Paul has been looked after for the past two years by French nurses, who had assumed him to be one of *their* heroes. When he wakes up, a motley crew of military and religious figures and an unspecified mayor rise to attention, then leave in disgust when they discover Paul to be "un allemand" – a German – in a scene that, within the first five minutes, defines the film's lack of realism and heavy-handed sense of humour.

Paul returns to Berlin by train and finds that his home city has changed drastically in his absence, the pre-war optimism and affluence replaced by a lack of jobs, a lack of money, and, crucially, a lack of men. An old neighbourhood sweetheart, Cilly, played by Sydne Rome, is pleased to see him back in one piece, but Paul is too shell-shocked to do anything about it. He drifts in and out of low-paid, demoralising jobs while being pursued romantically by Cilly and ideologically by Captain Hermann Kraft, played by David Hemmings, whose role is to embody the growing threat of Nazism. Eventually, Paul gives in to Cilly's advances, but when she runs off to Hollywood he becomes a gigolo – a plot development that might have been more interesting had it not been signposted in the film's title. Having been recruited by Marlene Dietrich's Baroness von Semering, Paul falls into a life of entertaining older women, including a sultry Kim Novak. In the end, however, before he can sufficiently reconcile any aspect of his post-war life, he gets caught in gunfire between Nazis and communists.

While the shooting of *Just A Gigolo* went by without too many major hitches, the editing and distribution of it were rather more problematic, as was the response by virtually all quarters of the press. Given both its purported subject matter and the fact that it had been, by all accounts, the most expensive film to have been made to date in post-war Germany, most people were expecting a lavish epic to rival Bob Fosse's 1972 big-screen adaptation of *Cabaret* – which had, of course, used Christopher Isherwood for its source material. When the initial, two-hour-plus cut premiered at the 1978 Cannes Film Festival, it was roundly lambasted for being overlong, overegged, plotless, and distinctly unfunny – no *Cabaret*, in other words. A frustrated Hemmings went back to the drawing board, beginning – but crucially not completing – the painstaking process of re-editing the film from scratch. Three quarters of the way through this second edit, he quit the project altogether, most likely because of a lack of additional funding for a film already well over budget.

In November, a second cut of *Just A Gigolo* was given its world premiere in Berlin with the entire cast and crew (apart from Bowie, who was mercifully on tour in Australia) in attendance. This new version, 20 minutes shorter than it had been when Hemmings last worked on it, was met with even more howls of derision than the first. Hemmings later claimed that the film's narrative arc and ironic sensibilities had been completely destroyed by the German assistants who took over the project after he left. Such losses in translation were, perhaps, at the root of quite a few of the film's problems: this was, remember, a film about Berlin, made in Berlin, with a predominantly German crew but British and American lead actors and director.

After the second version of *Just A Gigolo* was pulled from general release, Hemmings was given the green light, somewhat incredibly, to go back and edit the film for a third time. The resulting version is almost an hour shorter than the one that had aired at Cannes. It's debatable, however, whether this had any noticeable effect on the film's overall artistic merit. Both the English and German-language versions of the film, which are roughly the same length but assembled in different orders, are difficult either to follow or to engage with. There's nothing particularly remarkable about the direction; the actors are given little opportunity to show their worth; the plot is, at best, confused; and the dialogue routinely awkward. "There comes a time in every man's life," Bowie is forced to declare at one point, "where he has to avoid making the same mistake as Napoleon."

Even the soundtrack is a mess, comprised as it is of leaden pastiches of music-hall songs, a main theme that will likely remind any British parent or child of the 1980s of *Thomas The Tank Engine*, and modern-day contributions from The Village People and Manhattan Transfer. Bowie himself made one small contribution to the soundtrack (his unhappy experiences with *The Man Who Fell To Earth* perhaps precluding any further commitment), co-writing 'Revolutionary Song', which is used near the start of the film. It begins with him strumming a guitar and singing a vaguely Eastern, wordless melody. The film's musical supervisor, Jack Fishman, then added some additional instrumentation and some truly cringe-worthy lyrics, sung by an unidentified woman. The resulting curio, which is certainly not without charm, was released as a single in Japan, where it was attributed to The Rebels, but elsewhere it was only included on the film's soundtrack album, which has long since been deleted.

Further problems ensued even after Hemmings had completed his third and final cut of *Just A Gigolo*. Each of the major British distributors had passed on the project by this stage, and there was little interest from the USA either. The film eventually received its British premiere in London at the Prince Charles cinema in Leicester Square on February 14th, 1979. Despite being asked, like everybody else in attendance, to dress in smart, 1920s-style garb, Bowie turned up in a kimono, having spent the past couple of months in Tokyo (no doubt filling his head with Japanese influences). American audiences didn't get to see the film until 1981, but they clearly weren't missing much. Very few reviews even came close to being favourable, with most homing in on the word 'inept' to describe both the film itself and the performances of its lead actors. *Just A Gigolo* did nothing, in fact, for the reputation of anyone involved. Bowie seemed to be hit hardest. This was only his second major acting role, and there is nothing particularly redeemable about it. In fact, after this, it took him some time to gain any respect as an actor at all. Many critics took *Gigolo* as evidence that he simply couldn't act – *The Man Who Fell To Earth* didn't count, went the familiar refrain, because all he'd done there was play himself.

Bowie made a point of staying positive about the film in the immediate period after filming his role in it, but it didn't take too long for him to reveal his true feelings about the project. "You were disappointed," he told Angus MacKinnon of the *New Musical Express*, "and you weren't in it. Imagine how we felt." Describing the film, memorably, as "my 32 Elvis Presley movies contained in one", Bowie revealed his "great failure" to have been to accept the role on the basis of David Hemmings being a "terrific fella" rather than on "actually bothering to consider what the script consisted of – or rather didn't consist of, since it contained absolutely nothing".[11] Hemmings, for his part, remained admirably positive about the whole endeavour to the end. In 2001, in one of his last major interviews, he admitted, "I love *Just A Gigolo*, actually. I really, really, really do. But I think I'm the only person who does."[12] (Hemmings was similarly bullish about his subsequent work as a director of such lowbrow television series as *The A-Team* and *Murder She Wrote*.)

Bowie's second major project of 1978 was announced even before he had finished filming *Just A Gigolo*: a full-scale world tour, his first since 1976, taking in not just Europe and America but also Japan and Australia. This came as something of a surprise to most observers, who had anticipated, given the slowness with which he had returned to public life over the past year, that, if Bowie was to return to live performance at all, it would be with a handful of small, sporadic appearances. "Why are you returning to the circus?" asked Charles M.

Young of *Rolling Stone* magazine. "I need the money," Bowie replied, bluntly. And so, in mid March, he arrived in Dallas to begin rehearsals with the latest incarnation of his band.

The rhythm section, naturally, was the same, ever-dependable trio of Carlos Alomar, George Murray, and Dennis Davis. Bowie had expressed a rather optimistic wish that Brian Eno and Robert Fripp might complete an all-star sextet and join him in playing live the songs they had helped record. Neither, however, was willing to commit to five months, all told, on the road. "I gave it some serious consideration," Eno told *Zig-Zag*, "but the trouble was he was talking about a long tour … it would mean that I wouldn't be able to work again till the summer." Fripp was similarly disinclined. It's a measure perhaps of how much Bowie rated Fripp and Eno that he brought in four new recruits instead. Taking the Fripp role, as it were, were guitarist Adrian Belew and violinist Simon House; in place of Eno sat a pair of keyboardists, Roger Powell and Sean Mayes. All in all, this was the biggest and most musically diverse group Bowie had yet worked with.

Although each of the four new arrivals came from what was essentially a rock background, their musical paths and styles were quite different. Sean Mayes, of course, had been given a brief trial run at playing with Bowie when he joined the singer to perform "'Heroes'" on *Top Of The Pops* six months earlier. Mayes had in fact met Bowie five years earlier when his rock'n'roll revivalist group Fumble were picked as the primary support act on the Ziggy Stardust tour. His memories of touring and then recording with Bowie in 1978 were later compiled, posthumously, in a diary entitled *Life On Tour With David Bowie*. On the "'Heroes'" tour, Mayes handled both acoustic piano and synthesized strings, leaving the band's other keyboardist, Roger Powell, to concentrate on the more obviously electronic, avant-garde sounds. Powell was invited to join the band at the suggestion of Brian Eno, who was an admirer not just of Powell's playing in Todd Rundgren's group Utopia but also of his technical innovations. During the mid 1970s, Powell developed one of the first polyphonic synthesizer controllers, which he named the Powell Probe, and later created the pioneering sequencer program Texture. Since Utopia's split in 1985, Powell has concentrated on programming, and these days works in a senior creative capacity for computer manufacturer Apple.

Perhaps the most surprising addition to the "Heroes" band was Simon House, formerly of the progressive-rock group Hawkwind, on electric violin. The reasons for bringing in a pair of keyboardists (and a virtuoso guitarist) would have been clear to anybody who had heard either of Bowie's albums from 1977. Neither *Low* nor *"Heroes"*, however, is characterised by the sound of the violin, electric or otherwise. Nonetheless, House's contributions to the band were effective without being overly obtrusive, and make perfect sense within the context of the other musicians' playing. On '"Heroes"', for example, he would double up on the wailing, feedback-laden electric guitar lines, while elsewhere he might contribute frenetic, John Cale-like discords.

The best known of the new arrivals in Bowie's band (at least from a modern day perspective) was Adrian Belew, who had first made his name in Frank Zappa's band. This was also where Bowie first spotted him. As the guitarist has since recounted in numerous interviews, Bowie was in attendance at a Zappa gig in Berlin in February 1978. When, as was customary, Belew left the stage to allow Zappa to take a lengthy guitar-solo, Bowie took the opportunity to poach himself a new sideman. Belew was a more than capable substitute for Robert Fripp, but brought something of his own avant-rock stylings to the songs, too. (In a neat twist, Belew would also join a distinctly guitar-centric 21st century incarnation of Fripp's King Crimson.)

The tour rehearsals began without Bowie, who had celebrated completing his work on *Just A Gigolo* with a return trip to Kenya. By the time Bowie arrived in Dallas, sporting a healthy tan and sunny optimism, Carlos Alomar had taught the other musicians the bulk of the *Low / "Heroes"* material, on which much of the set would naturally draw. After a few days of practicing these newer songs, however, Bowie announced his plan, as Sean Mayes later recalled, to surprise his audience by doing "the whole of the *Ziggy Stardust* album". The band dutifully learnt all 12 songs on the album before Bowie pared them down to a more manageable seven: 'Five Years', 'Soul Love', 'Star', 'Hang On To Yourself', 'Ziggy Stardust', 'Suffragette City', and 'Rock 'N' Roll Suicide'. These blasts from the not too distant past would form the bulk of the second half of the 1978 setlist, which for some fans would come as something of a respite following an opening hour dominated by Bowie's European music.

The overall atmosphere of the 1978 tour rehearsals was much more relaxed and convivial than it would have been a year or two earlier, but the musicians involved were under no illusions about the fact that they were there to work. They would begin, most days, at 10am, and generally play right through until the early evening before retiring to their hotel. Only when it happened to be Sean Mayes's birthday did Bowie join the rest of the musicians for a few drinks in downtown Dallas. The only other extracurricular event of note came when band and crew gathered in Bowie's hotel suite for the first airing of Eric Idle's Rutles mockumentary *All You Need Is Cash* on the evening of March 22nd, which had the distinction of being the lowest-rated show on American television that week.

Exactly one week later, the tour opened at the San Diego Sports Arena. In the run-up to the first night, Bowie had told anybody willing to listen that this would, at last, be a showcase for the 'real' David Bowie, and that he would no longer be reliant on the costumes, masks, and characters of old. This was true to a certain extent: the show as a whole was certainly a world away from his big-budget trek across the States in support of *Diamond Dogs*. The stage set this time was essentially a more extreme take on the Station To Station tour, with huge banks of dazzling white light built up around and behind the musicians.

There was, however, still a general air of theatricality, something Bowie seemed powerless (or perhaps unwilling) to leave behind. While the other musicians were, unusually, allowed to wear what they wanted (with occasionally comical results), Bowie had a brand new wardrobe designed for him by Natasha Kornilof, who had been making costumes for him, on and off, since 1967, and who later devised the clown suit for his 'Ashes To Ashes' video. For the 1978 tour, she came up with a range of seemingly anti-fashion garments – high waisted, billowing trousers, GI-style t-shirts, vibrant, patterned shirts, and suchlike. These might not have been as extravagant as Bowie's Aladdin Sane look, for example, but were still rather striking.

The start of the show, too, was decidedly theatrical. As with the Station To Station tour, there was no support act; after the lights dimmed, the band took their places as though members of an orchestra, with Bowie standing behind his Chamberlin. Carlos Alomar, baton in hand, would then 'conduct' a rendition of the sombre, wordless 'Warszawa'. This was purely for effect – as became clear when he wasn't required to conduct the other instrumental tracks that peppered the set – but it worked. 'Warszawa' was a pretty perverse choice of opener even by Bowie's standards, but there was, equally, something quite fitting about it. It was this song, above all others, with which Bowie had unveiled his newly serious and decidedly European sound a year earlier. Kicking off with 'Changes' might well have got the crowds moving, but it would hardly have been representative of this year's Bowie.

After dispensing with 'Warszawa', Bowie moved to the front of the stage for '"Heroes"', which, whatever its true meaning, can't help but become a euphoric, life-affirming anthem when performed live. The spotlight for the next 40 minutes or so would remain almost entirely on *Low* and *"Heroes"*, with 'The Jean Genie' sandwiched somewhere in the middle as the only representative of Bowie's older material. Conscious of making the setlist as palatable as possible, however, he made sure that the slow, moody instrumentals were always followed by something more up-tempo, such as 'Be My Wife' or 'Beauty And The Beast'.

Once a taut 'Fame' had brought the first half to a close, Bowie and his band moved into the retrospective segment of the concert, running swiftly through seven tracks from *Ziggy Stardust*. These five-year-old songs worked remarkably well in the hands of Bowie's new band – perhaps surprisingly, given the marked differences in style and approach between the current line-up and The Spiders From Mars. Each of the songs was given something of a modern update by Carlos Alomar and the band, but never to the extent of losing sight of what made the material work so well in the first place. Often, in the case of songs such as 'Soul Love', it meant making more explicit the subtly funky undertones of the original, or adding a gentle wash of complementary synthesizer sounds to the mix.

The most radical change was to allow Simon House to play the opening riff in 'Ziggy Stardust' on his violin, but even that, incredibly, paid off. After an impassioned 'Rock 'N' Roll Suicide', Bowie gave one final nod to his recent avant-garde leanings with 'Art Decade' before closing the main set with the epic 'Station To Station'. Then came a three-song encore of feelgood tracks from the mid 1970s: 'Stay', 'TVC15', and 'Rebel Rebel'.

Bowie stuck fairly rigidly to the same setlist night after night as the tour wound its way across North America from west to east. From mid-April onwards, the setlist included a version of Bertolt Brecht and Kurt Weill's 'Alabama Song', which had famously been recorded, a decade earlier, by The Doors and included on the Los Angeles band's debut album. Everything else remained the same, apart from an occasional slight reorganisation of the *Low* and *"Heroes"* material. All in all the band played 31 shows in 26 cities over the course of six fast-paced weeks, during which they would regularly play four or five nights in a row. The band's performance at the Dallas Convention Centre on April 10th was filmed by a local TV network, with six songs from it later airing as *David Bowie On Stage*.

Midway through the tour, Tony Visconti flew out from England to begin preparations for the recording of what would become Bowie's second live album, *Stage*. Visconti had mixed Bowie's last live set,

David Live, but had been unhappy with the source material, so this time he decided to supervise all of the recording and engineering himself. "My plan was to record this album very carefully," he recalled in an essay included in the 2005 reissue of *Stage*, "as if it was a studio album." To that end he close-miked all of the instruments and placed four further microphones around the auditorium of each of the venues used for the recording. Using RCA's expensive mobile studio, he recorded four nights' worth of performances: two at the Spectrum Arena in Philadelphia, and a couple more at the Civic Center in Providence and The Gardens in Boston. According to its producer, *Stage* contains absolutely no overdubbing (which remains a surprisingly common practice on 'live' albums), partly because the performances were so good, but also because there simply wouldn't have been time, as Bowie was headed straight for Europe after completing the American leg of the tour. Visconti did, however, deploy a little bit of trickery on 'Station To Station': "The beginning and end are from Boston but the middle is from Providence."[13] It's a testament to how good the musicians were (and to Visconti's skilful editing) that the joins are imperceptible.

Visconti returned to his Good Earth studio in London, England, after the Boston show to begin mixing the live recordings, while Bowie completed his US tour with a three-night stand at Madison Square Garden. All manner of stars were in attendance across the three nights, including Andy Warhol, various members of Talking Heads, Bianca Jagger (with whom Bowie had reportedly been having an on-off relationship), and the two missing members of the *"Heroes"* team, Brian Eno and Robert Fripp. Bowie spent a valedictory night at Studio 54 and CBGB with Eno and Jagger before heading back to Europe for the second phase of the tour. The North American leg had been, it should be noted, an unqualified success. In six short weeks, Bowie had played to over 400,000 fans in the United States and Canada, and picked up rave reviews across the continent. Perhaps most noteworthy was the report by Robert Hilburn of the *Los Angeles Times*, who had, only a few months earlier, written off *"Heroes"* as a failed experiment by a musician too eager in his search for new ideas. Having attended one of Bowie's shows at the Inglewood Forum, however, Hilburn changed his tune, writing not just of how much he enjoyed the show, but how, of all the musical stars to emerge during the 1970s, Bowie "shook the rock'n'roll epicentre more than any other single figure".

In the brief period between Bowie's departure from New York and the start of his European tour, two interesting curios hit the shelves of record shops on both sides of the Atlantic. The first of these was the recording Bowie had made the previous December of *Peter And The Wolf*, released on RCA's Red Seal subsidiary on translucent green vinyl. The second, also issued by RCA, was *TV Eye*, a live album by Iggy Pop, on which Bowie plays on four songs: 'Funtime', 'Dirt', 'I Wanna Be Your Dog', and the title track. Each of these was recorded at the Agora Ballroom in Cleveland the previous March, except for 'I Wanna Be Your Dog', which was taped a few days later at Chicago's Riviera Theater. The rest of the material – 'Sixteen', 'I Got A Right', 'Lust For Life', and a ragged 'Nightclubbing' – was recorded later in the year, by which time Bowie had been replaced by Scott Thurston, and Iggy, from the sound of things, had slipped back off the rails.

David Bowie is listed as co-producer of *TV Eye*, but it's unlikely, in truth, that he had much to do with it beyond playing on half of the songs over a year prior to its release. Iggy used the album as a way of getting an early release from his three-album deal with RCA, the label that Bowie had urged to sign Iggy, but which had never really understood him or his music. While it is of some interest as a document of Iggy's return to the stage, and of Bowie's brief role as his keyboardist, *TV Eye* is ultimately a cheap cash-in by its principal author. Iggy even admitted as much himself in interviews around the time, in which he expressed his delight that he had been able to put it together (with the help of Hansa engineer Eduard Meyer) for only $5,000, despite having received an advance of several times that figure from RCA. None of the other musicians whose playing features on the album knew much about it, nor were they paid for their contributions; Hunt and Tony Sales reportedly only learnt of its existence when Hunt saw it in the window of a record store on the Sunset Strip.[14]

On May 14th the European leg of Bowie's 1978 tour began, fittingly, in his adopted homeland. The first date was in Frankfurt, and it was followed by performances in five more German cities, including one at the Deutschlandhalle in Berlin, and the filming of a 45-minute set for the nationwide television show *Musikladen Extra* (which didn't air until August). Bowie spent a month, all told, in continental Europe and Scandinavia, during which time he played to around 150,000 concertgoers in eight different countries. The majority of the 21 gigs passed without any controversy, with only two minor incidents of note to report on, both of which were entirely out of Bowie's control.

In Berlin, Bowie endeared himself further to his neighbours by demanding, in German, that a security guard stop manhandling a fan at the front; at the Palais des Sports in Lyon, France, there was a brief power cut almost immediately after the band played 'Blackout'. Sensing a growing restlessness in the crowd, Bowie and his band made a quick dash back to their hotel, only to return after the problem had, at least partially, been resolved. The concert resumed, but without its usual bright, white backing. "It felt like doing a show just for the troops just behind the front line," recalled Sean Mayes. "The neons didn't blaze but the music did."[15]

The second half of Bowie's European tour took the form of his first proper trek around the UK since that famous night in 1973 when he laid Ziggy Stardust to rest at the Hammersmith Odeon. The Diamond Dogs tour never even reached European – let alone British – soil, while in 1976 only the Wembley Empire Pool was granted a visit from the Thin White Duke. This time around, however, Bowie performed for 13 nights in total at venues in Newcastle, Glasgow, Stafford, and London. The shows received some of Bowie's finest write-ups yet. In *Melody Maker*, Chris Brazier felt it unlikely that he would "see a better concert this year", while Tony Parsons of the *New Musical Express* declared Bowie to be "the most compelling stage presence since Sinatra". Both journalists zeroed in on the potency of "'Heroes'": Brazier found it "predictably glorious", while for Parsons it was "the most moving spectacle I've ever witnessed at a rock gig".

The general feeling, too, was that, by shedding the costumes and masks and performing with a newfound authenticity, Bowie had regained his love for the stage; for Tony Parsons, the singer's persona on his triumphant return to the UK was "light years away from the contemptuous, contemptible Thin White Duke". Such a view is, of course, tempered somewhat by Bowie's regular complaints about touring and performing in interviews around this time. "I've decided really to cut it down to once every two years," he told Valerie Singleton on BBC TV's *Tonight* the following February. "I find it boring after the first ten shows. It starts to become repetitious." (Never mind every two years – after completing his 1978 tour, Bowie would only give worldwide audiences two opportunities to see him during the subsequent decade, in 1983 and 1987.)

It did, however, seem as though he particularly enjoyed these homecoming dates, perhaps in part because he could see light at the end of the touring tunnel. Having arrived in the UK from Belgium, Bowie spent the evening before the first Newcastle date in London, where he and some of his bandmates caught an Iggy Pop gig at the Music Machine in Camden. After the gig came a second meeting between Bowie, Iggy, and Johnny Rotten, who, according to Sean Mayes, "thought the gig was a load of rubbish". Bowie, Iggy, and the rest made their excuses, leaving the former Sex Pistol to complain to himself in the dressing room. Iggy then tagged along for some of Bowie's dates in northern England and Scotland, just as he had done a couple of years earlier on the Station To Station tour.

During the third of three nights at London's Earls Court arena – the venue at which Bowie had, in May 1973, been the first musician to perform – he gave 'Sound And Vision' a rare airing, declaring at the start, "This is last night stuff, folks!" A host of celebrities were in attendance that night, as might have been expected, but for Bowie the most important guest was his mother, for whom he reserved a seat in the royal box. All three Earls Court gigs were shot by David Hemmings as part of a planned documentary-cum-tour-film. Aside from a few clips shown the following week on the *London Weekend Show*, however, none of the footage has ever been released. Bowie later claimed that this was because he "simply didn't like the way it had been shot",[16] but other reports have suggested that it had more to do with the way *Just A Gigolo* was received, and Bowie's subsequent lack of enthusiasm for working with Hemmings.

After the last night at Earls Court, on July 1st, there were no further live dates scheduled until the Australasian leg of the tour, which was booked for November and December. But the intervening period, while quiet by the standards of the first half of the year, was certainly not one of inactivity. The day after the third Earls Court show, Bowie called all seven members of his touring band to Tony Visconti's Good Earth studio in London, hoping to capture the energy and enthusiasm of the live performances in a version of 'Alabama Song', which he had enjoyed playing onstage and which he intended to be his next single. The session was not quite as easy as might have been expected, however, as Dennis Davis struggled with the drums, which work against the central rhythm of the song. As a result, according to Sean Mayes, Visconti took the unusual step of recording everything else first, so that Davis could finally overdub his parts later on, "when his efforts couldn't disturb the beat".

Whatever difficulties ensued during the recording, however, were well worth it. 'Alabama Song' is one of the most unexpected and disorientating records Bowie made during the 1970s – and all the better for it. Its woozy, nightmarish feel serve as a useful signpost for much of the material on his next full-length effort, *Lodger*. Bowie had initially hoped to put it out as a single immediately, in order to maintain the momentum of his output, perhaps mindful of the fact that 1978 would be the first year since his rise to fame in 1969 without a new studio album. In the end, however, it sat on the shelf until 1980, at which point it was released instead as a stopgap between *Lodger* and *Scary Monsters*. It remains an interesting curio, particularly given its eventual status as Bowie's first new release of the new decade. (For the b-side, Bowie cut a stark reworking of 'Space Oddity', arranged for acoustic guitar, piano, bass, and drums, with the orchestral crescendo of the original replaced by 11 seconds of silence. It neatly reintroduced the story of Major Tom, to which Bowie would return on his next single, 'Ashes To Ashes'.)

Soon after recording 'Alabama Song', Bowie spent some time working with David Hemmings on ideas for the prospective film of the Earls Court gigs. The film, of course, was never completed to Bowie's satisfaction, and remains unreleased despite more recent suggestions that he might one day return to it. In fact, of all the projects that Bowie worked on in 1978 – including *Lodger*, which he began in August, and *Just A Gigolo*, of which Hemmings was still struggling to product a decent cut – only one would see the light during the same year, and thus go some way to satisfying the demands of Bowie's most rabid fans, who faced an unprecedented wait for any form of Bowie product, having been spoiled with two landmark albums in 1977.

That project was *Stage*, the live album Tony Visconti had recorded at the tail end of Bowie's US tour, and quickly mixed during the spring. Visconti had hit upon the idea, which Bowie apparently "loved"[17], of sequencing the tracks not in the manner of the live sets from which they were taken, but in a loosely chronological order. As such, the album opened with 'Hang On To Yourself', followed by four more *Ziggy Stardust* tracks and versions of 'Station To Station', 'Fame', 'TVC 15' – not exactly a fitting representation of Bowie '78. It wasn't until the second half of this two-disc set, in fact, that listeners got to hear any Berlin-era material, and even then the arrangement of the songs was decidedly questionable. Side three is made up entirely of instrumentals (all of which had been spaced out much more evenly during the concerts), leaving the sung songs from 1977, such as "'Heroes'" and 'What In The World', to side four.

Stage was ready for release during the summer but was delayed until September by a dispute between Bowie and his record label, RCA. Relations between the two parties had been deteriorating in recent times. Bowie had long been unhappy about the fact that, despite being the label's biggest star of the 1970s, he was, by his own estimation, broke; RCA, meanwhile, wasn't best pleased at the direction the singer had taken on his two most recent albums. In fairness to the label, *Low* and *"Heroes"* weren't selling anywhere near as well as *Young Americans* or *Station To Station*, particularly in America; and from a business perspective, simply making 'important' music isn't enough.

By 1978, Bowie was nearing the end of a multi-album contract, and it seemed increasingly likely that, upon completion of it, he would not re-sign. He assumed that, as a two-record set, *Stage* would count double, and thus allow him to chalk off two of the four albums he owed the label. But RCA disagreed, citing the previous example of *David Live*, which also filled four sides of vinyl, but which had only counted as one album on account of its being a live release.

There was little, in the end, that Bowie could do about this, aside from ensuring that he worked off his remaining three-album debt as soon as possible. The press evidently got wind of his disquiet, leading him – perhaps with a certain amount of coercion on the part of RCA – to issue a statement declaring his relationship with the label to be a "long and rewarding one". In reality, it was only a matter of time before he moved elsewhere.

In any case, from a purely artistic viewpoint, it would be difficult, really and truly, to argue that *Stage* (in its original form) has a comparable value to the two albums that preceded it. Like most live albums, it was released purely as a stop-gap between studio LPs, and an expensive souvenir of an experience that cannot really be reproduced on record – particularly, in this instance, when the sequencing is so ill thought-out.

Stage received little press attention of note, appearing only as a footnote at the end of the reviews sections in most music magazines and newspapers, and, despite breaking into the UK Top Five, sold poorly by comparison to the rest of Bowie's 1970s output.

Fortunately, when it came time to reissue the album 27 years after its original release, Tony Visconti did more than just deploy the usual remasterer's trick – that of simply turning the volume up. Instead, he returned to the original tapes, cleaned them up, and put the album back together in the order he really should have stuck to the first time around, beginning with 'Warszawa', and then '"Heroes"', and so on. The 2005 edition of *Stage* also includes three songs left off the original album – including a blistering version of 'Stay' – and is mixed superbly in both stereo and 5.1 surround sound. Few live albums sound as good as this one does, although Visconti's decision to mute the crowd noises everywhere except for at the start and end of the songs does sometimes leave you wondering whether you're actually listening to a live recording. But perhaps this is as much a reflection on the proficiency of the band, which barely puts a foot wrong throughout an hour and a half of music. Among the highlights are '"Heroes"', 'Alabama Song', 'Station To Station', and a radical reworking of 'What In The World', which starts off in lilting, reggae-inflected mode before launching, without a pause, into frenetic art-rock.

After a four-month break, during which Bowie laid the groundwork for *Lodger*, the *Low / "Heroes"* tour resumed for its last and most exciting leg. By 1978, Bowie must surely have lost count of the number of gigs he'd played across North America and Europe. Australasia was a different story altogether. He had spent a couple of weeks in Japan as Aladdin Sane in April 1973 but not been back since, and never once set foot in Australia or New Zealand. In the past, Bowie's fear of flying would have made any sort of tour of the Southern Hemisphere highly impractical. But since the spring of 1977 he had been flying regularly – to New York, Kenya, and beyond – thus opening up a whole new world of promotional activity.

The lack of personal attention paid to Australia by Bowie in the past had clearly done nothing to diminish his appeal there. During the next few weeks he played a series of outdoor shows to some of the biggest audiences of his career. Each passed largely without incident, although the high volume of the concert at Lang Park, Brisbane, drew complaints from residents in nearby towns, leading a local government minister, Russ Hinze, to investigate on behalf of the Noise Abatement Authority. Hinze's impartiality appeared somewhat questionable, however, when he complained to local reporters about the fact that, not only was this Bowie character noisy, he was also "a pommie".

At the end of November, Bowie flew across to New Zealand for performances in Christchurch and Auckland. The second of these, at the Western Springs Stadium, became the single largest musical event held in the country up to that point, when 41,000 turned up to hear his avant-rock songs in person. (Similar numbers had already attended the shows at cricket grounds in the Australian cities of Adelaide and Melbourne.) The final stage of the tour took Bowie to Japan, where he played three gigs in Osaka and two in Tokyo. The first of these was broadcast live on nationwide radio, and the last, on December 12th at the HNK Hall, taped for a later TV special.

Bowie celebrated the end of the tour at a 'Gigolo' party in Tokyo's Roppongi district, thrown for him by RCA to coincide with the Japanese premier of David Hemmings just-completed film, which Bowie also attended, wearing a kimono.

Having completed his professional obligations for the time being, he stayed on in Japan until the end of January, gathering thoughts and soaking up inspiration for future projects – chief among them his next album, *Lodger*, a strange musical travelogue already part-recorded in Switzerland that would, at least in theory, draw a neat line under his Berlin/Eno period.

DO SOMETHING BORING

Rock music criticism is written in lists, and driven often by an almost Aspergic desire to fit every singer, every song, and every sound into the neatest available tickbox. The received wisdom about the music David Bowie made in the late 1970s is a fine example. The three albums he recorded during 1976–9, in collaboration with Brian Eno and Tony Visconti, his rock-solid rhythm section, and a handful of guest musicians, are invariably grouped together as a 'Berlin trilogy'. But the notion that these records are all of a piece is rather misleading. It is true, of course, that each was made with much the same team (a notable distinction among Bowie records), and indeed that there are certain sonic similarities throughout. But while *Low* and *"Heroes"* are indisputably derived from similar experiments in sound and mood, *Lodger* – part three, as it were – is a very different animal, for all sorts of reasons.

Take first the idea of these three all being 'Berlin' records. While the majority of the *Low* sessions took place at the Château d'Hérouville, the album was at least completed in the city, and, moreover, is very much informed by Bowie's move towards it. *"Heroes"*, of course, was written and recorded solely in Berlin, and a great deal of it was derived directly from Bowie's experiences there. *Lodger*'s ties to Berlin are much more dubious. Although it contains faint echoes of Bowie's life at 155 Hauptstrasse, this last of three Bowie/Eno records of the 1970s was recorded in Montreux and New York City, and made up of songs either written on the spot or inspired by Bowie's travels during his 1978 world tour.

Moreover, by the time it was released, in May 1979, Bowie had for all intents and purposes bidden a fond farewell to Berlin. He had, in fact, not spent very much time in the city at all since completing his work on *Just A Gigolo* the previous spring, and had made clear his intention to explore new territories even earlier. Unlike his arrival in Berlin, which was based on so many complementary factors, Bowie's departure was largely unplanned, and driven by nothing more tangible than a continuing urge to seek out the new.

There was, by Bowie's standards, a huge gap between the making of *"Heroes"* and the completing of *Lodger*. *Low* and *"Heroes"* were recorded in the midst of a remarkably fertile 14-month period that also resulted in Iggy Pop's *The Idiot* and *Lust For Life*; a time in which Bowie did little else, career-wise, but make records. Between then and the completion of *Lodger*, a full year and a half later, Bowie had toured North America, Europe, and Australasia and filmed *Just A Gigolo*. It's well documented that neither Bowie nor Eno has ever had any desire to stay in the same place musically, or indeed geographically, for long. It's perhaps to be expected, then, that the third of the three Bowie/Eno records of the 1970s stands apart from its predecessors (the most obvious difference being the abandoning of the 'rock' side one / 'ambient' side two concept). Bowie had already acknowledged the fact that, with *Low* and *"Heroes"*, he had gone against one of his guiding principles by making, for all intents and purposes, two albums of "the same nature", so it would have been out of the question for him and Eno to follow the same pattern for a third time, even if they were completing a trilogy – or 'triptych', as they would have it.

Consider the difference in sound, mood, and approach between *Pin-Ups* and *Station To Station*, or *Here Come The Warm Jets* and

Discreet Music, and then the fact the recording of both pairs of albums was separated by less time than passed between the completion of *Low* and *Lodger*. Since working on *"Heroes"*, Eno had worked on all manner of projects with a wide range of collaborators, which included producing albums for Talking Heads and Devo – whom he later described as "anal" and "unable to experiment"[1] – and putting together the influential compilation album *No New York*. Clearly, neither he nor Bowie was likely to be in the same mood as they had been the previous summer – particularly now that a whole new wave of musical acts from The Human League to Gary Numan seemed to be basing their entire careers on the sound of *Low* and *"Heroes"*. Much the same had occurred a few years earlier, when pale imitations of Bowie's glam-rock records began to fill the airwaves. In order to stay ahead of the chasing pack, he would need to find yet another new sound.

Low and *"Heroes"* were both recorded in a vacuum of sorts. A physically and emotionally fragile Bowie had hidden himself away in the French countryside to make *Low* in 1976 while fighting his way through the most trying time of his life; a year later, while making *"Heroes"*, he was certainly more buoyant, but a comparable sense of conflict and anxiety came this time from an external source: the city of Berlin itself. *Lodger* was also recorded in a kind of vacuum, to some extent, but a very different one. This time around, not only was Bowie at his brightest and healthiest for the best part of a decade, but he also chose to record at a high-tech facility in the heart of tax-exile Switzerland – the country he had felt completely at odds with when his wife found them a house there two years earlier. Sean Mayes later described Mountain Studios in Montreux as being "right on the lake", and typified by "gleaming equipment, thick pile carpet, rough stone walls" – all "very chic".[2]

Bowie and Tony Visconti had put the finishing touches to *"Heroes"* in Montreux and were sufficiently impressed by the facilities that they ended up coming back to record *Lodger* there. Bowie had also struck up a friendship with David Richards, the in-house engineer-cum-producer, who would subsequently oversee three of the five albums Bowie has since made at Mountain, including *The Buddha Of Suburbia* and *1. Outside*. By strange coincidence, Richards's assistant during the late 1970s was a certain Eugene Chaplin, whose father was a rather famous silent comedian and whose mother had become a friend and neighbour of Bowie's at Clos des Mésanges.

Work on *Lodger* began in the first week of September, a couple of months after Bowie had finished the European leg of his 1978 tour, and exactly two years on from the commencement of work on *Low*. For the first few days, as had become standard, Bowie worked with Carlos Alomar, Dennis Davis, and George Murray on rhythm tracks.

Eno was also present from the start; Sean Mayes and Simon House came in a few days later, first to join in on spontaneous full-band recordings and then to add overdubs to backing tracks looped and edited by Bowie and Visconti. The last musician to arrive was Adrian Belew, who was put through the same ordeal Robert Fripp had been on *"Heroes"*: that is, he was simply told to start playing without having heard any of the songs.

One working title for *Lodger* was *Planned Accidents*, which serves as a useful description of the way in which much of the material was recorded. At the album's core is the concept of reinterpretation and repetition – a point Bowie hammered home by calling the ninth track 'Repetition'. Much of the material was built up from loops of the band jamming on the loosest of ideas. According to Sean Mayes, when Bowie then listened back to the tapes in search of a suitable section to loop, he would often "pick the part with the most mistakes, which when repeated would become an integral part of the song". The result of this, on songs such as 'African Night Flight' and 'Repetition', among others, is a tremendous sense of disorientation, as what feels at first like a false start gradually settles into a groove. (Eno would, of course, make highly effective use of much the same technique on the Talking Heads albums *Fear Of Music* and *Remain In Light*.)

The spirit of recycling and regeneration runs right through *Lodger*. Two of its songs were in fact derived from older Bowie material. 'Red Money' is at its core a slowed-down take on 'Sister Midnight', which he co-wrote with Carlos Alomar in rehearsals for the Station To Station tour and then donated to *The Idiot*. Bowie even used Iggy's version as source material for 'Red Money', lifting the bassline and several other backing tracks directly from the original recording. 'Move On', meanwhile, came about when Bowie happened to play a tape of 'All The Young Dudes' backwards. He and Visconti were quite taken with how the song sounded back-to-front, so set about rearranging it as such for *Lodger*, right down to the 'Dudes' vocal melody, which Bowie had to learn how to sing in reverse.

Two further *Lodger* tracks were derived from exactly the same source material, although in this instance it was something newly written by Bowie and Eno. Having already recorded the basic framework of 'Fantastic Voyage', the musicians swapped instruments – ostensibly to evoke the sound of a teenage garage combo, but perhaps also in response to the Oblique Strategy 'Use Unqualified People' – to re-record the same tune at a different tempo and in a much more ragged style. The resulting 'Boys Keep Swinging' has the same chords and overall structure, but a much more laid-back arrangement; according to Tony Visconti, a third song in the same vein was also recorded, but didn't make it onto the album.[3] (As with some of Bowie's other conceptual ideas of the time, including that of making albums with a 'rock' side and an 'ambient' side, this space-filling trick echoed something Neu! had done a few years earlier. Having spent most of the budget for *Neu! 2* on new instruments, the German group ran out of money midway through the sessions, so ended up padding the album out with sped-up and slowed-down versions of their previously released single 'Neuschnee' / 'Super'.)

Elsewhere on the album, Bowie and Eno brought together seemingly disparate musical styles to often striking effect. 'Yassassin' is a skilled crossbreeding of traditional Turkish music with reggae, a style

Bowie and his band had begun to experiment with earlier in the year with the live version of *Low*'s 'What In The World'. 'African Night Flight', meanwhile, pre-empts the world-beat style that Eno and David Byrne, and then Peter Gabriel and Paul Simon, would further develop in the 1980s.

Eno asserted himself much more on *Lodger* than he had on either of his previous collaborations with Bowie. On *Low* and *"Heroes"* his contributions were often reactive, and just as likely to involve manipulating the other players' parts as laying down tracks of his own. Here, however, he expanded his remit of instrumental contributions beyond his usual synthesizers and guitar treatments. On 'African Night Flight' he provides prepared piano and what is referred to in the credits as 'cricket menace' – actually a mangled drum machine – and he can be heard towards the end of the album tooting his 'horse trumpet' (readers of his 1995 diary, *A Year With Swollen Appendices*, might have their own theories about the provenance of such an expression).

Eno was also the instigator of quite a few of the songs, or at least their arrangements, with the other musicians regularly required to bow to his Oblique Strategy-like whims, some of which were better received than others. By all accounts, nobody much enjoyed his scheme of drawing up a chart of his favourite chords and pointing at a new one each time he wanted the band to change, all the while issuing instructions to 'play something funky'.

As Sean Mayes later recalled, this "'back to school' session" provoked quite a few grumbles, with Carlos Alomar in particular growing increasingly tired of what he interpreted as a condescending attitude from Eno. Bowie was unimpressed by the response of Alomar and the rest, and later complained, "These sulky, angry musicians were like children in a classroom."[4]

But it wasn't only the band who found cause to grumble. Perhaps the defining image of the *"Heroes"* sessions, aside from the idea of Hansa Tonstudios being in the shadow of the Berlin Wall, is that of Bowie and Eno adopting the voices of Peter Cook and Dudley Moore and bringing a sense of light relief to their work on what ended up being a tense, powerful record. This time around, however, the relationship between the principal collaborators wasn't quite so smooth. Each had a very different idea about the kind of record that they wanted to make, as perhaps would have been expected, given that they had seen very little of each other over the past year. "We've slightly changed our opinions about music and what we should be doing," Bowie revealed in 1979, but denied that this falling out of sync had caused any lasting problems while making *Lodger*. "We don't really get frayed tempers," he said, "but artistic temper sort of shows. I think the way we solve it is that one or the other of us will leave the studio for a couple of hours and let the other get on with it."[5]

For Eno, however, such an arrangement was less than acceptable. He later admitted that he and Bowie had "argued quite a lot" about how the songs should sound and that, in compromising their ideas, they ended up with an album that wasn't as good as it could have been. "[*Lodger*] started off extremely promising and quite revolutionary," he said, "[but] it didn't quite seem to end up that way."[6] Speaking more generally about his working methods in the late 1980s, Eno expressed his belief that "there's nothing more certain to kill an idea than democracy, as far as I'm concerned. … If you're going to make an experiment, just make it … either it fails or it doesn't."[7] He might just as well have been talking about making *Lodger*. That's not to suggest that Bowie and Eno had some catastrophic falling out – far from it – but there is a sense that the spark between the two men had largely been extinguished by the summer of 1978.

Carlos Alomar would later allude to the fact that, even before *Lodger* was released, a lot of people "[felt] that they were due for a trilogy".[8] Clearly, Bowie and Eno wouldn't have reconvened purely out of a sense of obligation, but it did seem as though their planned accidents sometimes took the form of experiments for experiments' sake – not least when Professor Eno took to pointing at random chords on a blackboard (from which, perhaps inevitably, nothing of worth ensued). And as intriguing an idea as it might have been to base two songs around the same structure, and another on a reversed 'All The Young Dudes', it's hard to have imagine that Bowie or Eno would have wanted to pad out an album in such a way a year or two earlier, when they were moulding such landmarks as 'Warszawa' and 'Sound And Vision' or '"Heroes"' and 'Sons Of The Silent Age'.

That *Lodger* was not made with the same fervent energy that drove its predecessors was made clear, too, by the wide span of time that was allowed to lapse between the start and end of work on the record. After three weeks in September, Bowie and his cohorts had effectively finished most of the ten songs that make up the album, with only vocals and a few instrumental overdubs left to be added. Five full months would pass, however, before he added these final touches. This can be attributed partly to the fact that Bowie had already arranged to spend most of November and December on tour in Australia, but that doesn't account for the rest of the time. He had very little on his agenda in October, but decided against completing the album then; and while one might excuse him staying on in Japan after the end of the tour, he seemed hardly to be in any kind of a hurry upon his return.

Eventually, Bowie, Visconti, and Adrian Belew reconvened in March at the Record Plant in New York City, where such landmark albums as *Electric Ladyland* and *Born To Run* had previously been made. According to Visconti, the New York session began with an attempt at recording some brand new material as an ad hoc three-piece, with Belew on drums, Bowie on guitar, and the producer on bass. Nothing of any real value ensued, however, so they refocused their attention on the songs cut in Switzerland in September, making minor alterations here and there. Belew added a bunch of new guitar-lines, and Visconti re-recorded the bassline on 'Boys Keep Swinging', which had originally been played, somewhat amateurishly, by Dennis Davis.

One notable absentee during this phase of overdubbing and ad-libbing was Brian Eno. Although he had, in fairness, chosen not to stick around for the latter stages of the *Low* and *"Heroes"* sessions either, he would almost certainly have been in close geographical proximity, having moved to Greenwich Village in 1978. One might have expected him to at least pop in to see what was going on at the Record Plant – in between shifts on his own current project, *The Plateaux Of Mirror*, which he was working on in the Bronx, or making preparations for his production of Talking Heads' *Fear Of Music* – but all indications suggest that he didn't. That's not to say that Bowie was short of visitors while at the Record Plant. The studio's location in central Manhattan made it hard to avoid other music-industry faces, familiar or otherwise. Mick Jagger stopped by on one occasion and, according to Visconti, "managed to criticise everything we played [him]";[9] a couple of members of Kiss also popped their heads round the door, but were reportedly given short shrift by the man who had done so much to inspire their post-glam look and sound. All of this was a far cry from Bowie's recent studio experiences in France and Germany, where he could work largely without interruption, except for visits from invited guests – Iggy Pop, Edgar Froese, and so on.

Once the various instrumental parts were completed to his satisfaction, Bowie moved on to *Lodger*'s lyrics and vocals. His songs had gone through several rather abrupt thematic shifts over the years. He had started out, of course, writing theatrical, character-based pieces from which, often, very little could be gleaned about their author. Then, during the mid-1970s, the songs, like Bowie himself, became more inward looking, culminating in *Low*'s catatonic gloom, which barely acknowledges the existence of any kind of outside world. For *Lodger*, by contrast, Bowie shifted his perspective all the way around again: he pops up from time to time, sliding into bars and learning to cope with "somebody's depression", but only in the briefest of allusions. Instead, the album's ten songs make up a kind of skewed travelogue of the places Bowie has been to over the past year, from Berlin to Tokyo to Nairobi, in which the author often plays only a peripheral role.

The first clue to the content of the album is its title, which casts

Bowie himself as the lodger: just visiting, not resident, and sometimes barely even present. Then there are the names of the songs on the album's first side. Four of the five – 'Fantastic Voyage', 'African Night Flight', 'Move On', and 'Red Sails' – make explicit the theme of travel and exploration. This being a Bowie record, of course, there's a little more to it than that. Apart, perhaps, from the rather forced couplets in 'Move On' about Africa's "sleepy people", Russia's horsemen, and sleeping on "matted ground" in Japan, Bowie does more than merely paint broad strokes about the places he has been to. He delves into the motivations of the people he met and observed on his travels, from migrant workers in Berlin ('Yassassin') to German fighter pilots living out strange, disconnected lives in Mombassa ('African Night Flight'), and also takes his first proper stab at the risky world of political songwriting on 'Fantastic Voyage', a not-so-veiled plea for an end to the threat of nuclear war.

Broadly speaking, if the first side of *Lodger* is Bowie's response to the various exotic climes of his recent travels, side two is his take – somewhat ahead of the curve, as ever – on apathy and consumerism in the western world. 'D.J.' lampoons the idea of the celebrity plate-spinner, 'Red Money' addresses the cost of responsibility, and 'Repetition' somewhat unexpectedly tackles the subject of domestic abuse. From a musical perspective, however, there's much less of a common thread. The opening 'Fantastic Voyage' is much more sedate than any of the 'rock' songs on *Low* or *"Heroes"*. Backed by Sean Mayes's rich, melodic piano and a trio of mandolins (played by Simon House, Tony Visconti, and Adrian Belew), Bowie offers a considered warning of how "our lives" are just as valuable as maintaining political loyalty and dignity. The subsequent 'African Night Flight', on the other hand, is a frenetic sound-collage of pianos (some prepared, some not), electric and acoustic percussion, animalistic sound effects, and short bursts of guitar. The vocal, too, is similarly feverish, with Bowie cramming so many words into each verse that he almost breaks into a rap – perhaps not by accident, given that he recorded it only a few miles from the Bronx, where rap originated. Track three is the stuttering, disorientated, and rather less remarkable 'Move On', which is probably more interesting conceptually, as a backwards reworking of 'All The Young Dudes', than as a song in its own right.

Up next is 'Yassassin', which sounds exactly as Bowie and Eno intended it to: a cross-fertilisation of reggae – represented by the loose, reverb-drenched rhythm section – and traditional Turkish music, symbolised here by Simon House's soaring violin.

The last track on Side One is made up of a similar intermingling of ideas, resulting in something akin to a less anxious, tape-warped 'Beauty And The Beast'. The rhythm is, as Bowie would later freely admit, another take on "that Neu! sound", but is counterbalanced by what he later described as a "contemporary English mercenary-cum-swashbuckling Errol Flynn".[10]

Side Two of *Lodger* begins with three warped attempts at pushing pop out beyond its usual boundaries, each of them co-written by Eno, and with mixed results. 'D.J.' is the latest in Bowie's line of seemingly straightforward, punch-drunk rock'n'rollers that are then gleefully perverted is some way or other (compare 'Be My Wife' or 'TVC 15'). This time, it's House's woozy violin that cuts into the boogie-woogie backing track, followed by a series of fragments of guitar solos, pasted roughly together to give the effect of a radio being detuned.

Next out of the blocks is 'Look Back In Anger', a so-so disco-rock track augmented by Eno's horse trumpet and a suitably theatrical Bowie vocal about an angel with "crumpled wings" come to take him off into the night. The third and final part of this oddball trio is 'Boys Keep Swinging', widely taken to be Bowie's latest paean to bisexuality, but perhaps a bit more considered than that. Although it was derived from the same basic structural elements as 'Fantastic Voyage', 'Boys Keep Swinging' has a very different feel. The arrangement is brash and callow, and the melody, driven by Visconti's bass, much more upbeat. The second half of the song, meanwhile, is dominated by another wild, multi-part solo from Adrian Belew.

The last two songs on *Lodger* offer further shifts in style and mood, and are among the album's strongest moments. A stark tale of suburban ennui that culminates in spousal abuse, 'Repetition' is one of the most unsettling songs in the Bowie canon; not just lyrically, but also in terms of the music, a woozy dirge of guitar, bass, drums, and treated violin. "Don't hit her," Bowie asks, but in a voice almost as devoid of emotion, one assumes, as that of the catalyst, a man named Johnny who "looks straight through you when you ask him how the kids are". The whole thing is rendered even more disquieting by its surroundings – only a minute earlier, Bowie had been singing about how, when you're a boy, "life is a pop of the cherry".

It's tempting to view 'Red Money', *Lodger*'s final track, as a comment by Bowie on the end of an era. The song on which it was based, 'Sister Midnight', was the first he wrote for *The Idiot*, which in turn was the pilot project of his 'Berlin period'. Now 'Red Money' brought that phase of his working life to a close. It brought a close, too, to his working relationship with Brian Eno – at least until they were reunited, in 1995, for *1. Outside* – but Bowie has since rejected as "mere whimsy"[11] the suggestion that the words "project cancelled" refer to a falling out between the two men. "Can you hear it fall?" might be taken to have a similar meaning, were it not for the fact that footage exists of Bowie singing it in January 1976, during a rehearsal for the Station To Station tour, a few months before he gave 'Sister Midnight' to Iggy. But it does, still, provide a tidy conclusion to Bowie's recorded output of the 1970s.

Lodger was released to the world at large on May 18th, 1979. Bowie had by then thrown himself back onto the promotional treadmill, appearing on a wide range of television and radio programmes, including *The Kenny Everett Video Show* in Britain, on which he sang the album's lead-in single, 'Boys Keep Swinging'. The single subsequently peaked at Number Seven on the UK Top 40, but was virtually ignored in the USA, where Bowie had not had a proper hit since 1975. *Lodger* itself, with its eye-catching gatefold sleeve of a besuited Bowie slumped across a tiled mortuary floor, limbs and nose bent out of shape, fared rather better, peaking at Number 20 on the *Billboard* albums chart and Number Four in the UK. But, like *Low* and *"Heroes"* before it, it wasn't a commercial success on the scale of Bowie's mid-1970s output, leading, no doubt, to further grumblings from RCA.

To make matters worse, whereas *"Heroes"* had been met, on the whole, with an abundance of superlatives, the critical response to *Lodger* was decidedly muted – worse, even, than the initial reaction to *Low*. "Another year, another record," wrote a bored Jon Savage in *Melody Maker*, summing up the overriding attitude to an album he also described as "nice enough" but "slightly faceless".[12] Greil Marcus's conclusions for *Rolling Stone* were similarly damning. Having hoped *Lodger* might herald "a major new move, or a major synthesis", Marcus instead hears "just another LP, and one of his weakest at that", full of songs "so drenched in irony that [they] cease to have any meaning at all".[13] In *New York Rocker*, meanwhile, Paul Yamada dismissed *Lodger* as "poorly thought out, callous, simple-minded, and complacent".[14]

Each of the three primary contributors to *Lodger* has since admitted that the album didn't turn out quite as well as it might have done. Eno, perhaps unsurprisingly, was the first to do so, and continues to lay the blame on his and Bowie's diverging intentions, and the fact, therefore, that the end result is a weakened, compromised take on two very different sets of ideas. He also suggested that its somewhat abrupt completion and release had more to do with the market's apparent need for new Bowie 'product' than anything else.

For Bowie, the problems lay not so much in the material, which he valued and continues to draw on in live performance, but in the final stages of the record's completion on New York. "I think Tony [Visconti] and I would both agree that we didn't take enough care mixing,"[15] he told *Uncut* magazine in 2001. For Visconti, the problems lay in part with the quality of equipment on offer to the pair of them in New York.

He has complained on several occasions that American recording studios of the 1970s were several years behind their European counterparts. Describing the time he and Bowie spent at the Record Plant, the producer writes, in his recent autobiography, of being "relegated to studio D because we booked at the last minute. 'D' implies the quality of the studio".[16]

Not having the right tools at their disposal does go some way towards explaining the muddied, everything-but-the-kitchen-sink sound of some of the songs, but Visconti also alludes to another possible reason. "The club life in the 1970s [in New York] was fuelled on cocaine," he writes. While he doesn't specifically implicate Bowie in this, there are enough mentions of nights out with John Belushi, and of not leaving clubs 'til midday, to suggest that Bowie might well have lapsed back into his old lifestyle, albeit fleetingly – which would certainly tally with the sound of *Lodger*. Over the years, cocaine's defining impact on music has been its sure-fire ability to produce murky, over-baked records. While a few such albums – *There's A Riot Goin' On*, or Bowie's own *Station To Station* – managed to succeed in spite (or even *because*) of this, the majority are overwrought, overindulgent, and overlong. Putting *Lodger*, an album of short, shared, mutated pop songs, into this category would seem a trifle unfair, but it does have the requisite fogginess.

In the end, *Lodger* seemed to be hindered more than anything by the weight of so much expectation, while today it floats in a curious limbo somewhere between being underrated and overburdened by its status as the trilogy's *Return Of The Jedi*. Most listeners came to it then, and come to it now, expecting some kind of resolution of the sounds and themes presented on *Low* and *"Heroes"*, but not really getting it. *Lodger* is, as Ian MacDonald wrote in a retrospective piece about the album, "always thought of as the anticlimax after *Low* and *"Heroes"*" – wrongly, in MacDonald's view, but it's easy to trace the route of that way of thinking. For all of its winning excursions into offbeat pop and what might be termed proto-world-music, *Lodger* does lack the pioneer spirit of *Low* or the sheer gravitas of *"Heroes"*. But, in a way, that's neither here nor there. Not every album has to be an overarching, mould-breaking, career-defining statement. It's enough, surely, to gather together ten largely excellent songs, peppered with intriguing sonic experiments. As MacDonald wrote, "[Even] if it doesn't add up to a single listening experience, its parts are rarely without quality."[17] Certainly, in terms of individual songs, some of the *Lodger* material – 'African Night Flight', 'Repetition', and 'Red Money', in particular – is up there with the very best of what Bowie produced during this phase of his career.

"In the '70s, I think I probably over-achieved,"[18] said the 21st century Bowie, with typically wry understatement, shortly after the release of the 24th – and, at the time of writing, most recent – studio album of his career, *Reality*. This is borne out in purely numerical terms: in the years between 1969 and 1980, he made 13 albums of his own (not including live albums and compilations), and co-wrote, produced, mixed, or played on yet more by Iggy Pop, Lou Reed, and others. In the three decades since, he has recorded ten further solo albums – an impressive enough number by most standards, but much less, and at a much slower pace, than before.

It might be more useful, ultimately, to view *Lodger* as not so much the end of one phase of Bowie's career as the start of another one. The album's closing track, 'Red Money', provides a subtle hint as to a change in its author's mindset. He was, he sings, "really feeling good" until "I got this small red box / And I didn't know what to do." The reference seems fairly oblique until it is coupled with Bowie's subsequent explanation in a British interview broadcast a few days before the album's release. "Red boxes keep cropping up in my paintings," he told Nicky Horne on London's Capital Radio, "and they represent responsibility."

Facing up to life's responsibilities had become an increasingly common theme for Bowie over the past few years – not least in terms of his son, Joey, who turned eight two weeks after *Lodger* was released. "Having a son made an enormous difference to me," he had told *Melody Maker* in 1977.[19] Bowie hadn't had a huge amount to do with his son's upbringing for the first years, but was now fast becoming as devoted a parent as can be. In 1980, after his divorce became final, Bowie was granted full custody of Joey, which inevitably had an effect on both his life and his career.

Lodger marked a change not just in the frequency of Bowie's albums, but also in the way that he took to promoting them. Up until *Station To Station*, he found himself stuck in a seemingly endless cycle of recording and touring – partly due to the fact that, under the terms of his deal with RCA, he wasn't actually making a great deal of money, so needed to keep working. Things began to change towards the end of the 1970s, perhaps in part because Bowie had found a new source of income: acting. He opted out of promoting *Low* altogether, but reached a more satisfactory compromise in time for *Lodger*. Instead of forcing himself back out onto the road for months at a time, he maintained his media profile by appearing on carefully selected television shows, such as *Saturday Night Live*, and, most crucially, by exploring the possibilities of the promo video.

Given that he is known, perhaps more than anything else, for his keenness to experiment and explore new media, Bowie took rather a long time to fully embrace the short-form music video. Those that he had made before 1979 were all fairly straight performance pieces, which, while enjoyable enough, do little more than any number of still images from the same period. Then, at the dawn of the 1980s, Bowie began all of a sudden to invest his music videos with as much invention and attention to detail as the songs they were designed to promote.

The catalyst, somewhat incongruously, was Bowie's appearance on *The Kenny Everett Video Show* in April 1979. The director of this late-1970s staple of British light-entertainment was David Mallet, with whom Bowie reconvened the following month to shoot videos for 'Boys Keep Swinging', 'Look Back In Anger', and 'D.J.', the three singles to be drawn from the album (the first of which was already on its way to becoming a UK Top 10 hit). None of them took the form that might have been expected of them on the basis of Bowie's previous videos. For 'Boys Keep Swinging', three gaudy drag queens, inspired by the performers at Romy Haag's, take it in turns to lip-sync along to the song. Only gradually does it become clear that each is actually a heavily made-up Bowie. The second video to be released, 'Look Back In Anger', is a fairly transparent retread of the end of Oscar Wilde's *The Picture Of Dorian Gray*, with Bowie putting on a look of overly theatrical anguish as his angelic self-portrait appears to cause his own face to melt away. The 'D.J.' video, meanwhile, is split between scenes of Bowie as the tormented title-character and more spontaneous footage of him being swarmed by admirers on the streets of London's Earls Court, including a burly man who showers the singer with kisses.

From a modern perspective, each of these videos looks rather quaint compared to the big-budget promos made for contemporary artists, but Bowie's partnership with Mallet didn't end there. The following year they collaborated on one of the most memorable, innovative, and, at the time, expensive short-form music videos of all time. 'Ashes To Ashes' made pioneering use, at a reported cost of £250,000, of the Quantel Paintbox, a computerised system that allowed for real-time manipulation of video footage, which in this case gave Mallet and Bowie the means to solarise the beachside scenes of Bowie and a troupe of New Romantic extras, including Steve Strange of the (then rather obscure) group Visage. Mallet subsequently directed a number of other noteworthy videos with Bowie, including 'Fashion', 'Let's Dance', and 'Hello Spaceboy', and went on to work with Queen, Def Leppard, U2, and others. It was 'Ashes To Ashes', however, that gave the first real indication of what this new art form was capable of.

In the meantime, Bowie hadn't given up on live performance altogether, but did reduce his onstage workload considerably, having decided to wait until he felt suitably enthusiastic about going back on the road. He didn't embark on another full-scale world tour until 1983, five years after the *"Heroes"* tour, and allowed another four years to lapse until the next one. That's not to say that he became idle, just that his priorities changed. Between making *Scary Monsters (And Super Creeps)* in 1980 and *Let's Dance* in 1983, for example, he starred for three months in the Broadway production of *The Elephant Man* and played the lead role in two films, *The Hunger* and *Merry Christmas, Mr. Lawrence*, thereby expanding his role of outsiders to include John Merrick, a 300-year-old vampire, and a prisoner of war. He also recorded an underappreciated five-track EP of songs written for a BBC production of Bertolt Brecht's *Baal*, which brought two more eras to a close: it was Bowie's final RCA release, and also the last record he would make with Tony Visconti for 20 years.

As the 1980s progressed and Bowie relaxed his once-frantic schedule, the quality of his work on record began to drop. *Let's Dance* brought him unparalleled commercial success, and is still fairly well-regarded, but has never quite been afforded the classic status of what came before it, while the albums that came immediately after it – *Tonight* (1984) and *Never Let Me Down* (1987) – reveal as sharp a decline in quality as one might care to find. *Let's Dance*'s predecessor, *Scary Monsters (And Super Creeps)*, is widely acknowledged to be the last 'great' Bowie album. It has become customary in recent times for each new album he makes to be rewarded with the rather backhanded compliment, "best thing he's done since *Scary Monsters*".

Scary Monsters is certainly a very fine album, and in some ways a more commercial crystallisation of the sound Bowie began to explore on *Lodger*. It laid the groundwork for Bowie's breakthrough into megastardom when it hit Number One in the UK and contains some of his most memorable songs of the period, among them the title track, the two-part 'It's No Game', 'Fashion', and 'Ashes To Ashes', which became Bowie's second chart-topping single in Britain. But as good as *Scary Monsters* is, to suggest that it so comprehensively overshadows everything that came after it is lazy and more than a little unfair. There have been plenty of high-points in Bowie's subsequent career, albeit more sporadic peaks than listeners had become used to during the 1970s. Even the much-maligned *Tin Machine* (1989) has a clutch of good songs hidden beneath its lumpen, over-compressed production, while the pair of albums he released in 1993, *Black Tie White Noise* and *The Buddha Of Suburbia*, suggested that there was plenty of life in the old dog yet. That was confirmed with the release over the next decade of two further albums that deserve, at the very least, to be considered in the context of the 'Berlin' records, *1. Outside* and *Heathen*. Perhaps not coincidentally, each reunited Bowie with a key collaborator from the late 1970s.

First up was 1995's *1. Outside*, for which Brian Eno returned to the fold, and which, like *Low*, started out purely as an experiment, and not necessarily an 'album'. In the summer of 1994, Bowie called an eclectic pool of musical collaborators to Mountain Studios, at the time his most widely used recording facility, among them guitarist Reeves Gabrels, drummer Sterling Campbell, bassist and multi-instrumentalist Erdal Kizilcay, and pianist Mike Garson, with whom he had not played since 1975. Eno took much the same role as he had filled on *Lodger*, directing proceedings and generating systems and 'laws' to shape the progression of the recording sessions. Bowie had been conscious, in assembling the *Outside* band, of the hostility with which some of Eno's schemes had been met during the late 1970s. "This time around I really handpicked musicians I knew would fall into the flow of things and anticipate each day with a degree of excitement," he explained at the time.[20] Perhaps the strangest of Eno's schemes was to devise a series of flash cards containing details of the character they had to adopt when they started to play. "It's 2005," began Erdal Kizilcay's. "You are a musician in a soul-Arab band in a North African role-sex club. … You play a kind of repetitive, atonal funk with occasional wildly ambitious ornaments to impress your future father-in-law, the Minister of Networks for Siliconia, who is in the audience."[21]

How great an impact Eno's cards had on the music that was produced is difficult to ascertain, but the end result is certainly one of the most unusual releases by a mainstream artist of the 1990s. Bowie and Eno had originally hoped to release the full, unedited three-hour jam with which they had kicked off the sessions for the album, but the idea was nixed by Virgin Records, the label to which Bowie had recently signed. The final product is certainly something of a curate's egg: at 75 minutes and 19 tracks long, it is by some distance the longest album in Bowie's catalogue, and also the only one on which the songs are interspersed by fragments of a narrative 'hyper cycle' about art and murder, complete with funny voices. To some it was a work of grand folly; to others, it remains one of the most expansive, experimental, and engaging albums of its time.

As its title suggests, *1. Outside* was initially conceived as the first part of a second series of Bowie/Eno collaborations, which it was rumoured might stretch this time to five albums and a play, to be directed by Robert Wilson. In the years since, however, nothing more has been heard of the project, aside from a handful of tracks that later surfaced on the internet, despite the fact that Bowie had at one point announced that the second part, *2. Contamination*, was well under way. Perhaps the muted critical and commercial response to *1. Outside* dulled his enthusiasm; certainly, by 1996, both he and Eno had moved on to other things. Bowie's next album, *Earthling*, was heavily influenced by British underground drum'n'bass, to rather more mixed results, while its follow-up, *hours*, saw him finally do what is generally expected of rock'n'roll musicians of advancing years: make an album of pleasant-enough songs that hark back to a bygone age.

In 2002, having recently become a father for the second time, Bowie released *Heathen*, his first album of the 21st century, on which he was reunited for the first time in two decades with Tony Visconti. Bowie and Visconti had in fact begun working together again in 2000, when they recorded *Toy*, an album largely made up of songs Bowie wrote in the 1960s. But despite being finished, right down to the artwork, by the end of the year, *Toy* was never released, reportedly because Virgin, Bowie's label of the time, was dissatisfied with the quality of the work.

As a result of this, Bowie quit Virgin and found a new home at Columbia, but by the time the ink was dry on his new deal he had turned his attention away from the still-unreleased *Toy*, having completed another new, Visconti-produced album, *Heathen*.

Heathen was assembled in a way that was very much reminiscent of how Bowie's albums of the late 1970s were made. During August and September, 2001, Bowie (playing a range of guitars and synthesizers, including an EMS Synthi A), Visconti (bass), and session drummer Matt Chamberlain recorded around 40 ideas – some of them full songs, others the tiniest of fragments – at Philip Glass's Looking Glass Studios in New York City and the newly built Allaire complex further upstate, just outside Woodstock. This second venue was suggested by David Torn, one of several guest musicians to contribute to the second phase of recording; others included Dave Grohl, Gerry Leonard, Pete Townshend, and the Scorchio string quartet. Surrounded by tranquil countryside, Allaire was very different to the type of studio that Bowie was used to. "I usually record in cities with lots of clash, like Berlin, New York, or Tokyo," he told Ingrid Sischy of *Interview* magazine. But as unfamiliar a setting as it might have been to Bowie, Allaire certainly brought out the best of him. *Heathen* is as pleasantly cohesive a record as any of his classic albums of the 1970s. A series of moving meditations on mortality and the state of the world, it frequently recalls bits of his back catalogue without ever trying to ape them. "I wanted to prove the sustaining power of music," Bowie explained, rather grandly, to Sischy – a bold claim, certainly, but one he was able to back up on record.

Unlike so many of his peers in the ever-growing field of heritage rock, Bowie is still capable, once in a while, of making records that, at the very least, compare well with the acknowledged classics of his earlier career. The best moments on *Outside* and *Heathen* – such as 'The Heart's Filthy Lesson' and 'I'm Deranged', or 'Sunday' and 'I Would Be Your Slave' – share many of the same qualities on display on the records Bowie made during the late 1970s with Eno, Visconti, Alomar, Davis,

Murray, et al. What they lack, of course, is the sense that wholly new ground is being broken at every turn, and the knowledge that, in years to come, whole generations of musicians will use them as a blueprint for their own creations.

Bowie himself is well aware of this, and more than happy to set *Low*, *"Heroes"*, and *Lodger* apart from whatever he has done, and continues to do. "For whatever reason, for whatever confluence of circumstances, Tony, Brian, and I created a powerful, anguished, sometimes euphoric language of sounds," he told *Uncut* magazine in 2001. "Nothing else sounded like those albums. Nothing else came close. If I never made another album it really wouldn't matter now; my complete being is within those three. They are my DNA."

THE HEART'S FILTHY LESSON

By the mid 1970s, David Bowie had established himself as one of British pop's leading players on both sides of the Atlantic. In the UK he had, between the summers of 1972 and 1976, released eight Top Five albums, including three chart-toppers, and 16 Top 40 singles, which between them spent 149 weeks on the Top 100. It took a little longer for him to break through in the USA, but when he did the results were similarly impressive. *Diamond Dogs*, *Young Americans*, and *Station To Station* were all awarded Gold Record certification (for sales of at least 500,000 copies) within a few months of release – as, indeed, were *David Live* and his first retrospective compilation album, *Changesonebowie*. These were no mere flashes in the pan, either. *Young Americans* stayed on the *Billboard* albums chart for five months, while the second single to be drawn from it, 'Fame', sold more than a million copies between July and October 1975.

The next phase of Bowie's career was, at least in commercial terms, markedly less successful. The first album from this period, *Low*, might now be viewed as Bowie's crowning achievement from an artistic standpoint, but for the accountants at RCA it was nothing short of a failure. Its initial chart peaks were comparable to those of *Young Americans*, but that only tells part of the story. The album's overall, long-term performance was much less impressive. *The Rise And Fall Of Ziggy Stardust And The Spiders From Mars* spent a total of 172 weeks on the British album chart; *Low* only managed 24. After an initial burst of interest, during which Bowie's most rabid fans – many of whom would have bought a record of traffic noise, were his name attached to it – rushed out to buy their copies, sales of the album were sluggish at best.

Prior to being reissued by EMI in the 1980s, *Low* sold only 176,000 copies in America, and had all but disappeared from the *Billboard* chart by the time Bowie arrived in the country, as part of Iggy Pop's backing band, in mid-March, 1977. The follow-up, *"Heroes"*, fared even worse, despite containing some rather more palatable material (not least its title track). It barely scraped into the US Top 40, and dropped off the charts altogether after three weeks. *Lodger* was slightly more successful, but only just. Needless to say, the two albums Bowie co-wrote and produced for Iggy Pop during the same time period, *The Idiot* and *Lust For Life*, had even less of an impact on charts, graphs, and tax returns.

But in this age of cult classics and 'undiscovered' gems, we know better than to assess a record's importance in terms of fiscal return and unit shifting alone. Almost anything you care to read about The Velvet Underground, for example, makes reference, somewhere, to Brian Eno's famous claim that although hardly anybody bought the group's albums in the late 1960s, those who did went on to form important bands of their own. A similar assertion can be made about David Bowie's output from a decade later. None of his records of the late 1970s set the charts alight, but they had a colossal effect on what followed, in terms of sound, mood, attitude, and more.

Most of the clearest examples of the impact of Bowie's 'Berlin' records came, perhaps unsurprisingly, in the five years or so after their release. "Tomorrow belongs to those who can hear it coming," was the phrase with which RCA trailed the release of *"Heroes"* in 1977, and while it might have sounded a bit like a line cut out of *The*

Man Who Fell To Earth, there was a fair amount of weight behind the claim. Bowie had already helped shape the sound of the early 1970s; now his latest move was about to inspire a whole new generation of bands and musicians.

From a musical perspective, the biggest impact Bowie had came with his adoption of the synthesizer as his primary tool for making music. Of course, using synthesizers in a rock or pop setting wasn't in itself a particularly revolutionary move. George Harrison brought a Moog back from America in 1969 and promptly used it to generate white noise and other such inorganic sounds for The Beatles' *Abbey Road*, while bands such as Pink Floyd and Roxy Music (thanks to Eno) had been decorating their songs with all sorts of otherworldly sounds since the early 1970s. And European pioneers such as Kraftwerk, Tangerine Dream, and Giorgio Moroder had already begun to make music that was arranged principally – and often exclusively – for synthesized sounds. But in the context of Anglo-American rock music, these ideas and concepts had yet to make any real inroads; even when established groups of the 1970s *did* use synthesizers, it was generally only as a means of embellishing what they had already created from the basic building blocks of guitar, bass, drums, and so on, and rarely as a truly integral element of their music.

Perhaps because of this, synthesizers were viewed by many musicians and indeed listeners with suspicion, as an example of the worst kind of prog-style excess. Even Queen, hardly the most modest of groups, proudly announced on the sleeves of their albums that "no synthesizers were used in the making of this record".

By 1977 there were a few British groups that placed synthesizers at the centre of their sound – notably Ultravox!, whose debut album was co-produced by Eno – but not many, and none of any great significance (at least not yet). The tide was still some way from turning. In a musical climate so dedicated to authenticity, it took a figure of Bowie's standing to begin to convince people that there was nothing phoney about working in so non-traditional a fashion – to show them that rock music, for want of a better umbrella term, could be driven by something other than the electric guitar. There was something revolutionary about the idea of synthesizer-based music in the 1970s that felt, to both musician and fan, like a crisp dismissal of what came before, and a journey into largely uncharted waters. But without Bowie's example to follow, it's debatable as to whether groups such as Soft Cell, Depeche Mode, The Human League, and so on would have achieved the level of success that they subsequently did – which in many instances greatly eclipsed the commercial success of *Low*, *"Heroes"*, and *Lodger*. Even Queen went back on their previous stance when they set up camp at Musicland in Munich, Germany, to record their synthesizer-heavy eighth album, *The Game*, in 1980.

The most brazenly determined heir to Bowie's throne was one Gary Anthony James Webb, a West London teenager better known to the world at large as Gary Numan. He first appeared in 1978 as the leader of Tubeway Army, but had shed his backing group by the end of the decade. Virtually everything Numan did during the first few years of his career smacked of a deep-seated interest in Bowie – whom he later described as having been "the biggest thing in my life"[1] – and his Berlin-era records. Even before you heard any of his records, such as the British chart-toppers "Are 'Friends' Electric?" and 'Cars', there was the Numan look, which seemed to be based, more than anything, on the cover of *"Heroes"*. The music itself, meanwhile, was a vague approximation of Bowie-meets-Kraftwerk, with much the same bleak, insular perspective as *Low*. A few years into his career, Numan even pulled a Ziggy Stardust-style retirement stunt.

All of this was too much for Bowie. He has a reputation, generally, for accepting with good grace those who proclaim him to be a key influence on their music, as demonstrated by the alliances he has formed over the years with groups such as Nine Inch Nails, Placebo, Arcade Fire, and others. But something – or perhaps everything – about Numan rubbed him up the wrong way. There are all sorts of apocryphal stories about Bowie having Numan removed from the bill of Kenny Everett's 1979 New Year's Eve television show, the veracity of which have never quite been confirmed, but Bowie had already made his feelings clear in the pages of *Record Mirror*. Asked his opinion of Numan's rise to success, he replied, testily, "I never meant for cloning to be part of the 1980s."[2]

While Numan was a little too transparent in his adoption of the sound and mood of Bowie '77, a lot of groups of the time used Bowie's experiments with minimal, synthesized art-rock as a springboard to other things. While he did, unquestionably, help inspire a whole heap of musicians to trade their guitars for synths, in other instances it was his ideological standpoint that had the greatest impact. The 'New School Of Pretension' Bowie and Eno had half-jokingly inaugurated during the *Low* and *"Heroes"* sessions now seemed to be overflowing with new students. All of a sudden, in the wake of glam, disco, and punk – which, despite their obvious stylistic differences, could all be generalised by their escapist, uptempo euphoria – came a more detached, thoughtful music with a decidedly European bent.

"When it came out, I thought *Low* was the sound of the future," Stephen Morris, drummer with Joy Division and New Order, told *Uncut* in 2001. Both of Morris's bands owed a clear debut to Berlin-era Bowie. Joy Division were originally called Warsaw in reference to Bowie's monolithic instrumental 'Warszawa' and were very much inspired by the bleak, icy feel of *Low* and *The Idiot*. The similarities are particularly noticeable on songs such as 'I Remember Nothing', with its sharp shards of guitar, sparse, metronomic drums, and general air of industrial unease. It's hard to imagine New Order existing without Bowie, either: so many of the group's songs are driven by funky, melodic basslines in the George Murray style or lit up by washes of synthesizer in the style of 'Sound And Vision'.

There are similar echoes in many other groups of the post-punk era. Consider Ian McCulloch's yearning, theatrical vocal on 'A Promise' by Echo & The Bunnymen; the funereal, 'Warszawa'-like pulse at the heart of Wire's 'Second K.O.'; the spidery guitar-lines woven through

Magazine's *Secondhand Daylight*; the twittering, Eno-like electronic sounds that cut into 'Slow Motion' by Ultravox; the ambient instrumental textures of The Human League's debut EP, *The Dignity Of Labour*; the fact that Japan were suddenly moved to write a song called 'Suburban Berlin'. With its icy extremes and unorthodox use of compression, noise gating, and so on, the sound-world that Bowie and his cohorts created on *Low* and *"Heroes"* quickly became the blueprint for left-of-centre record-making during the late 1970s.

The single most influential element of the Bowie sound, referenced at some point or other in the work of all of the bands mentioned above, was created by Tony Visconti and his Eventide Harmonizer. "When we were making the *Ideal For Living* EP, I remember we kept asking the engineer to make the drums sound like 'Speed Of Life'," recalled Stephen Morris. "Strangely enough he couldn't."

Morris wasn't the only one. Countless musicians, producers, and studio technicians of the time went to great lengths to reproduce the *Low* drum sound but were hindered by Visconti's reticence about exactly how he had created it. Nonetheless, all sorts of close-enough approximations began to appear almost as soon as *Low* hit the shelves, much to Bowie's dismay. "That depressive gorilla effect," as he put it, "was something I wish we'd never created, having had to live through four years of it with other English bands."[3] Indeed, by the dawn of the 1980s, it seemed to have infiltrated virtually every record in the charts, leaving Bowie indirectly responsible for the thumping backbeat heard on everything from 'In The Air Tonight' to 'Hungry Like The Wolf'.

In his review of *Lodger*, *Melody Maker*'s Jon Savage wondered, "Will the Eighties be this boring?" He didn't have to wait long for the answer, as the sound of Bowie's late-1970s recordings fed straight into the new decade's art-pop scene. It's there in the cold reticence of 'Fade To Grey' by Visage, whose frontman Steve Strange was one of the extras in Bowie's 'Ashes To Ashes' video; in the clash of rhythms and melodies at the root of Thomas Dolby's 'She Blinded Me By Science'; in the yearning, multi-layered vocals of 'Poison Arrow' by ABC; in the gated electronic drums and duelling synthesizers on Depeche Mode's *Speak And Spell*; and more.

"The Berlin period influenced me in many different ways," said Martin Fry of ABC, drawing specific attention to "the incredible economy of those records". The music ABC made was much brighter and more optimistic than anything Bowie did during 1976–9, but a clear line can still be drawn back to his textural, mechanised creations. The Bowie/Eno/Iggy albums had seemed, during the late 1970s, to provide the perfect aural backdrop to Fry's formative years in the "industrial heartland" of Sheffield. "Bowie was plugged into how my generation was feeling," he said. "[We were] alienated, nervous about the future, tense on amphetamines, saving up to buy synthesizers, paranoid and skint."[4] And so, for better or worse, the New Romantic scene was born.

Bowie's considerable influence on all of these groups, from Joy Division to ABC, is all the more striking when you consider the musical climate into which they were born. The late 1970s were as volatile a period as popular music, particularly in Britain, had yet seen. Almost as soon as the punk era began, great chunks of the 'old guard' of pop and rock found themselves ostracised and marginalised by a whole new wave of bands. Bowie, as noted elsewhere, was one of very few established stars canny enough to withstand this changing of the guard and maintain his relevance in this brave new musical world. Here was a man who had spent the best part of a decade changing the times (or changing with them) with an honesty and integrity that even Johnny Rotten couldn't sneer at – the same Johnny Rotten who, as Iggy Pop famously put it, "puts as much blood and sweat into what he does as Sigmund Freud did".

"I respected the nerve and the artistic commitment a massive change like [the one from *Station To Station* to *Low*] must have involved," said Martin Fry. "That alone shaped the way ABC would later approach things." Bowie's career is defined by a constant desire to evolve as both a musician and a performer, which has more often than not involved taking risks and avoiding the easy route to success. This is nowhere more apparent than in the context of *Low* and *"Heroes"*. Taking into account the success that his previous albums and persona had brought him, as well as his physical and emotional state at the time, it would have been very easy – and quite understandable – for Bowie to have done what his label most wanted in the autumn of 1976 and made *Young Americans II*. So many other musicians, finding themselves in such a position, would surely have taken that safer option and consolidated their mainstream popularity by recording another helping of plastic soul.

He opted instead to take the bravest and most rewarding left turn of his career, rebuffing RCA and tossing aside any sure-fire success that might have come his way in the process. There's a defiant integrity at the heart of that decision, which has in itself informed the career paths of several subsequent generations of musicians, even those whose work doesn't necessarily bear the influence of Bowie's. Bowie wasn't the first musician to follow his muse away from something that would, otherwise, have continued to bear commercially viable (if artistically unrewarding) fruit. There are all sorts of parallels in the careers of artists such as Bob Dylan, who hid himself away in Woodstock for a couple of years after hitting his commercial peak in 1966, and Scott Walker, who turned his back on sure-fire success with The Walker Brothers to make a series of brilliantly idiosyncratic solo albums. But none of them changed direction as frequently, consistently, and determinedly as did Bowie.

One example of a group taking Bowie's chameleonic lead is that of Talk Talk. In their earliest incarnation, the group made the kind of new-wave synth-pop that, like so much music of the late 1970s and early 1980s, bore the distinct influence of *Low* and its siblings. Bowie's influence on proceedings was such that Talk Talk frontman Mark Hollis asked Colin Thurston to produce their debut, *The Party's Over*, specifically because of his role in the making of *"Heroes"*. To begin with, Talk Talk were little more than a poor man's Duran Duran (note the similarity between the names), but Hollis clearly had much bigger plans for the future. "My idea is that a band should be able to develop constructively, like Bowie," he revealed in 1982. "Regardless of whether your next thing is considered better or worse, it must be a positive development."[5] And so it was that Talk Talk evolved, and by the mid 1980s were producing some of the decade's most affecting guitar-led rock. The singles 'It's My Life' and 'Life's What You Make It' and the album *The Colour Of Spring* brought Talk Talk to the precipice of superstardom. But rather than capitalise on that with more of the same, Talk Talk made their *Low*. *Spirit Of Eden* (1988) was a subtle, impressionistic masterpiece pitched somewhere between *In A Silent Way* by Miles Davis and John Martyn at his bleakest. Hollis refused to tour the album and all but disappeared until it came time to release Talk Talk's final album, the similarly ethereal *Laughing Stock*, in 1991.

Bowie's Berlin albums have continued to influence all manner of musicians in the decades since their original release, from the New Romantics of the early 1980s right through to contemporary groups such as Franz Ferdinand, Coldplay, and These New Puritans. Some bands, including Siouxsie & The Banshees and Depeche Mode, even went to Hansa Tonstudios in search of the essence of *"Heroes"*; others have resorted to calling in Brian Eno in the hope that he might have the same effect on their records as he did on Bowie's. U2 tried both, to varying levels of success, on their 1989 LP *Achtung Baby*, which was recorded just before the Berlin Wall came down.

In recent years, however, it has become more common for musicians to emulate Bowie's overall approach and sense of adventure than to borrow specific sounds from *Low* and the others. Moby is one such example of this. Although he stumbled a little bit too close to pastiche with the *"'Heroes'"* sound of 'We Are All Made Of Stars', he has tended, generally speaking, to create music that is informed by Bowie but not necessarily directly inspired by him. So, too, has Nine Inch Nails' Trent Reznor, who has often cited *Low* as one of his favourite albums, praising its "emotional content, that feeling of coldness and desperation, and the daring of the song structure".[6] It's these things, rather than specific guitar sounds or chord progressions, that Reznor then carried over to albums such as *The Downward Spiral* and *The Fragile*. Bowie, an avowed Nine Inch Nails fan, later wrote of how Reznor "unpacked his synth and threw away the manual" and "encouraged the computer to misconstrue input, willed it to spew out bloated, misshapen shards of sound that pierced and lacerated the listener"[7] – which is essentially what he and Eno did two decades earlier, minus the computer.

The British band Blur recall late-1970s Bowie in places, too, and indeed the group's frontman, Damon Albarn, has been heralded as the Bowie of his generation on more than one occasion. There are hints of *Low*'s icy desolation in songs such as 'He Thought Of Cars' (from *The Great Escape*) and 'Ambulance' (from *Think Tank*). But the most blatant representation of their admiration for mid-period Bowie is 'M.O.R.', which sounds so much like 'Boys Keep Swinging' that, after some gentlemanly legal manoeuvring, later pressings of the group's eponymous fifth album credit Albarn, Bowie, and Eno as co-authors of the song.

Perhaps the most striking contemporary example of musicians following the 'Bowie in Berlin' model is provided by Radiohead. Nirvana aside, the British quintet was the most influential guitar-band of the 1990s. While there's rarely much similarity between Radiohead's songs and those Bowie wrote and recorded for *Low* and *"Heroes"*, the band does seem to share his magpie-like talent for bringing disparate ideas and influences into a cohesive whole. Moreover, the path the band took at the turn of the millennium seemed, whether by accident or design, to echo almost exactly what Bowie did at the end of the 1970s. Having reset the boundaries of conventional 'rock' music with *OK Computer*, many expected Radiohead's next move to consolidate their status as one of the world's biggest bands. Instead, the five-piece group spent the next two years hidden away from the world at large, experimenting with sound before finally emerging with a pair of albums that bridged the gap – again – between rock and electronic music. Sound familiar? Like *Low* and *"Heroes"*, *Kid A* and *Amnesiac* were released within the space of a year; Radiohead refused to engage in any conventional means of promoting *Kid A* – which received decidedly lukewarm reviews at first but is now much more highly regarded – before throwing their weight more fully behind the spikier, more humanistic *Amnesiac*. (Without wishing to labour the point, one could draw similar comparisons between Radiohead's next album, *Hail To The Thief*, and Bowie's *Lodger*, each of them being more accessible but less artistically rewarding than what came before.)

There are countless other examples of ways in which Bowie, Eno, and Visconti's recordings from 1976–9 influenced what followed. But by far the greatest compliment paid to the music they made during that period came in 1992, when Philip Glass, one of the greatest composers of the later 20th century, unveiled his *Symphony No. 1 (Low)*. Glass took as his inspiration three songs from the *Low* sessions: 'Subterraneans', 'Warszawa', and 'Some Are', an outtake included on the 1991 reissue of the album. He then fashioned from them three movements of richly textured music that, while clearly derived from the original recordings, is full of new melodic and harmonic detail. Four years later, Glass did much the same with the *"Heroes"* material for his *Symphony No. 4*, which draws on six songs, including 'Sons Of The Silent Age', 'Sense Of Doubt', and '"Heroes"' itself, each arranged in rather more upbeat and sometimes melodramatic fashion than the often sombre *Low* symphony.

All of this seemed somewhat fitting, given that Glass had, along with Steve Reich, been a clear influence on some of the instrumental material included on the original albums. And it gave the strongest indication yet of the impact of Bowie's late-1970s works. "I first heard *Low* when it came out in 1977," Glass recalled shortly before the premiere of his *Symphony No. 1* in the summer of 1992. "I'd never encountered pop music conceived with that level of artistic ambition."[8] Later, in the liner notes to his *"Heroes"* symphony, Glass made clear his view that Bowie and Eno's synthesis of world music, experimental avant-garde, and rock'n'roll were instrumental in redefining the future of popular music. "The continuing influence of these works," he wrote, "has secured their stature as part of the new 'classics' of our time." Long may they remain so.

ENDNOTES

BLACK NOISE (pp22–30)

1 Roy Carr, Charles Shaar Murray, *Bowie: An Illustrated Record*
2 Bowie interviewed by Allan Jones, *Melody Maker* (October 29th 1977)
3 David Bowie interviewed by John Robinson, *New Musical Express* (December 2nd 2000)
4 Lester Bangs, *Creem* (January 1975)
5 David Bowie interviewed by Robert Hilburn, *New Musical Express* (November 5th 1974)
6 David Bowie interviewed by Allan Jones, *Melody Maker* (October 29th 1977)
7 Carlos Alomar interviewed by Colin McDonald (www.teenagewildlife.com)

THE YEAR OF MAGICAL THINKING (pp31–56)

1 David Bowie interviewed by Cameron Crowe, *Rolling Stone* (February 1976)
2 Maggie Abbott interviewed by Rob Hughes, *Uncut* (December 2005)
3 David Bowie interviewed by Cameron Crowe, *Rolling Stone* (February 1976)
4 Nicolas Roeg interviewed by Steve Stroyer and John Litflander, *Creem* (December 1975)
5 Domenic Priore, *Riot On Sunset Strip: Rock'n'Roll's Last Stand In Hollywood*
6 *Cracked Actor* BBC documentary (January 26th 1975)
7 David Bowie interviewed in *Hi Magazine* (June 7th 1975)
8 David Bowie interviewed by Cameron Crowe, *Rolling Stone* (February 1976)
9 David Bowie interviewed by Anthony O'Grady, *New Musical Express* (August 23rd 1975)
10 Anthony O'Grady, *New Musical Express* (August 23rd 1975)
11 David Bowie interviewed by Tony Parsons, *Arena* (May/June 1993)
12 David Buckley, *Strange Fascination: David Bowie: The Definitive Story*
13 Angela Bowie, *Backstage Passes: Life On the Wild Side With David Bowie*
14 Cameron Crowe, *Rolling Stone* (February 1976)
15 Nicolas Roeg interviewed by Rob Hughes, *Uncut* (December 2005)
16 David Bowie interviewed by Steve Stroyer and John Litflander, *Creem* (December 1975)
17 Si Litvinoff, Nicolas Roeg, and Candy Clark interviewed by Rob Hughes, *Uncut* (December 2005)
18 David Bowie interviewed by Steve Stroyer and John Litflander, *Creem* (December 1975)
19 Graham Fuller, 'Loving The Alien,' 2005 essay included in Criterion DVD reissue of *The Man Who Fell To Earth*
20 Mike Garson interviewed by Peter Gillman, Leni Gillman, *Alias David Bowie*
21 Tony Visconti, *Bowie, Bolan And The Brooklyn Boy: The Autobiography*
22 Harry Maslin interviewed by Jerry Hopkins, *Bowie*
23 David Bowie interviewed by Dave Fanning for *Planet Rock Profiles* (ITV, 1997)
24 Carlos Alomar interviewed by David Buckley, *Strange Fascination: David Bowie: The Definitive Story*
25 David Bowie interviewed by Dave Fanning for *Planet Rock Profiles* (ITV, 1997)
26 David Bowie interviewed by Tony Parsons, *Arena* (May/June 1993)
27 David Bowie interviewed by Russell Harty on *Russell Harty* (ITV, November 28th 1975)
28 Charles Shaar Murray, *New Musical Express* (January 10th 1976)
29 David Bowie interviewed by Allan Jones, *Melody Maker* (October 29th 1977)
30 Harry Maslin and Earl Slick interviewed by Richard Cromelin, *Circus* (March 1976)
31 Ian MacDonald, *The People's Music*
32 Paul Buckmaster interviewed by David Buckley, *Mojo: 60 Years Of Bowie* (January 2007)
33 Paul Buckmaster interviewed by David Buckley,

GOING ROUND & ROUND (pp57–71)

1   Michael Lippman interviewed by Timothy White, *Crawdaddy* (February 1978)
2   Angela Bowie, *Backstage Passes: Life On The Wild Side With David Bowie*
3   David Bowie interviewed by Stephen Dalton, *Uncut* (April 2001)
4   John Bate, *The Daily Telegraph* (May 18th 2004)
5   David Bowie interviewed by Cameron Crowe, *Playboy* (September 1976)
6   John Stewart, *Rochester Democrat And Chronicle* (March 26th 1976)
7   David Bowie interviewed by Bruno Stein, *Creem* (February 1975)
8   David Bowie interviewed by Anthony O'Grady, *New Musical Express* (August 23rd 1975)
9   David Bowie interviewed by Cameron Crowe, *Playboy* (September 1976)
10 Derek Jewell, *The Sunday Times* (May 9th 1976)
11 David Bowie interviewed by Fred Hauptfuhrer, *People* (September 1976)
12 Carlos Alomar interviewed by David Buckley, *Strange Fascination: David Bowie: The Definitive Story*
13 David Bowie interviewed by Cameron Crowe, *Playboy* (September 1976)
14 David Bowie interviewed by Allan Jones, *Melody Maker* (October 29th 1977)

DUM DUM DAYS (pp74–95)

1   Charles M. Young, *Rolling Stone* (May 19th 1977)
2   David Bowie interviewed by Jim Irvin and Paul Du Noyer, *Mojo* (July 2002)
3   Iggy Pop interviewed by David Fricke, *Rolling Stone* (April 2nd 2007)
4   Paul Trynka, *Iggy Pop: Open Up And Bleed*
5   David Bowie interviewed by Tim Lott, *Record Mirror* (September 9th 1977)
6   Michael Kimmelman, *The Accidental Masterpiece: On The Art Of Life And Vice Versa*
7   David Bowie interviewed by Charles Shaar Murray, *New Musical Express* (November 21st 1977)
8   Tony Visconti, *Bowie, Bolan And The Brooklyn Boy: The Autobiography*
9   David Bowie interviewed by Charles Shaar Murray, *New Musical Express* (November 21st 1977)
10 David Bowie interviewed by Stephen Dalton, *Uncut* (April 2001)
11 David Bowie interviewed by Angus MacKinnon, *New Musical Express* (September 13th 1980)
12 David Bowie interviewed by Stephen Dalton, *Uncut* (April 2001)
13 Christopher Hilton, *The Wall: The People's Story* (Sutton Publishing, 2001)
14 Tony Visconti, *Bowie, Bolan And The Brooklyn Boy: The Autobiography*
15 David Bowie interviewed by Kurt Loder for the *Sound + Vision* anthology (1989)
16 David Bowie interviewed by Kurt Loder for the *Sound + Vision* anthology (1989)
17 David Bowie on *VH1 Storytellers* (taped August 13th 1999)

WHAT IN THE WORLD (pp96–133)

1   Brian Eno interviewed by Stephen Dalton, *Uncut* (October 1999)
2   Brian Eno interviewed on *Chain Reaction*, BBC Radio 4 (24 May 2005)
3   Brian Eno interviewed by Michael Watts, *Melody Maker* (January 29th 1977)
4   David Bowie interviewed by Lisa Robinson, *New Musical Express* (March 19th 1977)
5   www.tonyvisconti.com
6   Tony Visconti, *Bowie, Bolan And The Brooklyn Boy: The Autobiography*
7   Tony Visconti, *Bowie, Bolan And The Brooklyn Boy: The Autobiography*
8   Dennis Davis interviewed by Ralph Denyer, *Sound International* (December 1978)
9   Rob Sheffield, *Rolling Stone* magazine (November 22nd 2001)
10 Ricky Gardiner interviewed by the author
11 Ricky Gardiner interviewed by the author
12 Tony Visconti interviewed by Stephen Dalton, *Uncut* (April 2001)
13 Ricky Gardiner interviewed by the author
14 Ricky Gardiner interviewed by the author
15 Ricky Gardiner interviewed by the author
16 George Murray interviewed by Ralph Denyer, *Sound International* (September 1978)

17 Robert Fripp interviewed by Dave Mandi, *Reflex* (February 5th 1991)
18 Carlos Alomar interviewed by David Buckley, *Strange Fascination*
19 Dennis Davis interviewed by the author
20 Tony Visconti interviewed by Stephen Dalton, *Uncut* (April 2001)
21 Dennis Davis interviewed by the author
22 Ricky Gardiner interviewed by the author
23 Tony Visconti interviewed by Michael Watts, *Melody Maker* (January 29th 1977)
24 David Bowie, 'My World', *Mirabelle* (August 11th 1973)
25 Ricky Gardiner interviewed by the author
26 Ricky Gardiner interviewed by the author
27 David Bowie interviewed by Stephen Dalton, *Uncut* (April 2001)
28 David Bowie interviewed by Brian Aris, *Hello!* (June 13th 1992)
29 Brian Eno interviewed by Glenn O'Brien, *Interview* (June 1978)
30 Brian Eno interviewed by Glenn O'Brien, *Interview* (June 1978)
31 Brian Eno interviewed by Glenn O'Brien, *Interview* (June 1978)
32 David Bowie interviewed by Stephen Dalton, *Uncut* (April 2001)
33 David Bowie interviewed by Michael Watts, *Melody Maker* (February 1978)
34 Tony Visconti interviewed by Michael Watts, *Melody Maker* (January 29th 1977)
35 David Bowie interviewed by Charles M. Young, *Rolling Stone* (January 12th 1978)
36 Brian Eno interviewed by Michael Watts, *Melody Maker* (January 29th 1977)
37 David Bowie interviewed by Tim Lott, *Record Mirror* (September 9th 1977)
38 Tony Visconti interviewed by Michael Watts, *Melody Maker* (January 29th 1977)
39 David Bowie interviewed by Timothy White, *Musician* (May 1983)
40 Carlos Alomar interviewed by David Buckley, *Strange Fascination*
41 David Bowie interviewed on *The Charlie Rose Show* (March 31st 1998)
42 Iggy Pop interviewed by Rob Tannenbaum, *Blender* (September 2003)
43 Angela Bowie, *Backstage Passes*
44 David Bowie interviewed by Stephen Dalton, *Uncut* (April 2001)
45 Angela Bowie, *Backstage Passes*
46 Angela Bowie, *Backstage Passes*
47 David Bowie interviewed by Charles Shaar Murray, *New Musical Express* (November 21st 1977)
48 Ricky Gardiner interviewed by the author
49 David Bowie interviewed by Charles Shaar Murray, *New Musical Express* (November 21st 1977)
50 Brian Eno interviewed by Glenn O'Brien
51 Nicholas Pegg *The Complete David Bowie*

NEIGHBOURHOOD THREAT (pp134–158)

1 David Bowie interviewed on *More Music* (1995)
2 Ian MacDonald / Charles Shaar Murray, *New Musical Express* (January 22nd 1977)
3 John Rowntree, *Records And Recording* (April 1977)
4 Michael Watts, *Melody Maker* (January 22nd 1977)
5 Michael Watts, *Melody Maker* (January 29th 1977)
6 Wesley Strick, *Circus* (February 28th 1977)
7 *Melody Maker* (January 29th 1977)
8 Iggy Pop, *I Need More*
9 Ricky Gardiner interviewed by the author
10 Ricky Gardiner interviewed by the author
11 Ian 'Knox' Carnochan interviewed by the author
12 David Bowie interviewed by Jim Irvin and Paul Du Noyer, *Mojo* (July 2002)
13 Nick Kent, *New Musical Express* (March 12th 1977)
14 Ian 'Knox' Carnochan interviewed by the author

15 Lester Bangs, *Psychotic Reactions And Carburetor Dung* (Anchor Books, 1987)
16 Iggy Pop interviewed by Charles M. Young, *Rolling Stone* (May 9th 1977)
17 Iggy Pop interviewed by Michael Watts, *Melody Maker* (March 5th 1977)
18 Nick Kent, *New Musical Express* (March 12th 1977)
19 Ian 'Knox' Carnochan interviewed by the author
20 David Bowie interviewed by Jean Rook, *The Daily Express* (February 14th 1979)
21 David Bowie interviewed by Charles Shaar Murray, *New Musical Express* (November 21st 1977)
22 David Bowie interviewed by John Tobler, *Zig Zag* (January 1978)
23 Marc Bolan interviewed by Robin Smith, *Record Mirror* (April 16th 1977)
24 Ian 'Knox' Carnochan interviewed by the author
25 Marc Bolan interviewed by Robin Smith, *Record Mirror* (April 16th 1977)
26 David Bowie interviewed by Lisa Robinson, *New Musical Express* (March 19th 1977)
27 Nick Kent, *New Musical Express* (April 2nd 1977)
28 Allan Jones, *Melody Maker* (March 5th 1977)
29 John Swenson, *Rolling Stone* (May 5th 1977)
30 Iggy Pop interviewed by RG Brickmaster, *New Musical Express* (March 5th 1977)
31 Harald Inhülsen interviewed by Michael Watts, *Melody Maker* (March 5th 1977)
32 Iggy Pop interviewed by Charles M. Young, *Rolling Stone* (May 19th 1977)
33 Ricky Gardiner interviewed by the author
34 Iggy Pop interviewed in *Q* (April 1996)
35 Ricky Gardiner interviewed by the author
36 Max Bell, *New Musical Express* (August 27th 1977)
37 Billy Altman, *Rolling Stone* (January 12th 1977)
38 Ricky Gardiner and Ian 'Knox' Carnochan interviewed by the author
39 David Bowie interviewed by Robert Phoenix, *Gettingit.com*
40 Ricky Gardiner interviewed by the author

FÜR EINEN TAG (pp159–187)

1   Tony Visconti, *Bowie, Bolan, And The Brooklyn Boy: The Autobiography*
2   Tony Visconti interviewed by Richard Buskin, *Sound On Sound* (October 2004)
3   Brian Eno interviewed by Ian MacDonald, *New Musical Express* (December 3rd 1977)
4   Dennis Davis interviewed by the author
5   Brian Eno interviewed by Glenn O'Brien, *Interview Magazine* (June 1978)
6   Brian Eno interviewed by Alan Moore, *Chain Reaction* (BBC Radio 4, February 3rd 2005)
7   George Murray interviewed by Ralph Denyer, *Sound International* (September 1978)
8   Tony Visconti interviewed by Richard Buskin, *Sound On Sound* (October 2004)
9   David Bowie interviewed by Timothy White, *Musician* (May 1983)
10 David Bowie interviewed by John Tobler, *Zig Zag* (January 1978)
11 Brian Eno interviewed by Ian MacDonald, *New Musical Express* (December 3rd 1977)
12 David Bowie interviewed by Tony Horkins, *International Musician* (December 1991)
13 Robert Fripp interviewed by David Fricke, *Synapse* (May/June 1979)
14 Brian Eno interviewed by Danny Baker and Kris Needs, *Zig Zag* (January 1978)
15 David Bowie interviewed by Stephen Dalton, *Uncut* (April 2001)
16 Brian Eno interviewed by Alan Moore, *Chain Reaction* (BBC Radio 4, February 3rd 2005)
17 Brian Eno interviewed by Ian MacDonald, *New Musical Express* (December 3rd 1977)
18 David Bowie interviewed by Timothy White, *Musician* (May 1983)
19 David Bowie interviewed by Allan Jones, *Melody Maker* (October 29th 1977)
20 David Bowie interviewed by Allan Jones, *Melody Maker* (October 29th 1977)
21 David Bowie interviewed by Stephen Dalton, *Uncut* (April 2001)
22 Tony Visconti interviewed by Richard Buskin, *Sound On Sound* (October 2004)
23 Brian Eno interviewed by Glenn O'Brien, *Interview Magazine* (June 1978)
24 Brian Eno interviewed by Ian MacDonald, *New Musical Express* (December 3rd 1977)
25 David Bowie interviewed by Charles Shaar Murray, *New Musical Express*

STAGE & SCREEN (pp190–220)
1   David Bowie interviewed by Allan Jones, *Melody Maker* (October 29th 1977)
2   David Bowie interviewed by Cameron Crowe, *Playboy* (June 1976)
3   David Bowie interviewed by David Quantick, *Q* (October 1999)
4   *The Starzone Interviews*, David Currie
5   Angela Bowie, *Backstage Passes*
6   David Bowie interviewed by Michael Watts, *Melody Maker* (February 18th 1978)
7   David Bowie interviewed by Valerie Singleton, *Tonight* (BBC1, February 12th, 1979)
8   David Bowie interviewed by Timothy White, *Crawdaddy* (February 1978)
9   David Bowie interviewed by Jean Rook, *Daily Express* (February 14th, 1979)
10 David Hemmings interviewed by Michael Watts, *Melody maker* (February 1978)
11 David Bowie interviewed by Angus MacKinnon, *New Musical Express* (September 1980)
12 David Hemmings interviewed by Stuart Jeffries, *The Guardian* (December 14th, 2001)
13 Tony Visconti, *Stage* sleevenotes (2005)
14 Paul Trynka, *Iggy Pop: Open Up And Bleed*
15 Sean Mayes, *Life On Tour With David Bowie*
16 David Bowie interviewed by Chris Roberts, *Uncut* (Novemmber 1999)
17 Tony Visconti, *Stage* sleevenotes (2005)

DO SOMETHING BORING (pp221–242)
1   Brian Eno interviewed by Andy Gill, *Mojo* (June 1995)
2   Sean Mayes, *Life On Tour With David Bowie*
3   www.tonyvisconti.com
4   David Bowie interviewed by Mark Rowland, *Musician* (November 1995)
5   David Bowie interviewed by Dave Herman, WNEW-FM New York (July 5th 1979)
6   Brian Eno interviewed by Charles Amirkhanian, KFPA-FM (February 2nd 1980)
7   Brian Eno interviewed by Charles Amirkhanian, *Reality Hackers* (Winter 1988)
8   Carlos Alomar interviewed by David Buckley, *Strange Fascination*
9   Tony Visconti, *Bowie, Bolan, And The Brooklyn Boy*
10 David Bowie interviewed by Nicky Horne, Capital Radio (May 14th 1979)
11 David Bowie interviewed by Stephen Dalton, *Uncut* (April 2001)
12 Jon Savage, *Melody Maker* (May 19th1979)
13 Greil Marcus, *Rolling Stone* (August 9th 1979)
14 Paul Yamada, *New York Rocker* (July 1979)
15 David Bowie interviewed by Stephen Dalton, *Uncut* (April 2001)
16 Tony Visconti, *Bowie, Bolan, And The Brooklyn Boy*
17 Ian MacDonald, *Uncut* (January 2003)
18 David Bowie interviewed by Richard Buskin, *Sound On Sound* magazine (October 2003)
19 David Bowie interviewed by Allan Jones, *Melody Maker* (October 29th 1977)
20 David Bowie interviewed by Mark Rowland, *Musician* (November 1995)
21 Brian Eno, reprinted in *Raygun* (October 1995)

THE HEART'S FILTHY LESSON ( )
1   Gary Numan interviewed by David Buckley, *Strange Fascination*
2   David Bowie interviewed by Paula Yates, *Record Mirror* (May 5th 1979)
3   David Bowie interviewed by Timothy White, *Musician* (May 1983)
4   Martin Fry interviewed in *Record Collector* (March 2001)
5   Mark Hollis interviewed by Tony Mitchell, *Sounds* (October 30th 1982)
6   Trent Reznor interviewed in *Mojo* (February 2005)
7   David Bowie, *Rolling Stone* (April 21st 2005)
8   Philip Glass, *Arena* (June 1993)

SELECTED DISCOGRAPHY

DAVID BOWIE ALBUMS

STATION TO STATION
RCA APL1 1327 (USA #3 /
UK #5)
January 1976

SIDE ONE
1. Station To Station
2. Golden Years
3. Word On A Wing

SIDE TWO
4. TVC 15
5. Stay
6. Wild Is The Wind

■ Produced and mixed by
David Bowie and Harry
Maslin. Recorded at
Cherokee Studios,
Hollywood, California,
October–December 1975.
David Bowie: vocals, guitar,
sax; Carlos Alomar: guitar;
George Murray: bass;
Dennis Davis: drums,
percussion; Earl Slick:
guitar; Roy Bittan: piano.

LOW
RCA PL 12030 (UK #2) /
RCA 2030 (USA #11)
January 1977

SIDE ONE
1. Speed Of Life
2. Breaking Glass
3. What In The World
4. Sound And Vision
5. Always Crashing In The
   Same Car
6. Be My Wife
7. A New Career In A New
   Town

SIDE TWO
8. Warszawa
9. Art Decade

10. Weeping Wall
11. Subterraneans °

■ Produced and mixed by
David Bowie and Tony
Visconti. Engineered by
Tony Visconti, Laurent
Thibault, and Eduard
Meyer. Recorded at the
Château d'Hérouville,
Pontoise, France, and Hansa
Tonstudio 2, Berlin,
Germany,
September–October 1976
(except °, for which some
instrumental parts were
recorded at Cherokee
Studios, Hollywood,
California, December 1975).
Mixed at Hansa Tonstudio 2,
October 1976.
David Bowie: vocals, guitar,
piano, sax, Chamberlin,
synthesizers, xylophone,
vibraphone, harmonica;
Carlos Alomar: guitar;
George Murray: bass;
Dennis Davis: drums,
percussion; Brian Eno:
piano, synthesizers,
treatments; Ricky Gardiner:
guitar; Roy Young: piano,
organ; Eduard Meyer: cello;
Iggy Pop, Tony Visconti, and
Mary Visconti: backing
vocals.

"HEROES"
RCA PL 12522 (UK #3) /
RCA 2522 (USA #35)
October 1977

SIDE ONE
1. Beauty And The Beast
2. Joe The Lion
3. "Heroes"
4. Sons Of The Silent Age
5. Blackout

SIDE TWO
6. V–2 Schneider
7. Sense Of Doubt
8. Moss Garden
9. Neuköln
10. The Secret Life Of
    Arabia

■ Produced and mixed by
David Bowie and Tony
Visconti. Engineered by
Tony Visconti, Colin
Thurston, and Eduard
Meyer. Assistant mix
engineering by Eugene
Chaplin and David
Richards. Recorded at
Hansa Tonstudio 3, Berlin
Germany, July 1977, and
mixed at Hansa Tonstudio 3
and Mountain Studios,
Montreux, Switzerland,
August 1977.
David Bowie: vocals, guitar,
piano, sax, synthesizers,
koto; Carlos Alomar: guitar;
George Murray: bass;
Dennis Davis: drums,
percussion; Brian Eno:
piano, synthesizers,
treatments; Robert Fripp:
guitar; Tony Visconti and
Antonia Maas: backing vocals.

STAGE
RCA PL 02913 (UK #5) /
RCA 2913 (USA #44)
September 1978

SIDE ONE
1. Hang On To Yourself
2. Ziggy Stardust
3. Five Years
4. Soul Love
5. Star

SIDE TWO
6. Station To Station
7. Fame
8. TVC 15

SIDE THREE
1. Warszawa
2. Speed Of Life
3. Art Decade
4. Sense Of Doubt
5. Breaking Glass

SIDE FOUR
6. "Heroes"
7. What In The World
8. Blackout
9. Beauty And The Beast

■ Produced and mixed by David Bowie and Tony Visconti. Recorded live at the Spectrum Arena, Philadelphia, Pennsylvania, April 28th–29th 1978, and the Civic Center, Providence, Rhode Island, May 5th 1978.
David Bowie: vocals, synthesizer; Carlos Alomar: guitar, backing vocals; George Murray: bass, backing vocals; Dennis Davis: drums, percussion; Adrian Belew: guitar, backing vocals; Sean Mayes: piano, keyboards, backing vocals; Simon House: violin; Roger Powell: synthesizers, backing vocals.

LODGER
RCA BOW LP1 (UK #4) / RCA 3254 (USA #20)
May 1979

SIDE ONE
1. Fantastic Voyage
2. African Night Flight
3. Move On
4. Yassassin
5. Red Sails

SIDE TWO
6. D.J.
7. Look Back In Anger
8. Boys Keep Swinging
9. Repetition
10. Red Money

■ Produced and mixed by David Bowie and Tony Visconti. Recorded at Mountain Studios, Montreux, Switzerland, September 1978, and The Record Plant, New York, New York, March 1979. Mixed at the Record Plant, March 1979.
David Bowie: vocals, piano, synthesizers; Carlos Alomar: guitar, backing vocals; George Murray: bass, backing vocals; Dennis Davis: drums, percussion, backing vocals; Brian Eno: synthesizers, treatments, backing vocals; Adrian Belew: guitar, mandolin, backing vocals; Sean Mayes: piano, backing vocals; Simon House: violin, mandolin, backing vocals; Tony Visconti: mandolin, guitar, backing vocals.

Each of these albums has been reissued several times on vinyl and CD. The 1991 EMI/Rykodisc CD editions contain between one and three bonus tracks; the current Virgin/EMI remasters, which were issued in 1999, do not. The expanded edition of *Stage* issued in 2005 replaces the original 'chronological' tracklisting with a new running-order that better reflects Bowie's 1978 live set.

SINGLES

'Golden Years' / 'Can You Hear Me'
RCA 2640 (UK #8) / RCA 10441 (USA #10)
November 1975

'TVC 15' / 'We Are The Dead'
RCA 2682 (UK #33) / RCA 10664 (USA #64)
April 1976

'Suffragette City' / 'Stay'
RCA 2726 (UK)
July 1976

'Stay' / 'Word On A Wing'
RCA 10736 (USA)
August 1976

'Sound And Vision' / 'A New Career In A New Town'
RCA PB 0905 (UK #3) / RCA 10905 (USA #69)
February 1977

'Be My Wife' / 'Speed Of Life'
RCA PB 1017 (UK) / RCA 11017 (USA)
April 1977

'"Heroes"' / 'V-2 Schneider'
RCA PB 1121 (UK #24) / RCA 11121 (USA)
September 1977; this was released as 'Helden' in Germany and as 'Héros' in France

'Beauty And The Beast' / 'Sense Of Doubt'
RCA PB 1190 (UK #39) / RCA 11190 (USA)
January 1977

'Breaking Glass' (live) / 'Ziggy Stardust' (live) / 'Art Decade' (live)
RCA BOW 1 (UK #54)
November 1978

'Boys Keep Swinging' / 'Fantastic Voyage'
RCA BOW 2 (UK #7) / RCA 11585 (USA)
April 1979

'D.J.' / 'Repetition'
RCA BOW 3 (UK #29)
June 1979

'D.J.' / 'Fantastic Voyage'
RCA 11661 (USA)
June 1979

**'Look Back In Anger' /
'Repetition'**
RCA 11724 (USA)
August 1979

**'John I'm Only Dancing
(Again)' / 'John I'm Only
Dancing (1972)'**
RCA BOW 4 (UK #12)
December 1979

**'Alabama Song' / 'Space
Oddity'**
RCA BOW 5 (UK #23)
February 1980

COMPILATIONS

PETER AND THE
WOLF
RCA Red Seal RL 12743
May 1978

SIDE ONE
1. Peter And The Wolf
    (Prokofiev, Op. 67)

SIDE TWO
2. Young Person's Guide To
    The Orchestra (Britten,
    Op. 34)

■ Produced by Jay David
Saks. Recorded at RCA
Studio B, New York, New
York, December 1977. David
Bowie: narration on track one;
with Eugene Ormandy and
The Philadelphia Orchestra.

SOUND + VISION
Rykodisc 0120 (USA #97)
September 1989

■ Six LP, three CD boxed

set, includes new mix of
'Helden'.

THE BEST OF DAVID
BOWIE 1974/1979
EMI 494300 (UK #39) /
Virgin 7243 4 94300 2 0 (USA)
April 1998

1. Sound And Vision
2. Golden Years (single edit)
3. Fame
4. Young Americans
5. John, I'm Only Dancing
    (Again)
6. Can You Hear Me
7. Wild Is The Wind
8. Knock On Wood (live)
9. TVC 15
10. 1984
11. It's Hard To Be A Saint
    In This City
12. Look Back In Anger
13. The Secret Life Of Arabia
14. D.J.
15. Beauty And The Beast
16. Breaking Glass
17. Boys Keep Swinging
18. "Heroes" (single version)

ALL SAINTS:
COLLECTED
INSTRUMENTALS
1977–1999
EMI 533 0452 (UK)
July 2001

1. A New Career In A New
    Town
2. V-2 Schneider
3. Abdulmajid
4. Weeping Wall
5. All Saints
6. Art Decade
7. Crystal Japan
8. Brilliant Adventure
9. Sense Of Doubt
10. Neuköln
11. The Mysteries
12. Ian Fish: U.K. Heir
13. Subterraneans
14. Warszawa
15. Some Are (Low
    Symphony Version)

■ *All Saints* brings together
instrumental tracks from
various stages in Bowie's
career. It includes
remastered versions of two
outtakes from 1976–7
('Abdulmajid' and 'All
Saints') and Philip Glass's
orchestral reinterpretation
of another ('Some Are'). The
album was originally
conceived by Bowie as a
Christmas present for
friends and family, and
included several tracks
missing from the 2001 edition
– 'South Horizon', 'Pallas
Athena', 'The Wedding', and
'Looking For Lester'.

IGGY POP
ALBUMS

THE IDIOT
RCA PL 12275 (UK #30) /
RCA 2275 (USA #72)
March 1977

SIDE ONE
1. Sister Midnight
2. Nightclubbing
3. Funtime
4. Baby

SIDE TWO
5. China Girl
6. Dum Dum Boys
7. Tiny Girls
8. Production
■ Produced by David
Bowie. Mixed by Tony
Visconti. Recorded at
Château d'Hérouville,
Pontoise, France, June–July
1976, and Musicland,
Munich, Germany, August
1976. Mixed at Hansa
Tonstudio 2, August 1976.
Iggy Pop: vocals, piano; David
Bowie: guitar, piano,
synthesizers, sax, drum
machine, backing vocals;
Laurent Thibault: bass, tape

loop; Michel Santangeli: drums; George Murray: bass; Dennis Davis: drums; Phil Palmer: guitar.

LUST FOR LIFE
RCA PL 12488 (UK #28) /
RCA 2488 (USA)
September 1977

SIDE ONE
1. Lust For Life
2. Sixteen
3. Some Weird Sin
4. The Passenger
5. Tonight

SIDE TWO
6. Success
7. Turn Blue
8. Neighborhood Threat
9. Fall In Love With Me

■ Produced by The Bewley Brothers (David Bowie, Iggy Pop, and Colin Thurston). Engineered by Colin Thurston and Eduard Meyer. Recorded and mixed at Hansa Tonstudio 2, Berlin, Germany, May–June 1976. Iggy Pop: vocals; David Bowie: piano, organ, synthesizers, backing vocals; Carlos Alomar: guitar; Ricky Gardiner: guitar; Tony Sales: bass, backing vocals; Hunt Sales: drums, backing vocals.

T.V. EYE (LIVE 1977)
RCA PL 12796 (UK)
May 1978

SIDE ONE
1. T.V. Eye
2. Funtime
3. Sixteen
4. I Got A Right

SIDE TWO
5. Lust For Life
6. Dirt
7. Nightclubbing
8. I Wanna Be Your Dog

■ Produced by Iggy Pop and David Bowie. Recorded live at the Agora, Cleveland, Ohio, March 21st–22nd 1977; the Aragon, Chicago, Illinois, March 28th 1977; and the Uptown Theatre, Kansas City, Missouri, October 26th 1977. Iggy Pop: vocals; David Bowie: piano; Ricky Gardiner: guitar; Tony Sales: bass; Hunt Sales: drums; Scott Heydon: guitar; Scott Thurston: guitar, piano, harmonica, synthesizer.

SINGLES

'Sister Midnight' / 'Baby'
RCA 10989 (USA)
February 1977

'China Girl' / 'Baby'
RCA PB 9093 (UK)
May 1977

'Success' / 'The Passenger'
RCA PB 9160 (UK)
October 1977

**'I Got A Right' (live) /
'Sixteen' (live)**
RCA PB 9213 (UK)
April 1978

COMPILATIONS

1977
Easy Action DNP001 (UK)
October 2007

■ Numerous live recordings of Iggy Pop circa 1977 have appeared over the years, with titles such as *Lust For Live* and *Heroin Hates You*, most of which should be avoided. This four-disc set, however, contains cleaned-up recordings of full sets in London, Paris, and Berlin – the first of which features Bowie on keyboards – and various other curios, including alternate mixes of tracks from *The Idiot*.

TOUR DATES

THE IDIOT TOUR,
MARCH–APRIL 1977
March 1st, Friars, Aylesbury, England
March 2nd, City Hall, Newcastle, England
March 3rd, Apollo Theatre, Manchester, England
March 5th, Rainbow Theatre, London, England
March 6th, Rainbow Theatre, London, England
March 7th, Rainbow Theatre, London, England
March 13th, Le Plateau Theatre, Montreal, Canada
March 14th, Seneca College, Toronto, Canada
March 16th, Harvard Square Theater, Boston, Massachusetts, USA
March 18th, Palladium, New York, New York, USA
March 19th, Tower Theater, Philadelphia, Pennsylvania, USA

March 21st, Agora Ballroom, Cleveland, Ohio, USA
March 22nd, Agora Ballroom, Cleveland, Ohio, USA
March 25th, Masonic Temple Auditorium, Detroit, Michigan, USA
March 27th, Riviera Theater, Chicago, Illinois, USA
March 28th, Riviera Theater, Chicago, Illinois, USA
March 29th, Leona Theater, Pittsburgh, Pennsylvania, USA
March 30th, Agora Ballroom, Columbus, Ohio, USA
April 1st, Oriental Theater, Milwaukee, Wisconsin, USA
April 4th, Paramount Theater, Portland, Oregon, USA
April 5th, Paramount Theater, Seattle, Washington, USA
April 7th, Vancouver Gardens, Vancouver, Washington, USA
April 13th, Berkeley Theater, San Francisco, California, USA
April 15th, Santa Monica Civic Auditorium, Los Angeles, California, USA
April 16th, Civic Auditorium, San Diego, California, USA

LOW / "HEROES" TOUR, MARCH–DECEMBER 1978
March 29th, Sports Arena, San Diego, California, USA
March 30th, Veterans Memorial Coliseum, Phoenix, Arizona, USA
April 2nd, Convention Center, Fresno, California, USA
April 3rd, Inglewood Forum, Los Angeles, California, USA
April 4th, Inglewood Forum, Los Angeles, California, USA
April 5th, Oakland Coliseum Arena, San Francisco, California, USA
April 6th, Inglewood Forum, Los Angeles, California, USA
April 9th, The Summit, Houston, Texas, USA
April 10th, Convention Center, Dallas, Texas, USA
April 11th, State University, Baton Rouge, Louisiana, USA
April 13th, Municipal Auditorium, Nashville, Tennessee, USA
April 14th, Mid-South Coliseum, Memphis, Tennessee, USA

April 15th, Municipal Auditorium, Kansas City, Kansas, USA
April 17th, Aerie Crown Theater, Chicago, Illinois, USA
April 18th, Aerie Crown Theater, Chicago, Illinois, USA
April 20th, Cobo Arena, Detroit, Michigan, USA
April 21st, Cobo Arena, Detroit, Michigan, USA
April 22nd, Richfield Coliseum, Cleveland, Ohio, USA
April 24th, Mecca Auditorium, Milwaukee, Wisconsin, USA
April 26th, Civic Arena, Pittsburgh, Pennsylvania, USA
April 27th, Capital Center, Washington DC, USA
April 28th, Spectrum Arena, Philadelphia, Pennsylvania, USA
April 29th, Spectrum Arena, Philadelphia, Pennsylvania, USA
May 1st, Maple Leaf Gardens, Toronto, Canada
May 2nd, Civic Center, Ottawa, Canada
May 3rd, Forum, Montreal, Canada
May 5th, Civic Center, Providence, Rhode Island, USA
May 6th, The Gardens, Boston, Massachusetts, USA
May 7th, Madison Square Garden, New York City, New York, USA
May 8th, Madison Square Garden, New York City, New York, USA
May 9th, Madison Square Garden, New York City, New York, USA
May 14th, Festhalle, Frankfurt, Germany
May 15th, Kongress Zentrum, Hamburg, Germany
May 16th, Deutschlandhalle, Berlin, Germany
May 18th, Graugahalle, Essen, Germany
May 19th, Sportshalle, Cologne, Germany
May 20th, Olympiahalle, Munich, Germany
May 22nd, Stadhalle, Vienna, Austria
May 24th, Pavilion De Paris Porte De Pantin, Paris, France
May 25th, Pavilion De Paris Porte De Pantin, Paris, France
May 26th, Palais Des Sports, Lyon, France
May 27th, Parc Chaneau, Marseilles, France
May 31st, Falkoner Teatret, Copenhagen, Denmark
June 1st, Falkoner Teatret, Copenhagen, Denmark

June 2nd, Kungliga Tennishallen, Stockholm, Sweden
June 4th, Scandinavium, Gothenburg, Sweden
June 5th, Ekeberghallen, Oslo, Norway
June 7th, Sports Paleis Ahoy, Rotterdam, Netherlands
June 8th, Sports Paleis Ahoy, Rotterdam, Netherlands
June 9th, Sports Paleis Ahoy, Rotterdam, Netherlands
June 11th, Voorst Nationaal, Brussels, Belgium
June 12th, Voorst Nationaal, Brussels, Belgium
June 14th, City Hall, Newcastle, England
June 15th, City Hall, Newcastle, England
June 16th, City Hall, Newcastle, England
June 19th, Apollo Theatre, Glasgow, Scotland
June 20th, Apollo Theatre, Glasgow, Scotland
June 21st, Apollo Theatre, Glasgow, Scotland
June 22nd, Apollo Theatre, Glasgow, Scotland
June 24th, Bingley Hall, Stafford, England
June 25th, Bingley Hall, Stafford, England
June 26th, Bingley Hall, Stafford, England
June 29th, Earl's Court, London, England
June 30th, Earl's Court, London, England

July 1st, Earl's Court, London, England
November 11th, Oval Cricket Ground, Adelaide, Australia
November 14th, Entertainment Centre, Perth, Australia
November 15th, Entertainment Centre, Perth, Australia
November 18th, Cricket Ground, Melbourne, Australia
November 21st, Lang Park, Brisbane, Australia
November 24th, Showground, Sydney, Australia
November 25th, Showground, Sydney, Australia
November 27th, Queen Elizabeth II Park, Christchurch, New Zealand
November 28th, Western Springs Stadium, Auckland, New Zealand
December 6th, , Kosei Nenkin Kaikan, Osaka, Japan
December 7th, , Kosei Nenkin Kaikan, Osaka, Japan
December 9th, , Banpaku Kinen Koen Hall, Osaka, Japan
December 11th, HNK Hall, Tokyo, Japan
December 12th, HNK Hall, Tokyo, Japan

BIBLIOGRAPHY

Bangs, Lester *Psychotic Reactions And Carburetor Dung* (Anchor Books 1987)
Bockris, Victor *Lou Reed* (Vintage 1994)
Bowie, Angela *Backstage Passes: Life On The Wild Side With David Bowie* (Orion 1993)
Bowie, David *Sound + Vision* (EMI 1989)
Bowie, David *Stage* CD booklet (Virgin/EMI 2005)
Buckley, David *Strange Fascination: David Bowie, The Definitive Biography* (Virgin 1995)
Cann, Kevin *David Bowie: A Chronology* (Vermillion 1983)
Carr, Roy, and Murray, Charles Shaar *Bowie: An Illustrated Record*
Cope, Julian *Krautrocksampler: One Head's Guide To The Great Kosmische Musik – 1968 Onwards* (Head Heritage 1995)
Eno, Brian *A Year With Swollen Appendices* (Faber 1996)
Gillman, Peter, and Gillman, Leni *Alias David Bowie* (Hodder & Stoughton 1986)
Hilton, Christopher *The Wall: The People's Story* (Sutton 2001)
Hopkins, Jerry *Bowie* (MacMillan 1986)
Kimmelmann, Michael *The Accidental Masterpiece: On The Art Of Life And Vice Versa* (Penguin 2005)
MacDonald, Ian *The People's Music* (Pimlico 2003)
Man Who Fell To Earth, The DVD booklet (Criterion 2005)
Mayes, Sean *Life On Tour With David Bowie: We Can Be Heroes* (Independent Music Press 1999)
Pegg, Nicholas *The Complete David Bowie* (Reynolds & Hearn 2003)

Pop, Iggy, and Wehrer, Anne *I Need More* (2.13.61 1997)
Prendergast, Mark *The Ambient Century: From Mahler To Moby – The Evolution Of Sound In The Electronic Age* (Bloomsbury 2003)
Priore, Domenic *Riot On Sunset Strip: Rock'n'Roll's Last Stand In Hollywood* (Jawbone 2007)
Strong, Martin C. *The Great Rock Discography, 6th Edition* (Canongate 2004)
Tamm, Eric *Brian Eno: His Music And The Vertical Colour Of Sound* (Faber 1990)
Taylor, Fredrick *The Berlin Wall: 13 August 1961 – 9 November 1989* (Bloomsbury 2006)
Trynka, Paul *Iggy Pop: Open Up And Bleed* (Sphere 2007)
Visconti, Tony *Bowie, Bolan & The Brooklyn Boy: The Autobiography* (Harper Collins 2007)
Wilcken, Hugo *Low (33 1/3)* (Continuum 2005)

WEBSITES

www.algonet.se/~bassman/
www.allmusic.com
www.alt-berlin.info
www.berlin.de
www.bowiewonderworld.com/
www.gettingit.com
www.glasspages.org
www.imdb.com
www.manzanera.com
www.moredarkthanshark.org
www.stuffem.wordpress.com
www.teenagewildlife.com/
www.tonyvisconti.com

PERIODICALS

Arena, Crawdaddy, Circus, Creem, The Daily Express, The Daily Telegraph, The Guardian, Hello, Hi! Magazine, International Musician, Interview, Melody Maker, Mirabelle, Mojo, Musician, New Musical Express, New York Rocker, The New York Times, People, Playboy, Q, Raygun, Reality Hackers, Records & Recording, Record Mirror, Reflex, Rolling Stone, Sound International, Sound On Sound, Sounds, Synapse, Uncut, Zig Zag.

INDEX

Words In Italics indicate album titles unless specified as something else; 'Words In Quotes' indicate song titles.

PICTURE CREDITS

Jacket SIPA Press/Rex. **2** Jan Persson/Redfern's. **6** Everett Collection/Rex; Roger Bamber/Rex. **7** Michael Ochs Archives/Getty; Jan Persson/Redfern's. **8** Ricky Gardiner. **9** Roberta Bayley/Redfern's. **10** Hulton Archive/Rex. **11** Ian Dickson/Redfern's; Michael Ochs Archives/Getty. **12** Michael Ochs Archives/Getty. **13** Sheila Rock/Rex. **14** Everett Collection/Rex; Ebet Roberts/Redfern's. **15** Sipa Press/Rex (2). **16** Richard E. Aaron/Redfern's. **Back jacket** Jan Persson/Redfern's.

THANK YOU AND GOODNIGHT ...

... to the Jawbone family – Nigel, Tony, Mark, Kevin, and the Jo(h)ns – for on-tap assistance and moral support; to Ian Carnochan, Dennis and Chie Davis, Billy Donald, Ricky Gardiner and Virginia Scott, for answering questions and plugging gaps; to Jack, for helping to resolve at least a hundred worthwhile dilemmas; to Joanna, for putting up with so many *Low* dinners; and to my mum, for many years of sound advice, and for naming me (inadvertently, she says) after the man who fell to earth.

"Discover your formulas and abandon them."
OBLIQUE STRATEGIES INSTRUCTION

ALSO AVAILABLE FROM JAWBONE PRESS